Glitter & Grit

Queer *Performance* **from the** *Heels on Wheels* **Femme Galaxy**

LIVE THE DREAM

HEELS ON WHEELS ROADSHOW

FEMME • FAG • FAG • FEMME • FAG • FEMME • FEMME • FAG • FEMME • FAG •

HEELSONWHEELSROADSHOW AXONDLUXE.CO

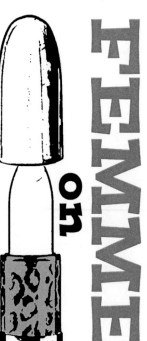

FEMME on FEMME

Heels on Wheels Roadshow * axondluxe.com

HOMO

BUTCHES N' BRE
HEELS ON WHEELS 20

Glitter & Grit

Queer Performance *from the* Heels on Wheels **Femme Galaxy**

Edited by Damien Luxe, Heather María Ács, Sabina Ibarrola

Publication Studio, Portland, USA
Second Edition - 2016

Glitter and Grit:
Queer Performance from the Heels on Wheels Femme Galaxy

Editors
Damien Luxe, Heather María Ács, Sabina Ibarrola

Anthology Curatorial Collective
Lizxnn Disaster
Andrea Glik
Mette Loulou von Kohl
Nicole Myles
Alejandro Rodríguez

Photographers
Nicole Myles
Sophie Spinelle
Tinker Coalescing
Laura Turley
Damien Luxe / Heels on Wheels Group

Cover Illustrator
Matthew de Leon

Book Designer
Hadassah Damien, femmetech.org

Publisher
Publication Studio, Portland
Printed in the USA.

ISBN   978-1-62462-127-7   **Edition**   2nd Edition, 1st printing, 2016

• •

"I have wanted to find you, to tell you that I am here, to invite you to remember me or add your own unique experiences to our common purpose, our collective tale. To come home with me. To join me in changing the world."

Amber Hollibaugh, *My Dangerous Desires*

Thank you to our tourmates and 300+ artistic collaborators! Thank you folks who have booked us, venues who've hosted us, people who've housed us, and everyone who's come to our shows!

Thank you donors who've ensured we're fed. Thank you volunteer photographers, videographers and writers who've made our work live longer.

Thank Trisha. Thank Pizza Slap. Thank you Shomi Noise for DJing many raging dance parties! Thank you Ketch who gave six of us matching tattoos. Thank you Laurence our first roadie. Thank you JP for sound tech & more. Thank you Lex Non Scripta for the Peepshow illustration. Thanks to The Stonewall Inn, JACK, and The Spectrum for hosting multiple Heels on Wheels Glitter Roadshows. Thanks to Branded Saloon for being a welcoming home to our Opentoe Peepshow salon & events for many years.

Thank you to all the other tours that have been holding it down over the years. We would not be here without you. Sister Spit, Mangos With Chili, Body Heat Queer Femme Porn Tour, Sins Invalid, and more.

Thank you femme sisters, allies, elders, and ancestors.

Audre Lorde, Dorothy Allison, Amber Hollibaugh, Cherríe Moraga, Adrienne Rich, Grace Lee Boggs, Gloria Anzaldúa, June Jordan, Ellen Stewart, Miss Major, Marsha P Johnson, Sylvia Rivera, Anna May Wong, Frida Kahlo, Jose Muñoz, Leslie Feinberg, Michelle Serros, Kate Bornstein, Lois Weaver, Minnie Bruce Pratt, Sandra Cisneros, Carmelita Tropicana, Joan Nestle, Aurora Levins Morales, Yoko Ono, Pratibha Parmar, Jennifer Miller, World Famous *BOB*, Felice Shays, and so many more...Femme Conference, Femme Family & the entire femmeiverse.

Thank you Mamone and Riot Grrrl Inc. for ongoing press support and providing carbon offset for our tours! Thank you to Jenny Romaine and Trudi Cohen of Great Small Works for fiscal sponsorship and being amazing political art leaders.

Thank you Queens, hustlers, escape artists, single moms, sex workers, anyone with multiple jobs, and wild ponies who can't be tamed.

Thanks especially to the lovers who have held us and the friends who've loved us. Thanks to Silas Howard for our motto: ***Keep Havin Fun!***

Thank you curatorial collective Lizxnn Disaster, Andrea Glik, Mette Loulou von Kohl, Nicole Myles and Alejandro Rodríguez for your endless work on this! Patricia and Publication Studio for being awesome to work with and believing in us.

Thank you everyone wearing a Heels on Wheels T-shirt or patch, with a cup in your cupboard, or a zine in your archive.

Sabina would also like to thank...
My ancestors of blood and of spirit. My chosen fam, especially Yumi and Alx, for keeping me here and loving me so hard. My HOW femmeily. Thank you most of all to my sisters Heather and Damien, the baddest bitches and biggest tenderhearts. Thank you for your love, trust, and grit. For adopting me into this pack of wild creatures. I love you.

Heather would also like to thank...
K. Connell, D. Mold, and M. Fleischer of Marymount Manhattan College for supporting my individual voice as an artist. My chosen family: Science McGhee, my big sister and biggest inspiration. Glenn Marla, Erica Cardwell, Sequinette Jaynesfield, Tennessee Jones. To Damien Luxe, my best friend and partner in action. To my mother. Without the foundation of her unflinching love, none of this would be possible.

Damien would also like to thank...
The sisterwives. All the lovers and friends - those still close and those no longer so - who supported this in order to support a world in which femmes of all makes and models matter. Extra to my queer fam for who that was multiple tours of femme ally awesomeness & coming to many shows! Bevin and Sarah Jenny thanks for letting sooooo many meetings happen in our apartment. Lizxnn Disaster you were the crucial axis, thank you for being so solid. Sabina, you are a sister and a warrior. Heather Acs I can't imagine who else I'd rather go on this ride with, you're a femmespiration to me. To my single mom who told me my creativity was a gift & taught me to work for what I want.

Thank you, book reader.

Table of Contents

4 The Show Must Go Wrong

5 Coming Into our Own

Because We Came From a Hungry Place

Damien Luxe

> "I never sat around waiting for permission to make my art or live my life. Why would I start now?"
> -- Heather María Ács

When this all started, all I wanted was to be weird, smart, queer -- and not lonely. I wanted hope and a place to put my ambition.

If we had just stayed home, watched internet TV, and waited for someone to discover us -- we never would have done all the things we did. We never would have had all the good and the bad experiences.

We never would have blasted our own hearts open, cried in each other's arms, made art, visited 34 states and three provinces, or partied as hard as we did. We never would have touched so many people, or fucked up and then challenged ourselves to do better. We never would have had people tell us we changed their lives, inspired them to femmeifest their dreams, or helped them get their ideas into the world.

I learned early on that if I wanted something, I was gonna have to work for it -- *ain't no one handing you anything, girl* -- refrained in my head. But something about that refrain was off, and creating a multi-year art project within radical, queer, feminist, anarchist, punk, and community art spaces shifted that story. People handed me things *all the time* when Heels on Wheels toured and performed: places to stay, dinner, appreciation, drinks, hugs, stories, handmade tokens like pins and patches, zines, confessions, photos, shots... As it turned out, as artists bold enough to tour complex queer femme stories, our bold generosity was exactly the key to getting to share in the best parts of many fantastic people.

The truth is: you can't buy this kind of interaction. You can't throw a bunch of money into a void and expect authenticity to emerge. *It was because we came from a hungry place that we got fed.* It was because we dared to live our dreams, legitimize ourselves as artists, and dive into the communities we knew were out there, that we got to do so: no dads, no masters, no waiting for permission.

In early 2010, I roped Heather, the other co-founder of Heels on Wheels, into working late into the night with me on a tour, and we ended up laughing and dressing up late nights too. Our vision was to put our art into the world on our terms: without waiting or compromising, and with fun and adventure. I had the design skills and van: Heather had the charm and coordinating skills. In part, Heels on Wheels is the story of our friendship, one that allowed us to be the magnificent beings we could be, of shining bright because we said so, of taking our working-class hustle and applying it for queer art.

Heels on Wheels is also a story of bringing as many people along for the ride as possible both because it's more fun that way and because broad impact, amplifying complex identities, and intersectionality all matter. Because we want a big queer family. It's a story of deciding that our world could be bigger, of making art and sharing it outside of NYC, academic, and gallery settings because those worlds were not offering space for us and damn if we were going to wait. It's a story of feminism, mutual aid, and solidarity in action: doing it together -- DIT -- instead of just doing it yourself -- DIY.

Now: imagine yourself in a room full of people each with their own story of how they got there, how their ancestors got them there. The lights go down as a few queer femmes in glittering attire come into the spotlit room's center, and your attention is taken into a story, an experience, a perspective, a surprise, a laugh: each of these a temporary walk into someone else's world, only for that moment. What do you do after? Are you the same or different? Are you willing to remember, to see the world differently, to shift? Years spent producing politicized queer live art has fed me with so many stories. It's led me to believe that space-making for queer voices is a daring act of persistence, and so too sharing my own stories. You never know for whom you are leaving the message: your life, too, is so valuable it deserves a stage.

I aim to inspire and encourage acts of daring self-preservation in others -- I do not know another way forward, but I know this one is possible. I can say for a fact: if you believe you are of value, you will find people to agree with you. For the love of your one short life, go find those people. If you have a vision, please share it. So many people are hungry, so many of us will come.

Living through Live Performance

Heather María Ács

Live performance can never be recreated or documented. What is shared in these pages is merely a shadow, a bone, a flicker of light, a symbol for something that was or will be. You have to be there. That is why I love live performance. In a remote world, live performance requires bodies breathing together in one place, hearts beating in the same space. We experience. We witness. We carve out time to feel, to celebrate, to grieve, to laugh. Live performance. Living. To live. And if some feelings are hard to access or covered up with the daily grind, don't worry, as an artist, I will try to access and feel aaaall kinds of feelings for you, with you - as an offering, as a gift. I am different with you in the room. I am more with you in the room. This moment is happening now, and it will never be the same. I will never be the same. We will never be the same. I don't ever want to be the same.

I am the most honest when I am on stage. I am the most myself. I lay my heart bare in front of you, because if the world were safer, that's the way I would live, all the time.

I picked up a book of feminist solo performance texts from the shelf of a tiny bookstore near St. Mark's Place within weeks of moving to New York City. That's it. That's what I'm going to do. I knew immediately without question. I had moved from West Virginia on a full scholarship to study acting. I loved my program and professors, but the work didn't speak to me. I was a freak, a punk, a weirdo. What acting roles existed for me in the late 90s? I didn't know political punks in West Virginia. I was just learning about d.i.y. as a subculture, but growing up with a working-class single mom, I'd been living it my whole life. That was it. This book. These artists. I'm going to do it myself. My own way. I began writing.

There were so few books that documented solo performance. I devoured Extreme Exposure, O Solo Homo. These books and the artists provided a clue, a key to a previously unknown door that would lead me down a path I did not yet understand. I read and reread the work of these artists. I watched videos where I could find them. I hustled my way into performance spaces like P.S. 122, Dixon Place (the old one), and WOW Cafe Theatre. I was mesmerized by artists like Karen Finley, Ron Athey, Whoopi Goldberg, Penny Arcade, Dred, Carmelita Tropicana, and Nao Bustamante.

Thank you Lenora Champagne for Out from Under: Texts by Women Performance Artists, Jo Bonney for Extreme Exposure, and Holly Hughes & David Roman for O Solo Homo. Thank you for creating these anthologies. For documenting what is impossible to document.

At the same time, my mind was being blown (and my life saved) by the work of radicals like Cherríe Moraga, Dorothy Allison, Angela Davis, Amber Hollibaugh, Gloria Anzaldúa, Sonia Sanchez, and many more. Self-education was an expectation in my radical communities and writers like these were considered foundational. The words of these artists and activists mentored and inspired me to create something...else. Something of my own. A new script.

I hope that some young femme, some forming creature of any age, who survived, who escaped, who decided to stay, who is scared to talk about their experiences, who feel they don't fit anywhere-that these characters and others will pick up this book and read, out loud. That they will perform these words for themselves, for their friends. There are so few scripts for us. So this is my gift to you. A collection of complicated, nuanced, and fearless writing by some of my favorite artists in the world. A script for you, and you, and you. To embody, to share. For you to lean on, devour, absorb. To invite you to create your own.

People say times are changing in media and art. Look at this show or that actor. But we have not yet arrived. Until people who are truly on the fringe are able to take center stage, consistently, sustainably, and with respect, there is still work to be done. So we make our own stages. In living rooms, warehouses, community centers, backyards. With Heels on Wheels, I performed on a bench in a tiny coffee shop in Richmond, Virginia for about eight people at a show organized by a friend I met at a protest ten years prior. I performed at an LGBT Center in New Jersey to an audience of five (including staff) because we reach out to small community spaces in towns on our route in order to stay true to the belief that art should be accessible.

These are real shows. This is what professional art looks like. This is survival. This is family. This is home.

We are the magic makers. We are the culture creators.

Introduction

Glitter and Grit are our Gay Agenda: The Heels on Wheels Story

Damien Luxe & Heather María Ács, Co-Founders & Artistic Directors
Sabina Ibarrola, Assistant Director

• •

The Heels on Wheels Glitter Roadshow

"Wait...they expected STRIPPERS?" The glares from the audience confirm that whatever they expected, this North Carolina lesbian bar audience is not happy with our fully-clothed arts. In the middle of touring the first annual Heels on Wheels Glitter Roadshow in 2010, our all-queer-femme-inine spectrum performance tour, we got an education in the social expectations applied to queer people who display femininity: just shut up and take off your clothes.

When we founded the Heels on Wheels Glitter Roadshow, Damien had a vision in which queer folks anywhere on the feminine spectrum -- fey fags, high femmes, hard femmes, dandy genderqueers & more -- could present high-quality interdisciplinary artwork that people would listen to and be inspired by that was not literary writing or burlesque, which have their own tours and niches. We, the co-founders, grew up poor and working-class, so we knew we'd have to find a way to get this work into the world on our own. So, like punks, we started independently booking and touring the U.S. (If punk dudes can do it, it can't be that hard, right?). We began in 2010, the year of this eye-opening encounter. We couldn't figure out why the venue and audience at this one gig was acting so strangely to us until we spotted the poster we'd sent them a few weeks earlier taped up on the front door. Upon further examination, we saw that Lesbian Strippers was written on it, and then scratched out.

Some of us on the tour have, in fact, been strippers in our lives and we support all sex workers. But that's not what we were touring. That's not what we told the venue we were touring. The simple fact that we sent a nice poster that featured four people of varying genders presenting a sparkly feminin-

Photo of Damien Luxe, Heather María Ács by Nicole Myles, 2011.

ity announcing a show was enough for a whole bar staff to assume that we would be naked at some point and to write that on our poster. This pervasive attitude, called sexism, is part of why we tour, why we made this show in the first place, and enough to keep us going into year seven and working on this anthology. Sexism shows up in all communities -- queer and otherwise. Making art that actively complicates what it looks like, sounds like, IS like to shamelessly and lovingly represent femininity, dandyness, fey, femme, queer, and beyond, confronts misogyny and can shift sexist assumptions. And that, my friends, is called social change: our Secret Gay Agenda, covered in glitter, powered by grit.

Heels on Wheels is working class-led and multi-racial, and our performances include artists across the spectrum of gender, sexuality, size, age, and ability, QPOC, mixed race folks, sex workers, immigrants, survivors: all fiercely political feminist queer artists who come together in a wild stage show of radical extravagance and thought-provoking glamour. Our mission emerges from an active anti-oppression, intersectional, liberatory standpoint boldly asserting: art can change our world. Sure, we put on a fabulous and fun art extravaganza that combines performing arts, music, multi-media, audience participation, and fierce looks onstage. But make no mistake, we are using cultural works to sabotage the status quo of gender, sexuality, and "feminine" appearance, replacing it with many visions and ideas of what thriving and surviving as femme folks can be. We are intentionally troubling the question: what and who are queer femmes? Queer femmes make art and organize in our communities to build power for historically-marginalized queer/lgbt stories and people. We create work about anything and everything from intersections of identity, trauma, and resilience to audacious characters and ridiculous acts of hilarity. Our femme artists are also educators, web designers, animal whisperers, sound engineers, healers, social workers, sex workers, scientists and more. Heels on Wheels is proud to highlight the expansive breadth of queer femme-inine talents.

Our shows – we've done 54 on tour plus a handful of one-offs and workshops -- are gorgeous, raucous, spirit-lifting, community-building acts of resistance that we're incredibly proud to be part of making happen. We toured annually from 2010-2014 with a rotating line-up of femme-inine spectrum artists, putting on sliding-scale, mostly all-ages and accessible, shows and workshops in community spaces, small theatres, galleries, book stores, colleges and universities, lgbt centers and youth organizations, warehouses, bars, and backyards. After a couple years of touring, and overwhelmingly positive responses, we realized it was necessary to bring our work home to Brooklyn in an ongoing format. In 2012, we decided to create a monthly artists' salon and expanded the call for performers to include artists of all genders, though we continue to center femme-inine spectrum voices. Thus, The Opentoe Peepshow: Revealing New Work by Queer Artists was born.

Sabina Ibarrola, Horrorchata, Heather María Ács, Shomi Noise, Lizxnn Disaster, Damien Luxe, Bryn Kelly, Bevin Branlandingham, Star Amerasu. Photo by Laura Turley @theglittertiger 2013

Opentoe Peepshow

Giving people access to high-quality art where they can see themselves reflected can be a transformative experience. There is a lack of financially-accessible spaces that nurture queer artists and engage queer audiences. Many of our community members are key players in a variety of art movements in NYC and beyond, but often lack the financial resources/institutional funding that allow artists to take risks in developing new work. So, we gathered in the back room of a bar called, Branded Saloon, in Prospect Heights, Brooklyn, on a tiny stage with an audience that could squish in 50 people if we got real cozy, on the first Sunday of the month for three years. Powered primarily by volunteer labor, HOW members bottomlined event logistics, stage management, tech, documentation, curation, and press/publicity, keepin it DIY and DIT: Doing It Together. We sought out new work and works-in-progress, and included a facilitated feedback session at the end of each show. This offered artists the rare opportunity to speak directly with audiences during the development stage of their work and audiences a chance to engage in the creative process. This exchange was educational and empowering. Our event even inspired some audience members to create new work themselves and go on to share the Peepshow stage!

We programmed 28 monthly events of work that was rigorous and impassioned from artists who are established and emerging, educated and self-taught, focusing on individuals who are often separated and/or overlooked by institutions in both the art world and society. Our curation and outreach is intentional in order to create line-ups that represent a wide array of intersectional identities and artistic mediums. The work we bring to our stages ranges from performance art, theatre, music, and literary arts, to puppetry, drag, acrobatics, comedy, dance and more. We always offer sliding-scale door fees with no one turned away for lack of funds, though we have had to turn people away due to lack of space! This is an issue of economic justice and access: Heels on Wheels is deeply invested in creating a community ethic in which events are financially accessible to audiences AND it is assumed/normalized that artists are paid for their work.

We have seen the impressive impact of HOW events and presence in the Brooklyn cultural landscape, ranging from increased femme visibility and intentional community, to a bolstered ethic of mutual support and collective care - resisting capitalist scarcity mentalities and heteropatriarchal tropes of feminine people in competition with each other. Our show has sparked other curators within our community to create new ongoing events using a simi-

lar workshop model. This speaks to the need and demand for these kinds of generative and creative community gatherings, yet HOW remains unique in our femme-centric gender justice mission and working class leadership, fulfilling an important role in nourishing feminine-spectrum community and increased engagement over time in issues of power and visibility.

BONUS: the Peepshow gave us a reason to wear themed outfits every month! Pizza theme was the best [see above]. Not to mention, all the ways it allowed us to make new friends and expand our artistic and social circles. Curating and promoting a monthly event is a great reason to approach someone you would like to meet. "Hey, you're so talented, I have this monthly event that I run, I'd love to have you perform!" "Check out my salon this month, the lineup is going to be amazing!" We felt like we always had something to offer that reflected the type of work we want to see in the world, and we would always have a seat to one of the best shows in town. Maybe it's because it was on a Sunday, but the Peepshow always felt like church to us. No matter how tired or exhausted we were, once we pulled our outfits and ourselves together and into that room, we felt like we were soaring. We had such an endless flow of impeccable, heart breaking and hilarious artists. Dimensions shifted, minds were blown and hearts burst open every month. At the end of every show, we left feeling tenderized and whole.

Community Events

A tour and a monthly? Why stop there!? In 2012 we co-produced an all-day event, called Beyond Visibility. Then, that June we started an Annual Cabaret to End Patriarchy, Fuck You Dad, on Fathers' Day -- which doubles as Damien's birthday party. In 2015 we added At Least You Tried, on Mothers' Day.

Anthology

That aside, organizing and touring a DIY art tour, while also curating and producing a monthly artists' salon isn't easy. Most of the work done to make it happen is volunteered, and since our door fees are always sliding-scale to make the events financially accessible we don't pull in a lot of money. Real talk: after five years of grassroots touring and events organizing, we were tired. We knew we needed to rest.

So, we took a year off from touring and decided to create a book anthology! How relaxing! Let's do something else we've never done before that takes an endless amount of planning, curating, and hours in front of the computer!

But we do it, because no matter how exhausted we were/are, we refuse to let all of this hard work and incredible, life-giving art pass by without being documented. And, we knew that if we wanted our work to be documented in any meaningful way, we would, again, have to do it ourselves. Our work and the work of the phenomenal artists that you'll find in these pages deserves the honor of being preserved as part of a legacy of fearless, vulnerable, risk-taking femmes and queer artists.

During our five years of touring and three years of a monthly salon we worked with over 300 artists and each of them brought vision and spirit to the stage. This anthology includes art in the form of writing and images from over 60 of those people.

Included you will find solo performance texts, poetry, photography, play scripts, creative nonfiction, sculpture, anecdotes from tour, pro tips, and more. Live art was, and is, the foundation of our project, so, to put that into a static form like a book is a challenge. These words are a gesture, a glimmer, a beginning, and an end. Who knows what the future holds for Heels on Wheels, but as of right now, this book marks the final project for our six years of organizing. Well, at least until the book tour...

Photo by Sophie Spinelle, banner by Lizxnn Disaster, 2012.

1

Doing it together

Creating & Making

Heels on Wheels

My Heels on Wheels Experience

by Shomi Noise

How do you describe magic?

We all experience magic differently and there are so many magical things in life so I guess answers are infinite. I'm not really talking about rabbits being pulled out of hats or witchcraft, even though rabbits and witches are pretty cool in my opinion. The magic I wanna talk about is more specific.

This magic is about sisterhood and travel. Or rather, sisterhood born out of travel. Hitting the road in a van with a bunch of rad femmes was one of the most magical things to ever happen to me.

I always dreamed of touring, but I was convinced that this activity was strictly reserved for bands. Hence, since I wasn't in a band and hadn't had the best luck being in bands in the past, the thought of touring seemed unattainable and out of reach to me.

At the time I was working at a nonprofit organization doing admin work and pretty much felt miserable on a daily basis. You know, life was kinda grey and I felt lost. Lost and wretched once again. I mean, not as wretched as when I was in college, but pretty close.

In addition to working my awful 9-5 nonprofit job, I was also DJing on the side. While fun sometimes, I must confess that DJing has never really fulfilled me creatively. My main passion has always been singing, since I can remember. For a long time, I was self-conscious of singing in public because I was never formally trained as a musician or a singer. Punk and riot grrrl did change that for me and it encouraged me to write my own songs, play guitar, write zines, etc. Yet, the hesitation to share the things I had created remained. For long periods of time I hid the things I had to say, didn't share my songs with anyone, and felt stifled by my own lack of confidence. There was also a larger narrative at play that has to do with race, class, gender, and depression. Ultimately, those are the things I would end up addressing in my art. Obviously, I had a story to tell, but I struggled to put it out there for a while.

College was a tumultuous rollercoaster of emotions for me, and on my last year of college, a few months before graduation, I tripped on shrooms, then acid, and I am convinced that these were the experiences that propelled me to write my zine titled, "Building Up Emotional Muscles." It felt good to do that, to be able to capture my story somewhere where it could be shared. Sometimes, I would go to basement punk shows and hand them out, sometimes I'd get drunk and hand them out at random college parties, or I would send them to some of my online message board queer punk friends and pen-pals. Basically I shared them with whoever was interested or whoever I was interested in when I wanted them to know more about me, and it felt good.I felt sort of accomplished and empowered.

But then, I graduated college and had to face adulthood so I briefly forgot about the zines as my young naive and idealistic self ventured into the grotesque and tragic world of the nonprofit industrial complex, ugh I'm not gonna get too much

Photo by Sophie Spinelle, 2013

in depth about that because it's a total buzzkill. Me and my best friend refer to these as the "dark years" because they were, they truly were. I was just a mess scrambling to get my shit together.

Then, I eventually met Heather and Damien through queer nightlife because I was DJing here and there all over Brooklyn, and I would see them partying or performing and I thought they were really fucking cool. I once saw them do a performance art number together where they were lesbian zombies and one of them had a pizza slice as a crotch and the other one was trying to eat it. To me this was hilarious and genius and I just thought they were the coolest femmes ever. I also saw Heather do a solo show titled "what the brain forgets and the heart denies, the body remembers..." at WOW Cafe and it was incredibly moving. She had a zine about it, which reminded me of my zine, so I went and dug out a copy and shared my zine with her at some queer party.

That same year I decided that I would push myself to be in a live band and get over my stage fright and I joined an X-Ray Spex cover band, we performed at the anti-valentine riot grrrl cover show at the now defunct Death By Audio. We had a blast and the audience got really into it. (Unfortunately the band disbanded shortly thereafter.) That night of the show though, Heather, Damien, and Lizxnn were in the audience and they loved my singing, so they decided to recruit me to go on the 2nd Heels on Wheels tour, I just didn't quite know this yet.

Heather began asking me to hang out, saying she wanted to be friends and get to know me, so we'd secretly go get hamburgers at an embarrassing fast food joint that shall not be named or instead we'd go to a Chinese restaurant by my job that gave out free wine. It was during one of these friend dates that she asked if I would ever consider touring. "Like as a DJ?" I asked. "Yeah as a DJ, but also as a singer and as a writer. You can read from your zines, which are so good, and you can sing songs," she replied.

This was a revelation to me. There was someone in this universe that believed in me, in my own words and my own sounds. But not just anyone, someone who I really thought was super talented and super cool. I just had to do it, I had to go. "Yes I'm on board. I have enough vacation time at work to do it." As soon as the words came out of my mouth I felt an excitement that is almost unexplainable. Heather was just as excited as I was. At that point I didn't even know what I would do while on tour or what to expect really. Little did I know that I was about to embark on one of the most life-changing experiences.

Travel changes you. Every time your body moves from point A to point B across large distances you become transformed. My entire life has involved a million transformations of this kind, since childhood, going from the US to Bolivia and back to the US several times. It was unsettling at first, disorienting, even traumatizing, but then in retrospect I learned to embrace it, because it made me who I am. I've also spent large amounts of time feeling stagnant and stuck in a particular place, and that feeling was even worse. In the end, deep inside my bones, I've always known that travel is there to save me. This is what happened when I joined The Heels on Wheels Glitter Roadshow.

I was embarking on a true adventure, a DIY Queer Femme Punk tour adventure full of all the glitter and sparkle you can imagine, with tons of laughter and joy, inspiration (or rather, femmespiration), solidarity, and dreaming. Of course, there were also times of frustration, rage, and tears, it is only natural. After all, magic is a complex thing.

My first tour was the most magical of them all. We went across the midwest to places like Pittsburgh, Columbus, Bloomington, Chicago, Minneapolis, Milwaukee, and Detroit.

At the time, I was having health issues and had to go on a super restrictive diet in which I couldn't eat gluten, grains, sugars, dairy, coffee, alcohol, or processed foods. Basically all I was eating was mostly nuts and greens, whenever I could find them, like a forest squirrel or something. (Forest squirrel because city squirrels be eating pizza and donuts those lucky bitches.) Anyways, while

Photo by Seth Walters, 2013

challenging and frustrating, this was also kind of comical, or at least I had to look at it that way to make it more bearable.

So I clearly remember having bought a ton of groceries to take on the trip with me. I had like two Whole Foods bags, my guitar, my DJ gear and small luggage, and I was waiting at a gas station by my house for the van aka The Dream. As I was waiting, some creepy cis-dude who worked at the station started to make small talk with me. I hate small talk in general, but small talk with cis-dudes is extra excruciating. Anyways, suddenly I saw the van coming down a hill like a unicorn flying in from the sky, down a rainbow, slide ready to rescue me. I was thinking "ok cis-dude byeeee, see ya never!" and I jumped in the van and off we went.

Lizxnn was driving, Damien was on the navigator seat. In the back were Heather and Amanda aka Panda Pong, they all welcomed me in with smiles and "yays!" At that point I really didn't know any of them that well, except for Heather who had been the one who convinced me to come along, but somehow I felt comfortable and at ease. It's like I finally belonged somewhere. Here, in this van of punk femme weirdos, I felt safe, I felt home, this was something rare for me.

On this tour my Zine, Building Up Emotional Muscles, came to life in a different way. I would narrate the contents of the Zine, but I would also sing and play guitar in between. I sang snippets of songs that had meant a lot to me growing up like "Como La Flor" by Selena, "Sliver" by Nirvana, and "Call The Doctor" by Sleater-Kinney, as well as an original song or two about resilience and self-love. I have terrible stage fright, so doing this was a challenge at first, but I also knew I had to push myself because deep down I wanted nothing more than to perform and tell my story. The more I did it, the easier it became, but also the entire Heels on Wheels crew always had my back and always gave me positive feedback and encouragement. That is a feeling that has no price. Especially since everyone else on tour was so fucking brilliant. Damien had an act where she was a pastor at the church of a femme deity named, Trisha, and she would enthrall the audience with her feminist sermons. Heather had this act called "this is what we have," full of narratives beautifully strung together where she talked about stars, stardust, life experiences, family and chosen family. Every time I would see her perform, it would bring tears to my eyes. Panda had a multimedia act where she dressed up as a consumerist robot who consumed "goods" excessively and then got sick and began puking money and at the end would break into song, singing Queen's "I want to break free." Lizxnn was like the badass manager. She would drive us everywhere, sell the merch, work the door and keep us on schedule, which sometimes was like herding cats, I'm sure. Sometimes, after our show I would bring out my DJ gear and we would have dance parties.

I would set up anywhere I could, from laundry machines to giant buckets of cat litter, and we'd dance the night away.

The show we put on was a blast, every city we went to people loved us. We were the dream team. I loved us. We were all falling in love with each other as friends and comrades. By the time we hit Detroit we became sisterwives in the backseat of the van. This is where our mutual platonic collective love was declared. A bond was made, and when we reached Philly by the end of tour we used whatever little money we had made to get matching tattoos of a heel over a wheel. It was just like that movie Foxfire, but maybe even gayer than that.

I was someone else, I felt confident, I felt like I could take on the world again. For once, I felt free. Having gone down highways from city to city with these amazing femme friends and having the chance of telling my stories to other queer weirdo freaks across the land really changed me. It fulfilled me, it made me feel validated, it gave me the strength and courage I had struggled to find elsewhere. It was then that I decided that no shitty job could ever break me, that I didn't have to put up with bullshit, there or anywhere, because in the end, this life is mine and it deserves to live the way it wants to live-making music, telling stories and being surrounded by talented magical radical creatures who share my worldview. I also learned that the world is so wide and vast and I shouldn't ever feel contained or limited by capitalism or the mainstream, which are things designed to break our spirits. It's like that thing Heather would say, "We are wild ponies that need to be free."

Not too long after the first tour I quit that shitty non-profit job and never looked back towards the Non-Profit Industrial Complex. I continued DJing and making ends meet however I could. Yes, there were many financial struggles, but I had peace of mind and less anxiety and now I also had a group of femmes who had my back.

I went on three more tours after that. There was a North-East tour where I once got really drunk in Providence and somehow ended on top of the van making a puppet talk about how she was independent and paid her own bills. Then there was a tragic and traumatic West Coast tour, which made me so much more aware about the fragility of life, but also the notion of human strength and resilience, and the final tour is where the lovely Sabina joined us and we went back to places like Detroit and Providence, and to cities in Canada like Toronto & Montreal. During that last tour I recall us running down the street in Providence on my birthday with fire sparklers in our hands, laughing and dancing in the night. That's the magic of tour, little moments like that, which become so huge in retrospect, even legendary.

We hung out at arcades and in hot tubs. Went to anarchist punk DIY spaces, youth centers, dive bars, bookstores, thrift stores, and cabins in the woods. People opened their homes and communities for us, made us dumpster-dived meals full of love, gave us amulets, let us play with their pets, sleep in their couches and beds, and gave us thank you notes for sharing our art with them. Thinking about it all makes my heart burst with joy every time. The Heels

On Wheels Glitter Roadshow has made me a better person, a stronger person, a less cynical person. It has taught me infinite things and equipped me with an arsenal of magical memories, but most importantly, it gave me friendship, femme friendships that I will cherish my entire life.

Shomi Noise, 2013. Photo by Laura Turley @theglittertiger

To Count Myself Among You

Sabina Ibarrola

When I first became a part of Heels on Wheels, I had some Very Serious Performance Artist Ambitions. I also had more than a little inner shygirl anxiety about infiltrating this gang of tough, sequined badasses. How had I fooled them into thinking I was cool enough?

Well, the truth is that if you hang around and make yourself helpful (read: available for grunt work) often enough, sometimes wonderful things can happen. After performing and volunteering at the Opentoe Peepshow in 2013, I was invited to join Heels on Wheels as one of the "Kitten Heels," part of an initiative to expand the group's leadership and offer professional development. I soon became one of the co-curators of the Opentoe Peepshow and in early 2014, Heather and Damien invited me to assistant-produce, stage manage, and perform on the 5th Annual Glitter Roadshow.

I could never have anticipated what I was getting myself into. The magic and laughter and late nights, and especially the many, *many* Google docs that would come to fill my life. Mentorship is one word for it. Sistership is another.

Over these last two years (has it only been two?), you've taught me how to write a grant, book a venue, and craft a press release. You've taught me how to curate a kick-ass lineup, as well as stage manage a bevy of artists, each with their own Very Special Feelings and detailed tech needs. You've taught me how to host a show with confidence, grace, and humor. How to make something out of nothing. How to make everything out of nothing. You've taught me how to be a Good Queen, showing up with integrity and class (even and maybe especially when inside you feel like dying). You've taught me how to layer patterns and how to tease my hair. How to pizza slap!

Together we are time witches, stretching hours and days to pack them so densely: part necessity, part pure desire to juice this life for all it's worth. We worked our asses off to make that tour come together, and even at the most difficult moments, I felt sure that it was worth it. I loved our show and felt proud of it, and I loved the in-between moments perhaps even more so. The conversations before bed, as the makeup comes off and hair goes up, or in the morning over scrambled eggs and coffee: recounting the night's adventures, and what we want to dream possible, what we love about each other, teasing and laughing. I don't know how to write it without gushing, without mixing

Photo by Mée Rose, 2014, Toronto.

my metaphors. This is my femme mentorship, and I'm fully aware of how lucky I am.

So many things spoken and unspoken. So many things that pass between us by osmosis or electricity or some other unseen hand we might call Spirit.

You've taught me about tenacity, about showing up and showing up and showing up for each other, about making a way for myself through this world. You've taught me how to keep my heart and my dreams wide open, even as this world tries to shrink us every day, tries to tell us that we are *too much*. You've taught me that too much is exactly how much I want.

You've taught me how to fix my face so that I can stare unblinkingly into all that we are up against. You have become my family. In a world poisoned by the deadly lies and power of white supremacist, ableist, capitalist heteropatriarchy, it feels like nothing less than magic, nothing less than divine protection to have found my way into this tiny pack of fierce creatures, to count myself among you. This is what we have. I don't think it can be overstated.

My Time Touring with Heels on Wheels Glitter Road Show

Bevin Branlandingham

In Early Spring, 2013 I had the opportunity to attend two gigs with Heels on Wheels at a couple of colleges in the Northeast. I have known about HOW since its inception, mostly because two of my besties (Heather Ács and Damien Luxe) conceived it. Much like the Sister Spit tour, I always wonder what it would be like to "get in the van" and bring my work around. I'm lucky that part of my income comes from going to colleges to do workshops and performances, so I get a bit of that, but never in the big group. Getting to do those two gigs was a little taste of the road-trip-meets-art-adventure without ever having to forsake a shower because there were too many people / too few showers available / too little time (the greatest road show complaint I hear from everyone who goes on any tour).

Ever relentlessly documenting my life, I made a little photo essay of our trip to Hampshire College to present a workshop on confidence (Femme-powerment–from the stage to the street) and perform as the evening entertainment for the Five Colleges Queer Conference. I had a really great time and it was an honor to be in such extraordinary company for our 16 hour adventure.

We got-in-the-van. All nine of us, Femmes, in some way or another.

There was the HOW Production team, Heather and Damien. The HOW touring artists, DJ Shomi Noise and Lixznn Disaster. The folks on the East Coast leg of the tour (me and Kirya Traber). The photographer for the day, Nicole, and the amazing Cristy Road, catching a ride with Heels on Wheels to go to her own workshops/readings.

Our fearless driver & navigatrix was Lixznn disaster & our road photographer was Nicole Ayla Myles.

I learned early on that Lizxnn drives that van like a boss. Seriously, not at all intimidated by the size and power of that huge van, as we rolled over curbs as needed and got where we needed to go (Northampton, MA) safely.

I went with Damien Luxe when she bought "The Dream," the name given to this huge light blue beast of a conversion van with bucket seats, a fold down queen bed in the back and track lighting for ambient evenings. Oh, and a VHS tape player with a mini TV and a whole collection of old movies and porn. Thrift shop treasures!

Being in the van was a pretty amazing experience. Imagine how wonderful, inspirational and loud it is to be surrounded by chatty Femmes. It is the most at home I ever feel. When my "too much" is exactly as much as everyone else's. We learned that all of us had been raised with working class single moms. We had a spontaneous performance art moment where those of us who had no dad were told by those who had bad dads all the things we wished we'd heard growing up.

For example:

"You're so pretty exactly as you are."

"Here, let me show you how to build a bookshelf."

"I support you growing up to be a working artist."

"I love you unconditionally, no matter what."

(As an aside, it's really powerful work to reparent yourself as an adult when you learn what unconditional love can look like.)

We decided we were going to perform that at "Fuck You Dad," Damien's annual father's day/birthday party performance show.

Ever multi-faceted touring artists, Shomi Noise, who would DJ later that night, did some casual community organizing using the wifi hot spot on her phone.

As a former drag king troupe producer, I am familiar with traveling with a group of folks and creating itineraries. We were given explicit timing instructions of when we would leave and could expect to return. We knew it would be a long day. Our lunch stop ended up being a Dunkin Donuts in the middle of who-knows-where Massachusetts because of timing.

They were pretty amused with us flowing in and out, getting breakfast sandwiches and using the bathrooms in turn. It was just so incredible to roll up to the various pit stops we made with this group of Femmes nine deep. Being a weirdo out in the world is pretty usual for me, but being a weirdo with other weirdos is a spectacle is empowering beyond words. That's Femme visibility.

We used our time in the van to work through the workshop we were going to give that day on finding self-confidence using the stage, assigning who would present which parts. It was great to get to create with those amazing minds.

Bevin Branlandingham, 2013. Photo by Laura Turley @theglittertiger

There was considerably less gear in the back of the van than we would have had if the tour was for more than a 16 hour trip with no overnight.

After getting to the college early, we went to a crazy natural foods store in Northampton (though I'm not really sure which town we were in since I wasn't navigating or paying attention) that had more fruit and Easter candy than I expected to see. After snacks we got into the conference and set up for our workshop.

I always like to give folks the option to follow us on the internet, so I created this intensely detailed situation on the white board during our workshop with all of our hashtags and usernames on social media.

At the beginning of the workshop we each told a two minute story of our journey to self confidence. I like to begin my workshops and performances at colleges telling people how glad and grateful I am to do this work. I explain that when I was in college if I had access to seeing a queer fat femme teach me about self-confidence (or, let's be honest, just seeing a queer fat femme) it would have changed my entire life.

After the workshop we made our way over to this barn where there would be the Heels on Wheels performance and a QUEER PROM.

We spent some time backstage eating dinner and getting ready. Heather and I did yoga stretching where their financial aid office is. No doubt, where a lot of stressed out students line up every semester like I once did. I tried to invoke some healing and patience energy to those students.

Being a performer means that the term "backstage" is a loose idea that includes kitchens, storage rooms, alleys behind bars, bathrooms, a sheet tacked up to the ceiling bisecting a part of the room that is the performance space and many, many other weird permutations.

Buying merch at shows is a fabulous way to support touring artists. Heels on Wheels always includes a merch mall staffed by Lizxnn.

It's impossible to summarize the work presented by the HOW artists that night, but here's my attempt to give you the diaspora. Heather did her performance "This is What We Have," about adventures, freedom, longing and stardust. Damien did her piece "Exorcise" a comedic act about a process for embodiment from trauma. It's very empowering. Shomi did some singing and storytelling about immigrant adolescence and coming out. And Kirya did this incredible piece using Beyonce moves about growing up, gender and body hair. My piece is about what it is like to spend 34 years in a body bigger than what society deems "average," and I think it's a good piece for college shows because it's very body oppression 101, personal and empowering.

After the show we hung out listening to DJ Shomi Noise on the decks. We went out to the van for a brief hang out and imagined that we were sailing through the air in the van with Cristy Road's illustrations of the night sky floating by us.

We arrived home at 5:30 in the morning. Getting a little lost in some giant state park and only had to stop once so someone could pee behind a car.

I can't tell you how much love I have in my heart for all of the artists involved with Heels on Wheels. They mean so much to me personally and as a queer femme in the world. Heels on Wheels is an amazing organization that is working-class led, feminist and femme empowering. I'm so glad I had the opportunity to mini-tour with them!

This is the Moment

Andrea Glik

· ·

This is the moment. This is the moment when everything comes together and I make sense. On this block, in this bar, in this world. This is the moment when the magic begins.

This is the moment, is when I see them. Jumping off their bikes in kitten heels. Thrusting open the doors of the van with wigs whiskey leather boots tumbling out behind them.

It happens for the first time.

I'm 20 years old and haven't been to a gay bar outside my hometown. I'm nervous I won't get in because I'm underage. I'm nervous because I haven't met anyone who felt like my people yet. I'm nervous because I don't know who my people are because I don't know who the fuck I am yet.

It begins. A glimpse of glitter down the crowded block. And I am hit with it. It is sequins and eyeliner and suitcases full of costumes and tinctures and treasures. It is wrapped in a leopard print scarf and is shoving a man out of the way to get to me. It is femme-ily.

"Hey. Let's get inside away from these normals" she says.

We walk into the bar. It's too early for the bouncer to be there so I get in no problem.

Up a flight of stairs. It's a dark lit room with a stage. My first of many.

"This is Andie, she's doing merch."

I feel underdressed in my black hoodie. I'm hiding in it.

I think maybe I'm done hiding.

I sit behind the merch booth and watch explosions of femininity on stage that open something up inside me and make room. Make room for feeling. For magic.

Being taken in by a queer family is like coming home to people who have always been waiting for you, you just didn't know it yet. It is an old practice, survival strategy.

That moment. That moment I was taken in by a wolf pack of powerful femmes opened up a world for me.

This is the moment.

When I walk into the bar/coffee shop/ party/ art show/ restaurant and look around the room for them. "Hey you must be with them" someone says and points to a table of colorful hair and laughter and hands pounding on the table and something magical in the making. "Yeah, I am."

Bring Us The Dime, our beginnings

Damien Luxe

· ·

After the 2010 Heels on Wheels Glitter Roadshow, Heather and I were hanging out with our friend Helaine and recounting the tour.

"We drove all the way to Austin! It ruled, except everyone but Damien paid their own way to fly home."

"We had a night off in New Orleans, and I took a makeout break in the van with my lover, the merchpup, and laid them out on a crinkly bed of trader joe's bags." I grinned at Heather.

"Yeah but we were so glad to have those snacks because we were barely scraping through, moneywise, on the tour, but we made it work. Damien did not trash the snacks, at least." Side-eye from Heather anyway.

Helaine was beloved to us because she was both enamored with queer performance artists, and she also came up working class/poor like Heather and I. She wanted to know everything -- and by everything, she meant: How much and how?

As the resident dad and financial executive of Heels on Wheels, I was thrilled to go into detail. (As a raised-poor person, I love talking about money.) Well, I explained, to create the March 2010 tour, Heather and I had started in January of the same year. Fuck it, we're doing this, she said. Fuck it, I'm not working right now, I'd said: Unemployment Insurance has been the best artist grant I could have ever hoped to receive. Fuck it, it's time, we said.

We got on our email, facebook, myspace, and phones, and started researching venues, calling friends of friends and booked, promoted, and planned a tour that drove from New York City to Austin. We got one university gig that included two people who weren't on that tour and got them flown in. We got a speaking gig! At Duke University! Everything else was community venues, local lesbian bars, and art galleries. We sent press releases and phone and email spammed the south to the best of our ability.

At some point, we realized we needed to bring in the grown femme tools, though: IT WAS TIME TO CROWDFUND THIS THING!

I'd calculated our gas costs for the van at around $400, and our food costs per person for five people for eight days at $80 per person. What could go wrong with a tour paying $10/day for food and covering travel one way?

That's good, we'll ask for $800 -- it's exactly what we need to make sure we don't have to spange for gas or eat each other's makeup on the road. Yeah! I'd argued, "We're not trying to be like those people who fundraise and don't earn the trust of their donors by like buying excess things like toilet paper. We're gonna deliver on our crowdfund promise!"

In my first-year never-done-this-before calculations, I didn't think about prosaic things like oil changes or the fact that people eat more than once a day or that we'd need pens and to print. In my resolute scarcity, I didn't calculate in the scale of work, or the time put in to make the tour, or the time on the road. We'd get paid at our sliding-scale shows! I figured. Art's about adventure not profit! After debating if we should even do a fundraiser, Heather agreed, and we kept moving.

At this point in the retelling, Helaine asked something to the effect of how much we worked on the tour -- and so we did the numbers. We figured we hovered over our laptops 20-30 hours a week for seven weeks, and then were on call as organizers and logistics and performers and bookers for 12-15 hours a day for ten days

... wait that's like 280-380 hours of work.

"But, you all made money, right?" Helaine asked.

Heather and I looked at each other. "Weeeeeeellllll."

Between costs and splitting profit between the other performers, we'd each cleared about $40.

As the resident dad and financial executive of Heels on Wheels, I am very fast at math: Wait, that's means we made $0.10 an hour for tour.

A dime! Heels on Wheels profited us one dime, per hour, for starting it. That's the real DIY story my friends.

The three of us looked at each other, the way people who understand the wealth that was in that $40 we walked away with, how precious that income was, how it was spent with pride. We looked at each other knowing that was more than just ten cents, even if it was just a dime....

"You know, Helaine," Heather began, "Someday we're going to do something with that dime."

"Yeah, someday, we'll be sitting in our office," -- we both began talking,

-- "on the top floor of a tall building --

-- looking out a wall of windows --

-- sitting at a polished mahogany desk --

-- with a tiger skin rug --

-- no, with a real tiger who likes us! --

-- no, a real submissive in a tiger outfit who wants us to step on them --

-- and we'll be meeting with some femmes who are coming up --

-- and we'll want to explain this story --

-- and I'll stand up and ring a buzzer --

-- no, I'll swirl around in my chair and clap twice and say *Helaine! Bring us the dime!* --

-- and it will come out, in a glass container --

-- laid on a bed of velvet and gold --

-- and we'll look at it --

-- we'll touch it --

-- and we'll laugh."

Photo by Ally Picard, 2009. Used for the first, 2010 tour poster.

2
Making Something out of Nothing

The Invocation

Kama La Mackerel

• •

I invoke our mothers, our grand-mothers, and our female ancestry—

I invoke the caretakers, teachers, mentors and warrior women of history—

I invoke the women and femmes of history, those who suffered, those who died, those who lived, those who fought, and those who resisted —

I invoke the femmes of all genders, bloods, ages, lineages, generations of witches and fighters who infuse the universe with love, rage and magic—

I invoke my great-great grandmother, and all those women who came on a ship, from the continent to the island, hands tied, bodies battered, minds resilient—

I invoke the women who never made it to the shores, the warriors who had to die, their dark flesh an offering to the creatures of the sea, their blood a sacrifice that continuously flows in our oceans, our seas, our rivers and all our water bodies—

I invoke my transcendent Hindu lineage and those generations of women who navigated patriarchy and colonialism on sugar-cane plantations—

I honour my mother, Vimala Devi, teacher, mentor, nurse, care-taker, inspiration and embodiment of femme power—

I honour her mother, Danapakion, woman whose resilience knew no bounds and whose story still remains untold, repressed, forgotten, chained to the silence of history—

I invoke strength and wisdom from Goddess Kali Ma, redeemer of the Universe, Goddess of Time, Change and Destruction, Goddess with bloodied eyes and a black tongue, who cuts patriarchy and wears it as an accessory around her neck, who steps on misogyny and crushes it with the strength of her foot...

That real, imagined, spiritual lineage, past, present and future, those women and femmes who push the universe to be always greater than itself, better than itself, I invoke, and I honor.

this is what we have...

Heather María Ács

- -

Preset: large brown paper bag with collected items, chair USC (up stage center), coupons taped under chair, faerie/xxxmas lights wrapped in a ball, paper bag with star coupons

Begin-I walk among the audience with a crumpled, brown paper bag, and ask people if there's anything they want to get rid of or don't need in their pockets or purses. I take whatever they will give me, and put it in my bag. I walk to the center of the playing space and dump out the contents. I play the game "this is what we have." I hold up each object, examine it, and say, "this is what we have." After I've gone through ten objects or so, I end with a final, "this is what we have. this is all that we have," referring to everything that is spread across the playing space. I do not throw out items after a performance, so the items accumulate over the course of tour.

1

Quite a long time, and not so very long ago, I moved from West Virginia to New York City to study theatre. I was obsessed with New York City and wanted, more than anything, to escape the small-town mindset that had been making me miserable for my entire angsty, teenage life. The fear of being trapped in my hometown propelled me forward, and despite my wild and unruly teenage ways, finally manifested, no femmeifested, in the scholarship my single mom incessantly reminded, would be my only ticket out of state. Fuck yes. This was actually happening. My best friend from West Virginia grew up in a holler where she was made fun of and harassed for her light skin and mixed race background. As she puts it, she was constantly reminded by all sides, that she didn't belong anywhere. By the time I met her she'd dropped out of highschool, moved in with a musician friend of mine, and I thought she was the smartest, coolest person I knew. She moved to New York City 3 months after I did-basically, to hang out with me. I had a full scholarship to study acting. She had a G.E.D., a sic Chelsea cut, and a suitcase we hid under my bed. We were escape artists-ready to break free from the gravitational pull of the mountains where we'd grown up and make our way into the unknown universe.

2

(pick up tangle of faerie lights as the nebula)

Nebulae are the birthplaces of stars. A nebula is basically a cloud of dust and gas. Inside the nebula, gravity causes the dust and gas to "clump" together, forming a "proto" or baby star.

A developing star is not very stable. In order to achieve life as a star, the forming star will need to achieve and maintain equilibrium, a balance between gravity pulling atoms toward the center and gas pressure pushing heat and light away from the core.

3

(wrapping lights around chair)

We told my new college roommates that my best friend lived in Bensonhurst, Brooklyn, so it was too far for her to take the train home late at night from the school housing where we lived in Manhattan. That's why she stayed over a lot. They had no idea where Bensonhurst was, so it was the perfect lie. Bensonhurst is a neighborhood deep into Brooklyn, almost at the end of the line near Coney Island. I only knew this because I'd met these spooky, punk girls on St. Mark's Place and that's where they lived. They were sisters and their parents went back and forth between Brooklyn and São Paulo, so they had the house to themselves part of the time. The younger sister was the responsible one and some nights she would drive us from whatever bar or show we were hanging out at on the Lower East Side back to their place to sleep. *(Sit on chair as passenger seat, looking out the window.)* If I could keep from passing out long enough, I would be rewarded with a vision of the glittery city slowly disappearing on the other side of the river as we crept our way into Brooklyn

For a while we were into playing this game we called, "this is what we have." At any point throughout the evening, someone could call out, "this is what we have!" We'd stop whatever we were doing, run to the middle of the room, and start emptying our pockets and bags *(do this)*. We'd look at all the items and say "this is what we have, this is all that we have," pretending that the pile in front of us were our only known possessions in the entire universe. We were weird girls who hoarded tiny items anyway, so at any given point we might have a pile that included a handful of safety pins, some rubber bands, several tiny dinosaurs in various colors, a plastic chicken nugget with purple eyeshadow (a femme), a laser keychain, and change that usually equaled less than 2 dollars. New people would join and disperse throughout the evening, so our little constellation of items was a new surprise every time.

4

Scientists identify the birth of a star as the moment that nuclear fusion begins and the star begins to radiate energy into space. Basically, the moment the star begins to shine is the actual moment that it's born.

5

Our favorite bar, of course, was the Mars Bar, a notorious dive bar on the lower east side, which at that particular moment in time, mostly consisted of construction workers, punks, and british dudes. It had the grossest bathrooms I'd ever seen in my life. We loved it. We went there almost every night. One night, we were trying to see some band play on the west side of town. They wouldn't let us in because they were checking id's for once. After getting in a fight with the door guy, we said fuck it-let's chug some 40s and go to the Mars Bar. On our way, we passed a parking lot full of grocery carts surrounded by a fence that was 4 or 5 feet tall. It's clear what happens next, right? We scramble over or crawl under the fence, and somehow liberate one of the carts by hoisting it over the fence and onto the sidewalk. *(Use chair as shopping cart here. I play my friend pushing the cart.)* I jump in the grocery cart and my friend proceeds to run as fast as she can, pushing me in the cart from the west village to the east village to the amusement and annoyance of the people on the streets of New York City on some random, magical night. We went faster and faster, picking up speed, the air hit hidden spots on my teeth cuz I was smiling so big and laughing so loud. The wheels on the concrete started giving off sparks. Things began to burst and snap, little synaptic explosions firing off through my whole body, and suddenly there was light *(plug in faerie lights, which light up around the chair)*, so much light, we'd become luminescent. *(Climb up to stand on chair and spin in a slow circle.)*We flew through solar systems, multidimensional atmospheres, and horsehead nebulae. Our tiny hooves tucked tight in our black leather boots. Kicking up dust across the concrete cosmic sky, destination: Mars...

6

(abrupt change, jumping down off of the chair to sitting, pull coupon section of newspaper from underneath the chair, begin tearing and ripping the paper. The movement is not exact, it gives only gives the essence.)

My mother sits, alone in the house, perpetually clipping coupons. She does this for me. She does this for us. It is an act of survival, an act of love. I know this, but...inside the most shame-filled part of my teenage heart...this image, is a gravitational field from which I fear I'll never escape...

The thought of sitting, waiting, wishing-not even wishing. *(Pause ripping. More conversational to audience.)* My mother didn't play the lottery-she was too practical, pragmatic. There was no reason to waste money-this is what we have, just this.

There's no Prince Charming on the way, no miracle. No one is coming to save us. You do what you have to do. This is what we have.

(Begin ripping the coupons again. The emotion informs the rhythm of the tearing. The pace builds.) You should feel lucky to go to the same job every day, where someone else tells you what to do. You do their tasks, help with their career, their dreams, putting your good face on, smiling, mmhmming them. You come home to no one but your children, watch television with the cats. No social life, no lovers, no one to say "you're special," "you're beautiful," "I love you," "Let's dance...." And no matter how much or how hard you work, it's never enough. Work. You work for your children, you work for your boss, the heat and light energy leaving your body by the moment, the hard, reflective work of shining your light on everyone except yourself, leaving you with a core of iron and rock...

I would rather, I would rather do anything...

No. I am going to do everything....*[Throw scraps into the air.]*

7

I was scared. Which meant I had to do it. In the last days of one summer, quite a long time and not so very long ago, I hitchhiked along Highway 1 from LA to San Francisco, San Francisco to Eugene, Oregon. I'd been traveling on fake greyhound bus passes my friend made for us, but this was different. Truly free. We traveled in 2s or 3s, I never traveled alone, and if anyone felt sketched out at any time, we trusted our guts and waited for the next ride. Lots of people picked us up cuz they saw us as "girls," out on our own. Sometimes, they were relieved to see that one of us was a guy once we got in the car, other times, they referred to all of us as "she."

Sometimes they'd just motion for us to jump in the back of the truck and we wouldn't have to talk to anyone. Sometimes that was the best. Just wind. And open sky.

There were crazy hippies, religious fanatics, a Hollywood stuntman turned trucker, and a guy who gave us a freshly caught, 4 ft salmon when we were just about to run out of food. One time, we got picked up by a limousine! (I am not making this up!) The guy who drove it gave romantic sunset tours along the ocean. We got to ride in the back like a real limo ride! The ceiling was covered with glow in the dark stars and planets, and when Guns n Roses came on the radio, he smiled at us in the rearview mirror and cranked it all the way up, as loud as it would go! *(Move to sit in chair, leaning back.)*

One night, along the Oregon coast, I laid on my back, staring up at a night sky full of stars. So many stars and constellations crowning my head. I thought about how my mother would tell me the story of stardust....

*****Quite a long time, and not so very long ago, we were born of a massive star. After shining for billions of years, a star's core turns to iron, and it explodes as a Supernova. Gold, lead and uranium are produced, and shoot off into space with the force of the massive explosion. *(Reach for small paper bag and pull out a chain of paper stars, cut from the same coupon section of the newspaper.)* The remaining parts of the dying star mix with other matter and form new stars, some with planets. That's how our earth was formed and why it is rich in these heavy elements. *(Begin tearing stars from the chain and giving them out to the audience.)* The iron in your blood, and the calcium in your bones, were all forged in such stars. We are born of a massive star. We are made of stardust.*****

I thought about all the people I know and love, the ways we're connected, the space in between. The stars move, and so do we. I could see us up there, recognize our faces. The night sky, an obsidian mirror of our sparkling lives lived on the simple water and clay of the earth below. Our destinies constantly in motion, intertwined, shared.

On the bluffs above us, I could see the lights from the windows of the rich houses-sprawled mansions looming over us on the coastal cliffs, teetering on the edge of nothing. They had no idea we were down there, that we even existed. I thought, I will never be famous. I will never be rich. No one is coming to save me, to discover me. I will not break. I looked up at the night sky, a symphonic movement of planets, stars, constellations. I breathed in ocean and dozing firewood, feeling so very lucky to be alive. So thankful to be my mother's daughter. So very happy, to be exactly where I was, in that salty, luminous night.

8

(Wrapping glowing faerie lights around my body)

This is what we have. This is all that we have.

We are excavating the dust of stars.

We are the magic makers.
(ask audience gently, "Right?", urging them to respond, "Yes.")

We are the culture creators.

This is what we have.

sometimes what we have is not enough.

sometimes what we have is far too much-we cannot bear the weight.

sometimes what we have, is just right.

sometimes we have absolutely no idea what we have.

but others do. and don't. and do. and so do we.

the stars move, and so do we.

we are their mirror, and they ours.

we are excavating the dust of stars.

hold each other tightly

this is what we have

Illustration by Cristy C. Road, 2012.

My first performance

"You ain't nothing but a hound dog, crying all the time."
Does anybody, recognize that? Recognize that? Elvis? Elvis Presley?

That was from my repertoire from when I was six years old. It was 1977, San Francisco, I was six years old, and I was a ham. I was the youngest of nine children and we lived in a poor neighborhood in a hotel in San Francisco, the Tenderloin. My mom, Dorothy, grew up in the '30s and '40s and was obsessed with movies, with movie stars. She read all the gossip magazines, she knew every movie star, she took me to old movies all the time. And, I was a ham. And so those two things came together. And she really believed in my talent because I was always performing for my family, these impressions, one of which was Elvis. And you know, and so, one day, you know she really believed in my talent she always was like, "Oh maybe you should go somewhere, talk to that guy, go somewhere, you'll get discovered!" She was like, "Go do this, you'll get discovered." You know, it was like in the movies in the 40s, they're going cross country and they're doing a musical and they "get discovered." So that was in her head, that was in my head.

So one day I said to my mom, "I don't want to go to school today." Six years old. She says, "Fine with me." But, she said, "You can't go to work with me, you're going to have to go to work with your brother." This was the same brother that would let me put shaving cream on my face next to him in the mirror and he would shave and I would pretend to shave. My brother Gerry. So, he worked as a janitor in a night club, in a sort of seedy part of San Francisco. It was called The Palms. I don't know why my mom didn't have a problem with me going there and missing school...that's a whole other story we'll get into another time.

So I go to work with my brother and I, you know, I'm hanging out, looking for stuff to do. I've helped him clean a bit, done a little labor and I'm getting a little bored. I've downed about three Shirley Temples by this time, I'm starting to feel it, I'm a little amped. I see there's a stage at the Palms. And I have in my head, "You might get discovered." In my own little workings, I don't talk about it with anybody, I got this going in my head, I got my Shirley Temples in my system. And I see that the owner has shown up, the owner of The Palms. So I decide, I march right up to the stage, I get on stage, I don't tell anybody, I don't warn anybody, I don't discuss. I do my whole act. My whole act that I've been entertaining my family with for some time. And you know I'd never performed on stage at this point. And I get up, I'm doing my act, I do Elvis, I do my Mae West and I go,

"My left leg's Christmas, and my right leg's New Years, why don't you come up and see me between the holidays."

Yeah. Yep. Yes. I never knew why that was so funny at that time, I just knew that whenever I did it, it killed. And I got a lot of laughs, and all my brothers and sisters would be like, "Do the thing with the Mae West," all the time. I think it was extra funny, perhaps because I was such a little tomboy. A tiny butch, if you will. I think it was and still is one of my most convincing performances of femininity, so to speak. So I was like, I'm doing my Mae West, I'm doing my whole thing. Then I get into the impressions of the men, which I was at ease doing as a tiny masculine. So, I do my Chuck Berry rock and roll bit, "Go Johnny, Go." Keep in mind this is a six year old doing this. And I do my John Wayne. So I'm doing it!. I'm up on stage! I'm up on the stage at The Palms! I'm sweating, the owner's like, "What the hell is going on?" My brother's holding a broom and looks up like, "What the fuck? She just skipped a step, I'm over here sweeping the floor and she goes right to the stage."

So the owner comes up to me and goes, "Listen kid, I want to book you. For Valentine's day. You're going to open for a rock band called Pearl Harbor and the Explosions." Now, Pearl Harbor and The Explosions was a San Francisco semi-famous punk bed led by a Filipino and German woman who went by "Pearl Harbor." It's an honor to be associated even in a small way with a tiny bit of 70's punk history. I always wonder if she remembers that night... So, my name's Drae but when I was little, I went by my birth name, Andrea. So the owner said, "We're going to call you, "San Andrea's Fault, San Francisco's own little earthquake. AND I'm going to pay you five dollars."

Woah. So I was like, "Woah, ah, I've been discovered. I have been discovered!"

So i'm very excited, obviously, and you know, we're very poor, and I'm thinking like, I'm going to get us all out of that situation, with my talent, my impersonations, my three or four minute act.

So I go home, tell my mom, "I'm doing a show! "

So now, this is like, to us, my 'big break'. So, we're getting ready for it. Some weeks go by, we're going to some thrift stores, buy some feather boas. We're preparing, talking about, you know, all these things.

So it comes , the night of the show comes. I go on, it's a packed house, packed house, San Francisco 1977 or 78? Polk Street. My mom's way in the back. She can't even get in. My brother's at the bar, incredulous, shaking his head, like, "Are you serious? What the hell?" You know, I get on stage, I do my act, and I close with my John Wayne, "Round them chairs in a circle, pilgrims, and get ready for "Pearl Harbor and the Explosions!"

And it kills! They go bananas, the whole place. It's very exciting!

So, I get off stage and the owner says, "I was going to give you five dollars, but you did so good, I'm going to give you twenty dollars."

And it was, you know, I didn't even know twenty dollars existed at that time. You know, it was the 70s, that was like a hundred dollars at that time, and I was six years old, so I didn't even get the concept.

I ran back to my mom, I'm waving the twenty dollars in the air excitedly. So then I took the twenty dollars and I took my mom and brother out to a diner for Valentine's day dinner that night. And that was my very first performance, and I don't know if I was discovered or if I discovered performing, but I'm here right now, still doing it, so "come up and see me sometime."

Photo by Nicole Myles, 2013

Maiden, Sexy Aunty/Shark Mom, Crone: Working Class Femme of Color Elderhood

Leah Lakshmi Piepzna-Samarasinha

I am almost 40. I look in the mirror and like what I see. I look kind of like Amber did when I met her. I look prettier than I did when I was 21 because I have made it all the way to this earth. Even though there are still times suicide visits and I wonder about taking root amidst the stars, I have chosen to stay. Figured out how to stay. This is not an automatic. I put on weight, put meat on my bones, enough to enjoy a spanking and survive the lean years and lean into them with my fat. It has been a long, long time since I have had to see my abusive family. There have been stormy years and shining ones, ones where everything lined up and fell apart again. ones where everything was full of success on the outside and struggle on the inside and I was still living the questions. I sure did get to know myself.

I spent a lot of the month of October being almost 40 and lying on my bed clutching my sheets in a panic. I'd thrown my back out so bad just before I had to move. I was used to white knuckling my back pain when it hit every few months and I am a master at breathing with my chronic pain, but I was in this new big pain every.single.day. and it made everything harder in a new way than it'd ever been.

I took my friend's T3s and I breathed and I walked very carefully and I lay in bed and thought- I am almost 40 and I am not gaymarried and I do not work at a social service nonprofit or a university and I have no family money and I have never had access to any and I am disabled and even though by the grace of the goddess of hustle I have been able to make a living I do not have a retirement fund, my wealth has gone to paying my time off when I am sick and everyone's rent when they are about to get evicted and even still there have been plenty of times when I have had 47 dollars to my name, or overdraft, or nothing. I do not own a house or much besides a beautiful old busted car and a computer and wardrobe and my own freedom and independence. And though I have a sweetheart, I am unpartnered. I had all the feels of undesireability, all my oldest ghosts about being ugly and undesireably dancing hard in my head. Saying, I am almost 40 and not "cashed in", which is such a horrible term with such deep roots when you pull them apart.

I don't talk to my parents but I have a big family. I have at least six people who call me akka (big sister in Tamil.) I have one person who calls me Magic Shark Aunty. I have one person who calls me Shark Mom. I have a lot of brothers, sisters, siblings, cripfam, femmefam, little sisters, cousins, a life-twin, sweethearts, exes and enemies. I have fam I've never met in person but we trade tips and meds and lifegiving survival on online sick and disabled queer groups. I take my responsibilities to my family very seriously. In season 2 of Sons of Anarchy (SPOILER ALERT) when Gemma tells Tara, "God put me here to be a fierce mother" after she survives her gang rape, I related.

One thing I figured out along the way is that family means just about everything to me. This might seem ironic to some who know that I walked away from my abusive parents almost 20 years ago, or it might make perfect sense. My birth family still means everything to me, even if the choices I made to walk out of hell mean we don't talk or celebrate birthdays or Christmas. My chosen queer family- the ones I chose, the ones who choose me, the ones where we chose each other for a time and then parted, the ones who are family in the way that you just can't stand them because of what they remind you of, including yourself, family like family who hasn't talked for 10 years or will always have a fistfight at the same dinner table- they mean everything to me. They mean it in how I throw Thank God We Have Each Other Parties for 45 with my sister, how she and I look like white and brown versions of each other from behind, same curls, same laugh. They mean it in how I hold and let go of people I have loved deeply who didn't stay forever. It is not the same way I dreamed queerfam when I was newly free, 22 years old and run away, pinning all my hopes on those strange ideas of family and community I had never seen.

It is not automatic, the revolution will take care of it. I know how we can and do betray each other. But I also know how we are learning not to.

I can remember being 21 just fine. Skinny girl, big boots, sharp mind with lightening and thunder in it, barely here, no guarantee or clue how I was gonna stay.

When I was 21, I was Amber Hollibaugh's intern. I don't remember how I got that job, but there were definitely no backroom deals or connections because I was way too depressed and awkward to know how to do any of that and I don't think any internet because it was 1995. I think I probably called up the Lesbian AIDS Project, where she worked, and left a message asking if I could volunteer. I wanted to do whatever I needed to do in order to hang out in the same room and help out this sexworking working class Roma daddy in a motorcycle club femme AIDS activist whose words felt the most like home and heaven when I read them than any other queer theory. She was 49. I was 21. I was way too small, barely on the planet, tight black slip and jeans and big boots and a huge clot of brown girl curls I didn't know how to manage. I didn't know how to put on eyeliner and, surrounded by clones shaved headed dykes and depression, I didn't have anyone to ask. I knew how to read books in my tiny room, smoke cigarettes, write, haltingly, on a Mac Classic with 2 megabites of memory, poems I didn't show anyone, read books standing up in A Different Light's poetry section. I had found the femmes-found Minnie Bruce Pratt's S/he and shoplifted my copy from the Tower Books on 4th (I knew all the tricks from working shipping and receiving in another bookstore.) I read Stone Butch Blues and related to Jess's depression and loneliness. I found Chrystos' poetry and hung out tight to every volume.

Amber blew me away. She was everything I wanted to be- so femme and so fierce and so on it and such a great organizer. When she opened her mouth, gems fell out and kept waterfall dragoning. She definitely knew how to put on her eyeliner. I just wanted to sit at her feet and try not to fuck up. I fucked up a few times. Of course I fucked up. In the meantime, I was happy to just buy the tokens and hand out the condoms and safer works kits and listen to her. I remember one time when I said, "You're like a mother to us all" and rearing back as she snapped her eyes at me. I had fucked up. She didn't want to be the mother of anyone. She was probably sick of being called "elder" in her 40s, the same way many folks who are part of my grown up 90s generation feel now. Our elders are all too often disapeared or dead. We don't want to be elders in our 30s and 40s partly because of internalized ageism, but also because we mourn the elders who disapeared and are scared shitless we will become one of them. And as femmes we fear that getting older means losing any of the desireability we have fought hard to carve out for our bodies.

I fucked up. But Amber still quirked the side of her mouth at me when she looked at me. She bought me coffee sometimes. Said hey, why don't we do a joint interview for this femme book that's coming out, where we do an older femme/ younger femme thing? and got me the very first time I got published in a book, ever. When we went to the Barnes and Noble next door to the office and turned on the tape deck, she opened her mouth and all the words she'd lived came waterfalling out. Femme and class and mixed race and abuse and SM and Roma and stripping and organizing for the Communist Party and being lovers with Leslie Feinberg in Toronto in 1971 before there was a trans movement and crossing the only picket line she ever crossed in her life, a picket line of anti sex feminists with signs with her name on them at the Scholar and the Feminist conference in 1983. And I just shut the fuck up and listened and said thank you jesus yes, thank you for letting me be in the same room as you.

Now I am 39 and Amber is 68. We co keynoted at the Sydney Femme Conference last year. She has diabetes and I have fibro. We talk- about writing, about revolution, about class and books and the impossibility of getting funded if the purpose of your organization is to destroy capitalism. She had to move. I had to move. We changed the world. A little. A lot. Some things haven't changed. Sime things we don't know about yet. I have people who look at me like I looked at her, and I have lots of advice and stories and an ache inside where I know how much I still don't know.

We were never meant to survive, and no one taught us how to age. Our families work til they're dead. Our queer family die in their forties, fifties, sixties, twenties, teens. I have been wondering about queer working class femme disabled life maps that do not involve buying into the system and do not end in poverty, loneliness, alone, nursing home lockup, death too young. What does it mean- to not cash in and settle job/ gay marriage/ house in the east end with a mortgage you have to pay? To not be like your cousins who are working at Walmart, but not to have some fancy university job either and to not know what the in between is? If you work at Walmart or have a university job, to worry about when you will be fired from it for being too Black, too fat, too crazy? To know that that job may make you more disabled or crazy? If you are sick and disabled, to know that you may get sicker and more disabled as you age? If you have a little bit of money, to know that it is not yours, you are holding up your whole family and community and also the debt that got you there?

In the midst of my fear about the future, I went to a working class femmes group on Facebook for wisdom. 29 likes. Of course everyone could relate. One femme, Sossity Chiricuzio, said,

"Now i'm about to turn 44, and i'm still working poor, still dealing w/ chronic pain, treading debt waters and trying to hang on to an 'affordable' rental. however, i've also learned to center my worth on my own well being (whatever that is, and however well i can manage it day to day varying, of course), and to spend my time and energy w/ people who loop it back to me... i choose yes family (created and some born to), no children, yes radical, no traditional. i buy a lottery ticket now and again, but have no expectations of owning a home and no plan for retiring. i am surprised to have lived this long, and at how many people i've gained and lost along the way. i am going to do my best to live as long as i can, as well as i can, having the best sex and food and effect on the world as i possibly can. my birthday present to myself when i turned 40 was to grow out my beard - something that has presented a challenge to me almost every day since, but it felt right. felt magic. crone magic. fuck you it's my face magic. fuck your beauty standards magic. fuck me cause it'll be the ride of your life magic. i guess what i'm saying is that the way that works for you is the right way to do it. we have to be our own role models, and mirrors for each other. i want to count your silver hairs like shooting stars, trace your scars and wrinkles like a sonnet, kiss all the places gravity is in love w/. i see you femme, and i think you're just right."

I repeat to myself: I intend to figure out how to live my life as long as I can, as well I as can, on my own terms, as part of my lifelong work to build communities of liberation- ones that center Black and Brown femme working/poor sex working sickos, with all our fear and all our genius. I am going to keep figuring out how to support myself and my communities, putting money in my retirement fund and donating one day of my intutive healing practice's income to Black queer freedom dreamers in Ferguson. I am going to trust in our crip broke femme of color science to figure this one out, because it is the one thing that has never let me down. I am going to remember that since it is a collective problem, it needs a collective solution.

I'm freedom dreaming on the idea that the disability justice communities that have saved me and each other over and over and we are still building will keep freedom dreaming in the future. That the ways we sick and disabled queers have fought and cum to redefine what beauty, desire and sex are can take me and us into my 40s, my 50s, my 60s, 70s, 80 and 90s thriving and on my own terms. That my one model of queer femme of color elderhood does not have to mean dying in my 40s or 50s like Glora Anzaldua, June Jordan and Barbara Cameron. What will it mean if we don't die, and if we keep burning for the next fifty years? What do we need to get ourselves there?

Again, I am struck by how much able bodied communities and movements lose when they don't perceive the voices of sick and disabled genius. Many able bodied queer fears of aging are disabled already realities. And we are organizing our ways out of nightmare nursing homes and shitty isolated housing, figuring out the real deal of crip cohousing and mutual aid, figuring out how to rig accessible bathrooms and care collectives now. How to have sexy queer communities that do not just live in an inaccessible club, party, meeting and protest culture now.

That month, I walked and lay on my crip bed into the hurricane and through the eye of the storm. I came out the other side. I got picked up at a coffee shop. I look at myself in the mirror, my grey side shave, no-time-for-bullshit almost 40 eyes, breathe in to the movements that have my back- and the self that does too- and say, I see you femme and I think you're just right.

Dig. (para mi vida.)

Meliza Bañales aka Missy Fuego

I want to tell you about my grandmother and planting roses. How getting the soil just right for the seeds requires your whole body, crouched, hunched, both hands, both arms—working,massaging,

rotating. My abuelita didn't use a shovel. Just some water, her hands, patience. She waited for the ground to invite her. And when the black mud slid through her fingers she went in. And in this story, I am eleven-years-old and I go with her. Though it

starts slow, it quickly gathers momentum. And there we are pushing, sweating, all smells, all dark and thick. "It's always an ugly business, getting to something so beautiful," she would say, "can you turn the earth, mija?" I keep going, find my chest to the ground, my neck bent—I'll be honest with you. I was holding back then because I was afraid to get dirty, afraid I wouldn't get the stains out of my knees. Afraid to be surrounded, to be held. I didn't know if I'd make it back from the black mud, "Effort," she'd whisper, "keep going." The sun to my back I'd push to get through, the moment when the seeds

could drop was so close and I wanted it to happen but didn't know if my hands could get the job done. But we kept going and before I knew it I felt something give and I stopped. Took a shallow breath in my flat girl chest and pulled out, "Now just sit, just for a minute," Tita said. I couldn't hear the freeway over my

Tita's house in North Hollywood or the wires buzzing with electricity or someone's favorite show or a phone call good-bye. I only remember the sky—it was so blue. And a small wind found my face. I want you to know this is how you make me feel. When I'm thick in you—when I fall into you like a fool who only knows trust and this moment—when the whole of my-self lets loose. I am up to my arms in you. Can I put my chest to the altar of your heart. I'll be honest with you: I'm not holding back. I'm here to make a mess of you because only the brave aren't afraid to get lost—they live to be consumed. So let me get lost in you. Can you turn the earth, mija—can you let me use both hands to see inside your pain your past your desire your hurt and write a different ending. I enjoy the dark. The quiet. It's always an ugly business getting to something so beautiful—I want you to know

I come from a long line of growers. And I am not afraid to dig.

To my van, the Dream

By Damien Luxe

Van <>Van Photo by Najva Sol, 2012. L to R: Dee W., Shomi Noise, Najva Sol, Damien Luxe, Myloh Bones, Lizxnn Disaster, Valentino, Heather Acs.

Dream: I love you, no vehicle replaces you, no tour will be the same without you.

Heels on Wheels touring was made possible in part because I aquired a resource: a van. A seven-person, sweet-driving, gas-guzzling eight-cylinder conversion van with a TV and comfy-ass seats. My magic in vehicle form. I bought her in 2009 after I was laid off my dayjob and restless for adventure. I knew she'd be perfect for any dream I could imagine: I just didn't know it would be DIY art touring. She was all possibility.

It's important to describe The Dream to outsiders. I hear that for other tours renting vans and dealing with vehicles has been challenging. We, however, always had a reliable and comfortable ride that could buckle seven and move nine or more. This was major in making travel, and therefore shows, possible for Heels on Wheels.

In short: gas + oil changes + one month insurance (the touring deal we ended up making with me) is way less money than bus or airfare for six anywhere you go within one time zone. So, we drove, were able to pay artists more/at all, and rolled deep in a babemobile. We drove from from NYC to Austin; to Minneapolis; to Detroit; to Toronto; to Baltimore; to Providence; to Montreal; to colleges and lesbian bars and community centers near

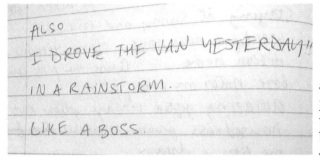

ALSO
I DROVE THE VAN YESTERDAY!!

IN A RAINSTORM.

LIKE A BOSS.

and far. We drove gear & people to Branded Saloon, the queer-run country bar a mile from my house where we had our monthly Opentoe Peepshow for 2 ½ years, just because it was comfortable.

The Dream took us on four of our five cross-country tours, and all of our local stops. While she and I had lots of other adventures, which I wrote about in my zine Vanifesto, the Heels on Wheels ones are especially precious to me. Lizxnn Disaster masterfully took charge of driving us from 2011-2014, after our first tour taught us I could not both run a tour and drive. There was a snowstorm heading out of Minneapolis I'm sure she saved our lives by driving so well. I was second driver, since I got the van so often otherwise. Occsaionally other folks got the job -- as seen above from Sabina Ibarrola's journal after her first time driving the Dream, it was a special honor. Even when the passenger door handle broke off in the Hampshire college stop before the 2013 tour, Heels on Wheels made it fun, as Shomi Noise yelled

out "Mi'lady wants to get out of the front!" once we realised no door handle meant being stuck inside.

Like all precious yet irratio-nal loves, the Dream was shat-tered in January 2015 when she was stolen. Luckly, no tour was planned the following spring.

RIP van, we did absolutely everything imaginable.

3

Putting Your Face On: Survival, Struggle, Resilience

Strange Fruit

Bekezelah Mguni

A letter to myself about not going back

Cut the noose
You wove
Around your neck
Calling it love
    - A case of mistaken identity

Drop from this branch breaking
And kiss the ground for letting you land
On your feet again

Be grateful
You survived
An almost successful attempt
To suffocate
Your own desires
...a superficial exercise in pretense and flattery

An accumulation of empty years
Is not impressive
Though it might count for endurance

Mind you don't
Climb that tree again.

How Whitney Houston Saved My Life

(Excerpt from "Building Up Emotional Muscles: Part 4")

By Shomi Noise

It feels as if I have always been depressed. Perhaps it's as a result of my background, you know, the back and forth between US and Bolivia, all those culture clashes, my parents' divorce, just feeling misplaced all the darn time, and all those crazy intense and nameless emotions that came about as a result. The drug use and drinking didn't help either. I've always been an intense creature, and all my feelings are intense and crazy. This sometimes freaks people out, and it freaks me out too sometimes, although not so much lately, I've come to terms with my intensities somewhat.

Growing up I just felt so ugly, inferior, awkward and disgruntled. As I mentioned before, I now realize that the intersectionality of oppressions faced growing up totally had a direct effect on this. As a result of all that confusion and self-hatred, the thought of suicide accompanied me all throughout middle school and high school. Of course back then when I was a child these were just fantasies, mindless angsty thoughts that came from time to time. Until I finally tried it.

#1

Once when I was in 8th or seventh grade tried to cut my wrist with some dull shaving blade. Of course, I did it the wrong way and only managed to make a tiny scratch. My sister did notice it though and confronted me about it in the bathroom and began to cry so hard as she held my puny wrist. It sort of broke my heart to see her cry like that, so my idiotic teenage self promised to not do it again at home, even though I kept fantasizing about it all through high school.

#2

Then I came to college, still lost in self-deprecation, I started to drink and do self-destructive things to cope with my depression, but it just made things worse. At this point all my identity crises began to really peak. The notion of oppression became quite clear to me by then. So I began to realize all the race and class disparities and unfairness my family and other Latino and people of color, and working class and single parent families go through as I interacted with more and more privileged white kids who just had it so easy their whole lives and who didn't even have a clue what being brown and poor was like, and worst of all, they truly didn't care or empathize, they just didnt give two shits, which drove me nuts. So I became really angry and started to feel so powerless and hopeless. Also, my queerness just seemed so wretched. That one girl in college I liked so much rejected me and I felt like a loser, and no other gays on campus seemed interested in me so I was convinced I was going to die alone and be wretched forever.

I had just moved to that dorm- the gay/artsy/stoner dorm. But I isolated myself because I felt alienated and I was too shy to socialize unless I was shitfaced. Everything felt just so wrong wrong wrong.

During my first year at said dorm, I would try to drink my sorrows away and then I'd make an ass out of myself and then I'd feel so mortified and angry at myself about it. I was caught in a terrible vicious cycle. So one night I was at my lowest low and after having a meltdown and crying in my dorm room for hours, I decided that my life totally sucked and that there was no point in even trying anymore.

So I went after a bottle of codeine pills that a dentist had prescribed to me after i had my wisdom teeth taken out, and just erratically swallowed ALL of them. Five minutes later I panicked and decided that I perhaps didn't really want to die. So I ran to the bathroom and tried to make myself puke but I just couldn't and this made me panic even more.

Things began to slow down and my body just felt sooo weird. I was roaming through the halls when I bumped into that geeky kid who called himself Ziggy. I had met him at an LGBT meeting, and at the time he was a math major who was into d&d and other uber geeky role playing games, he loved progressive rock, and was also obsessed with David Bowie, hence his nickname. He was nice and pleasant and I liked him because he was approachable and down to earth and he happened to also be latino and queer. When I bumped into him that night in the dorm room hall, he did not notice my distraught self and invited me to go see "This is Spinal Tap" in his dorm room. I agreed because I was freaking out about possibly dying and could use some company, so i went to see this movie and I sat there silently panicking as things just got slower and slower and my breathing felt shorter and shorter.

Finally I just couldn't take it anymore and I just got up and said, "need bathroom" and ran out of there and back to the bathroom where I tried to puke again and failed. I said to myself, as I hugged the toilet bowl, "I'll just walk it out, I wont fall asleep, I'll just walk it out" and stumbled out of the communal bathroom onto the dorm's hall. This is when I bumped into my crush who looked at me and said, "hey, what's wrong with you? Are you drunk???" and I slurred back "nooooo ssssstuuuupid bitchhh, Iiee just tooka buncha pills cuz I wuzzz trying to kill ma self.....ooops."

She was all like "WHAT!!!!?" and freaked out of course, then Ziggy showed up in the hall asking if I was ok because I had ran out of his room quite abruptly, My crush replied, "She's SO NOT OK! She took a bunch of pills and is trying to kill herself!!!!! ohmygod what should we do??????" they both took me to my room, and I began to cry and asked them to not tell anyone about it, "please, I beg you, don't tell anyone, I don't want to go to the hospital, I don't wanna go. Please!!!!!" I sobbed so hard. Ziggy sympathized with me and said, "yeah the hospital is not a good idea, they'll call your parents who will get upset and if it's a suicide attempt then they can even have you put in the loony bin. I've been through this."

My crush interrupted, "so what should we do? What if she dies?" "She wont die, we'll give her lots of water, and I'll look after her," Ziggy said.

"Good cuz I can't deal with this, I'm leaving" said the girl I crushed on so much, then she left. And that is how my crush on her began to end.

She is not an asshole though, i think she was just scared at the situation and did not know how to deal at the moment, which is totally understandable. We are still great friends till this day and we always have a laugh about how i once puked on her and how much of a hot mess i was. Me and Irene have gone a long way and I totally cherish our friendship.

That night I was lucky I had Ziggy looking after me. And I'm not sure if I ever told him, but I am forever grateful for what he did for me that night, I barely even knew him that well and he stood beside me the whole night talking to me, giving me water, and making sure I was ok. After drinking lots of water, the puking eventually began and breathing stopped hurting.

That is how I survived my second suicide attempt, which was more like a cry for help than anything else.

3, third is a charm: How Whitney Houston saved my life.

That same year towards the end of the semester, I had another massive meltdown. This time it happened in public.

One evening, after much thought and consideration, I decided to go to that Take Back the Night March thingy at the women's campus by myself. All the hip Rutgers lesbians were there. Now I look back on it and they weren't all that cool or hip really, but at the time little gay me felt so intimidated and alienated by them. Needless to say, barely any of them ever gave me the time of day. So I went and I was standing there and no one was talking to me and I felt as if I was the only dork who was there by herself standing all alone. So suddenly this wave of sadness, melancholy, and darkness just hits me like a really bad high and I just wanted to cry so badly. But I obviously didn't want to be seen crying in public so I began to look around for a bathroom when suddenly I tripped on something and fell on my face. Everyone just stared, some even laughed, then one girl came up to me and asked if I was ok. "DOES IT LOOK LIKE I'M OK??? OF COURSE I AM NOT OK!!!" I said, and ran away crying. It all feels so juvenile and dumb now, but back then I felt mortification that induced the most erratic feelings in me. It had been a crappy semester. Life was unfolding but it didn't seem so fair or hopeful.

I took a bus in my moment of despair, and cried all the way until I got off on the main avenue stop. Disgruntled and sad at my loneliness and depression, I entered the local pharmacy/convenience store. I walked to the aisle where they sell insecticides, bug repellents, and.....rat poison.

I was on a mission, and this time I was gonna do it, and no one would stop me because

"life is cruel and it sucks," I thought to myself, "this is not a cry for help anymore. I just want to get the fuck out." I grabbed a box of rat poison and I stared at it with my tear-soaked eyes full of anger and despair. "Maybe I should mix this with something sweet so that it doesn't taste bad and goes down easily. Maybe I should just get drunk tonight and then eat this shit so that I pass out unnoticed and never wake up, or maybe......"

And suddenly, my thoughts were interrupted by a song that was coming on overhead through the store's speakers. I thought to myself "this sounds so familiar," as I began to listen. It was Whitney Houston and CeCe Winans singing that cheesy gospel song about friendship, "Count on Me":

Count on me through thick and thin
A friendship that will never end
When you are weak, I will be strong

Helping you to carry on
Call on me, I will be there
Don't be afraid
Please believe me when I say
Count on me...

I can see it's hurting you
I can feel your pain
It's hard to see the sunshine through the rain
I know sometimes it seems as if it's never gonna end
But you'll get through it
Just don't give in cause you can...

Ok, yeah cheesy to the maxxx. But this shit seriously saved me.

Suddenly I stared blankly into space and my eyes widened. And as I listened to the lyrics I just began to think about the people that I love, and who love me unconditionally. And about what they would do if I did indeed die. I thought about my mom, who despite all the adversity she's faced, has done so much for me and my sis because she adores us. I thought about my sister and the time she saw my puny little wrist scratches and cried so much because she really loves me and does not want to see me dead. I thought about my best friend Aurora who is so funny and so kind and who has been there for me always through thick and thin, during good times and bad times. I thought about all those nice folks I've encountered in my short immature and inexperienced life like Ziggy.

I thought about all those people I was and still am yet to meet, but whom perhaps I'd grow to love as well. I thought about a lot of things while that song played in the background. Killing myself would just hurt all those people I loved, and suddenly I felt like an asshole for even trying to do it. And I realized that I had been kind of selfish by drowning in my self-hate and self-deprecation and not thinking about or appreciating those who do love me unconditionally.

I realized that the world is rough but that we are here to face it and learn lessons from it. And I realized that I could be so much more to the world than just a premature corpse. I realized that there are all these things that I want to learn and do, and all these dreams and goals I have, and if I work really hard and act bravely, I could totally achieve them.

So at that moment, I put down the box of rat poison, dried my tears, and walked back to my dorm room breathing with much more ease.

Even though hard times have not ceased and I have had several more panic attacks, breakdowns, and meltdowns, ever since my encounter with the Whitney Houston song, I have not attempted to kill myself again, and I am not planning to. That song also made me realize that I need to always appreciate those who love me.

So let this be a lesson to all of you who are reading this. Because sometimes, we lose sleep and get all bent out of shape because certain people reject us or ignore us, meanwhile we perhaps ignore or forget about those people who will always be there for us and who will love us no matter what.

Please try to be aware of this. There are folks who will be your buddies and party with you and have superficial fun with you, but when the party is over and the shit hits the fan and times are rough, they are nowhere to be found. I say keep those folks at arms length and appreciate the people in your lives that you can really count on at all times, who are kind to you, loyal, and to whom you don't need to put up a front for. Seeing through the bullshit and learning how and who to trust is an important lesson I came to learn and that I am still learning.

Anyways, so that is how Whitney Houston once saved my life.

WELLING :: 6

· · · · · · · · · · · · · · · · · · ·

Don't marry marry

My lot
a fragile mind
gleaming strange cut
a shifting setting.

Look back
turn to
face lifted from the wall
a salt mine relief
stakes on fire held high to
ward off unbreathable air.

Eight stories
deep
earth mineral rich
shackled to a contract.

A salt mine
standing licking lips
the hair at the nape
solid strands of gold
a damp the lungs bare easy for
    the salt.

Johnny Forever Nawracaj vel Joachim Magdalena

It was I
what is done
one hand over the other
over and over
under the tap.
Don't marry
marry
who is to know
how well
a coin beyond seer's reach
stone fountain.

Youth eternal
womb saturated
revelation given breath
a hormonal self-knowledge
wed to the blood
to the bone.

A lack
not mine
the world come forth
loin to bind in iron
leafy greens to whet the dark
come after lazur each evening.

Good night
learn in your sleep
all that comes
the many open lidded hours
gleaming
strange cut
you've mined [your mind] not diamond
but salt.

//////////////

Leda's revenge

headstrong
    owe solid piss-stream

be youth, be an
    angel

a fucker out of
    luck

we do

experiment

experiment's on you

be Leda

flax, moat

be sweet,
    vegetable,
    rot.

be swan's down,
    serpent's throat,
goat committing
    tight arches
    her whole
    body
over and over

head angling horn
fore hooves raise
gauge the earth

then back
    that pair of legs
fly.

fuckface,

you brought a friend

let teeth plant your

sons,

the trees.

//////////////

Brain Poison Heirlooms
(with instructions)

Samantha Galarza

(backwards statue of liberty pose)

On my tongue I absorb the shock of complacency- A sting that is ever-present.

This world - where commodity substitutes fulfillment. And the illusion of freedom blinds, deafens, and numbs.

(draw island out)

Puerto Rico, my heart's devotion, let it sink back in the ocean.

(grab island and put it down. Then kick it)

Always the pop-u-lation growing (pregnant bump). And the money owing. "I like to live in Americcaa"

(turn around very slowly still in statue of liberty position. Drop hand that is up and write 1917 on face. Put hand back up and shake body as if a boat has just crashed into her)

The Jones Act states that anyone born in the colony of Puerto Rico is a US citizen.

STEP FORWARD

(drop hand again to write 1947 on arm. When putting arm back up grab hair and do round head motion with crippled fingers drag down thing)

Luis Muñoz Marin launches Operation Bootstrap. In an effort to make people un-poor, women are forcefully sterilized and farm and factory work-ers are heavily recruited from the colony to the states.

STEP FORWARD

(write 1957 on arm)

My grandpa, a 17 yr old black Puerto Rican with a 5th grade education, is pushed and pulled to move to Newark, NJ - leaving behind domestic abuse and extreme poverty only to get chased out of parks, apartments, jobs and streets; arrested for not breaking any laws; regularly stalked and beaten by gangs of white boys and the police; denied further schooling because there were no bilingual programs.

(Smudge all the dates that were written on body)

My grandpa, a 17 yr old black Puerto Rican, develops a hatred for everything black

¿Cómo se gana una guerra política?

Si lo sabes dime tú

¿Cómo?

Cuando empezó con Mama Juevo y Fulano Gusano entregandome dos vidas llenas de mentiras sociales y odio

Corriendo por las venas que sustienen mi cerebro

Apoyado por los brazos que me dan cariño

Los ojos que me adoran

Labios que me besan

Que me critican cuando dudo

Mamaaaa Ooooh

(hands over chest and leg over womb in moment of silence)

You're so numb.

Numb to the body that you created.

Is it my queerness that offends you?

Or is it what other people would think if they knew?

And they would, if you acknowledged it or let me speak for myself.

(rubbing black away)

On my head I carry the burden of explanation.

How do I explain to my younger sister that her Afro-Puerto Rican, Afro-Brazilian curls of plight should not be flat ironed away because of her white-washed conception of beauty

When, until this day, both my abuelitas utilize what little energy they have in their 70 year old arthritic bones to comb and recomb their natural kinks until every strand has taken on a foreign composition.

(start to roll hair up very slowly)

The darkest one on my father's side and reminded of that whether my cousins were making fun of me or my grandma was lovingly calling me negrita, I managed to combat feeling ugly and worthless purely because I was born with Paris-Hilton-over-confidence. But that subliminal shit still fucks with you.

(2 full and then the rest in mid crunch position)

6-8-12 pack from the core muscles I'm using

Putting so much intention, focus, and energy to get by as I was taught

Follow as intended

See only what's in front of me

No peripheral, no behind

Palante siempre palante

Walking on a wire in which there is no easy route

With each clench my skeleton decalcifies

In spite of pain and blood and sorrow

I dig my feet deeper

Imagining that when I hit the bone,

If I can just hit the bone I can skate on it

But the straight path doesn't give the security it promises

My eyes lose their perception of depth, color

Spine is curved unwillingly

Every time I defy the wind it takes me so that I remember

The relentless persecution of walking a lie

Every time I defy the wind it takes me so that I remember

Making it harder to return to a life in which constriction of breath is sport

(BALLERINA UP & FALLING)

I yearn for your approval; for the unrequited, unconditional acceptance I'm entitled to as your daughter. Oye mi canto.

(Sit Up)

It wasn't until collegeeeee that I was FINALLLY given the context and language to express pride in the things that other people didn't value.

(face audience with blowy sound)

(low narrator voice) Identity Politics—the beginning of your new motherfuckin life. An explosion where all the shit you never understood finally makes sensee!!!

Que viva la patria Puerto Rico. Que viva la revolución! Pedro Albizu Campos. Que viva la raza baby!

Round up the people of color. Round up my gays. Round up the other anti-oppressionists!

(celebratory and big) I love myselffffff. Y te amo a ti tambien porque tú, te aparaces como yo. Porque los dos amamos lo mismo. Porque, aunque no tenemos nada en común, you reject constructs too! We have so much to teach each other. So much to de-con-struct. You know we're bout to change the world right?

But soon things started to change.....

• •

Heels on Wheels in Detroit, 2011. Photo by Lizxnn Disaster

Anniversary

Leah Horlick

It has taken you five years and fifteen hundred
      kilometres to get you away, and closer

to the mountains. You can see them—
      every day, like you always wanted. Near,

and distant. Every day you can ask people
      not to touch you—

   on the bus, on the beach, or in your new kitchen.
      Or, you could ask them to—

which lately, is harder. How can it still
      feel so soon? She has never been

near this new body of yours—
      short-haired, tattooed, very strong

and very, very fast, now. You carry a chunk of rose
      quartz the size of your thumb for safety.

You have sworn to yourself a life of people
      who know when to stop. You promised—

and spent your first night in the new apartment drawing
      circles in salt and rain, whispering

to your old self, come here. I built this
      for you. I promised.

First World Bullshit

Cristy C. Road

• •

I had this vision--- where I would move to NYC and become AN ARTIST....
AND AN ACTIVIST..... And I would feel SAFE... at the protest.

A queer latina artist with a big punk community. A queer Latina in the
anarchist black block at the protest. A community where respect was the
foundation of our interactions. Where call-out culture was synonymous with
accountability and our eagerness to transform was plain old common sense.
A community where visions didn't always intersect, but racism, sexism, clas-
sism, ableism, ageism, and mental health were a consistent dialogue, therefore, allowing our separate visions to intersect in a magical cadence of glitter
and unicorns and consensual orgies and a third eye in the backs of our heads
reserved for one another's insecurities, vulnerabilities, and MORE GLIT-
TER!!! AND CUTE DENIM VESTS!!!!!

BUT THAT JUST HAPPENS LIKE ITS ORGANIC AND NATURAL to
communities that are built upon the fractured.... we've actually suffered. One
cant force inclusion and diversity when one has been forced into isolation
their entire life. It's a pipe dream, a bad dream, a childhood ideal, a moment
in time that I hold onto through abiding by the ones I trust, or a fake moment in our brain manifested through the habit of saving face--- and even
that face crumbles in the face of trauma. Im 32 now, and I can no longer trust
a community. Its not just the fault of the systems of authority that destroy
us---- but of the support systems that fail us.

Remember when you lost your family and you forgot where your home
was and you lost your mind and it was the only time you were able to com-
promise with the one you loved and the one you hurt the most? When the
world was at war and it was global---or interpersonal---it didn't matter---be-
cause you were fucked, and you were able to hold yourself and others ac-
countable for the rough patches: THANK GOD. But it took a minefield.

Now, I forage in a conflicted universe where money buys love and safety
scales passion because Im scared to be alone---but ide rather be alone than
bored. Ide rather talk to my therapist about the commodification of love that
makes it easy for me to cross romantic intersections based on deep spiritual
purposes---or an internal need to conform.

When were alone, everyone could hear us scream if we try hard enough,
but no one could hold us while we suffer. We're taught to elevate romantic

love on a pedastl, so when we have it, we choke it---Then power could be abused and diffused and after 6 years of deep bonding and deep drowning in an inability to communicate---all we are left with are blatant reminders of the institutions that told us how to love, the abusive ex lovers we hopped trains with in 2002, a tattered suitcase of daddy issues, and defensively REAL insecurities that allow us to participate in love---just a little awkwardly. Between the self-persecution of not being radical enough, and the self-persecution of having chosen those lovers who broke us in the first place.

Now, in lieu of hope of actually finding a ground where love and revolution could truthfully co-exist---INSECURITIES become the global insurrection----NOT the orgy I participated in on Friday night. But the urge to be free, that came from the orgy that made me feel uncomfortable. The one that made me hate myself and my body; and moved me to cut off a slew of racist anarchists.

VULNERABILITY---it's what no one wants and what everyone needs. I gave up my original quest. I came to NY, I did the art and the rummaging and the spanging and I just wanted to be me because frankly, feeling like the only brown person in the anarchist block at the protest made me sad...

And so I found myself...in a nightclub. At the hole on 2nd ave and 2nd st. --before it was the cock. I found friends, I found revelation, I found femme visibility and the potency of fanplastico by MAC cosmetics--- especially when its stolen. I found spirituality, a divine connection to the ocean and the sky and the plants and my ancestors who answer to powers higher than industrialized power, ramones-style pop punk, and the anarchist block at the protest--- BECAUSE THEY. WERE. THERE. FIRST. I Found an interest in self care outside of the cocaine agenda that kept me together when I became frayed and dismayed, and I found it at my own pace. Because being forced to believe in no gods and no masters felt RACIST. BECAUSE TELLING ME WHERE TO SHOP AND WHAT TO EAT FELT CLASSIST. Because telling someone what to do in the face of trauma was tacky.

You don't know what I need. I need "community" where cops stay cops. I need "community" where activists are not going to police me for my choices and my vices and my complicated needs. My community is going to understand that we are who we are because colonialism and systematic queerphobia got us here, and transformative justice is not justice if we are not allowed to bleed.

I found that sore spot---the one that told me love and community were not real because I tried it once before and I could count the scars that left me tough but left me breathless. I found vulnerability---the magic ingredient that enabled a lifetime of self-awareness but yet a magnitude of self-hate, and 6 hour house meetings where we collectively drowned in our own tears.

I smile sometimes and ask if this is all bullshit---the quest to find safety within a fraction of a system that I've accepted as unsafe. The first world bullshit we can engage in because we can. The privilege of having the free-dom to love. I have the freedom to seek community despite failed attempts. I have the freedom to fuck and assembly and dissent I had the space to vent about safety and accountability to the 3 or 4 co-conspirators who let me. I have the resources that could help me participate in social justice while simultaneously crying about my ex. I have the freedom to live in an all queer, all femme of color, all bitch slapping cave in Brooklyn---No matter how far we had run from the homes that layed out our foundations.

But in the end, once we own the privileges that make our destiny easier--- how could we sustain the constant fight against detriment and oppression, if we can't even get along? If we can't even get out of bed in the morning? If we keep finding the time to hurt one another and the time to hurt ourselves? If we keep silencing one another for being too weak, too jealous, too poor, too incapable, too drunk, to stoned, to tired, too abused, or too oppressed?

So I'm just sitting here---waiting for someone to silence the racist, tacky person who keeps telling people of color how to actually fight a war. Like "sit here this my definition of peaceful protest". Because frankly---It's been almost 10 years since I moved to NYC to be an artist and cover myself with unicorns and astrology and queer punks and glitter and MORE GLITTER---- and I'm currently too busy unlearning my chores, and re-learning self-preser-vation.

I don't even even personally like glitter on my person tbh.

I could live my life looking for baggage that looks like mine, and I could live my life reiterating the same stance on abuse for the 6 thousandth time--- OR I could listen and learn from your baggage, and you can learn from mine- -- because I am fucking tired of feeling guilt. Guilt for the weight I carry in the "community" as a queer Latina abuse survivor with anxiety problems. As a wingnut Gemini with a profound interest in motherhood and cars, but yet a frivolous inability to learn how to drive. And as a loner---an underdog with a hometown too far away to feel like I could ever go back; but too close, to feel like I could ever conform to a new culture.

My baggage is NOT a burden to your community---but the precious little dents in the fabric of my existence that sparkle when they're facing a sharp angle towards the sun. And maybe if our city was at war or our stability was taken away we could submit to some kind of silence---some kind of forgiveness---because FEELINGS suddenly overshadowed facts, and vulnerability became a weapon to stay grounded and empathetic towards the community that naturally forms when we are able to suffer, love, and heal.

And then the first world bullshit stays at the round table discussion about poly that happened Friday night at the queer potluck, because we finally felt strong enough to leave it there, because we finally learned how to respect our lovers, so we can tend to more universal battles. And hopefully we will someday feel strong enough to look one another in the eye and say "I'm sorry" or "I love you" or "lets check in with one another's boundaries and then, perhaps, we can tear the system down"---and it would only happen on those sporadic hours---like the sunset or the sunrise---when our baggage gets lit like a flame---those sporadic hours when we're not fighting another war.

Girl

Muggs Fogarty

I was too afraid to jump

off the rocks

to the cold

forgiving water.

I thought my top would come off

the breasts I didn't want,

or that my friends would see

my tampon string—

a grenade pin along my thigh.

I had no towel,

no change of clothes.

I would have to show

my underwear, my legs

I didn't shave clean.

So I called from the rock

that I couldn't do it,

that I was afraid.

But I was never afraid,

I was always just

ashamed

of my body

body body.

My girl's body body body.

Queered Paradelle (On Neutral Pronouns)

Nobody wants you, or "them/their/they're."

Nobody wants you, or "them/their/they're."

So many eyes sometimes—just mirrors.

So many eyes. Sometimes, just mirrors.

Them", just language nobody wants.

There, there. They're nobody. Or, mirrors.

Dark shroud, cover this body.
    Block the unstable light.

Dark shroud cover.
    This body, block the unstable light.

Both sides of the coin shining,
    becoming one image.

Both sides of the coin.
    Shining, becoming one image.

This body, shining, becoming both—
    this unstable image.

Dark becoming, shroud this cover.
    Coin, block the light.

It is a boy.

It is a boy.

No, it's a girl, nevermind.

No. It's a girl, nevermind.

Nevermind, a boy, a girl. No, it's "it".

Girl, nevermind.

Unstable girl becoming boy,
    cover this body of light.

Nobody wants "it" in their mirror.
    Block the dark.

So many coins in their eyes.
    They're becoming eyes.

Block their mirrors.

They want you unstable,

Both Sides.

When our own kind aren't ready for each other

Here's the thing, if we're no longer talking,
if we parted, if we lost one another in a frenzy
of calendar dates or indifference, I'm sending
you compassion because you've built me & in
spite of ache, you've created shifts in this world.

We've ached together at least once. We have.
We've been the offbeat song, the hiding place
where together we kept secrets tucked in our
own pores for warmth. We've scrawled goofy
smiles upon subway platforms, cemeteries, taxi
cabs that kicked us out for being ourselves,
just leaning & in love. I would never erase this.

I must accept and love you for this. That deep
breath over windowsill stares. Yeah true, this is all we know: lost photo-
graphs and family from migration stories & the stories we must tell ourselves.
I want us to not let go, not replay the last times until they are the mouths of
myths and tectonics.

I want for us to be something different.
Guess what? I've been eating all the foods you hate, so I could learn to hate
you back too. Guess again? My fingertips have had your sweat on them &
they can't help but map all that we've built so beautifully to demolish.

Let's not be colonial. All I wanna know is:

Can we learn something else?

Survival skills

Sossity Chiricuzio

· ·

I know the secrets of hand stitching patches into the inner thighs of second hand leggings. Of clear fingernail polish on runs in my stockings, to stop them above the hemline. Except when I don't care and let them run anyway, because fuck those classicist beauty standards anyways.

I know not to open my legs to anyone that would judge those patches, those runs, or me. I learned this the hard way, with dropped poor kid eyes hiding shame, and anger at you for that shame. I learned after inadequate sex and horrid goodbyes. After stellar sex and heartbreak. After 2.5 down-wardly mobile lovers and half of my twenties.

I know, far more clearly than lots of people who share my faint melato-nin and expensive education, that I am lucky to have needle, thread, and light to stitch by. That my belly is full and my feet are warm. That I have leggings at all.

I owe $150,000 for that education. My original loan was $30,000. I make $13,000 a year. My degree isn't in math, but I can see the sum of those numbers.

I will be in debt for the rest of my life because I wanted to know more than public school was authorized to tell me. Because I believed the story that a degree was a ladder. Because I knew everything important didn't happen to rich, white men.

I know that even though poor, queer, female and disabled are relevant, everyday I reap the privilege of being white. I know how to make room and be quiet and listen and learn. I know how to support and leave my ego out of it. I know it's still not enough. I know to keep trying anyhow.

I know that many weeds are actually food or medicine that are so resil-ient, they spurn farms and profit margins entirely.

I want brand new leggings. Bras that fit. Socks that match. I want underwear that hasn't a single rip and a coat nobody wore before me. I want streaks of color in my hair, and to pay the electric bill, from the same paycheck. I want a bigger paycheck.

I want to not care about a paycheck at all. I want to trade skill for skill, time for time. I want to work for joy and survival, but not in survival mode.

I know the running tally of prices of everything that goes into the cart. At the register, I'll know within $3 what the total is. This is because I know exactly how much money I have, but also, because figuring out which $5 worth of food to put back with a line of waiting people and a fistful of food stamps in your 12 year old hand sticks with you.

I always carry a knife. Except in airports. And federal buildings. I know how to use my keys, instead, if I have to.

I have my reasons. A whole other list of them, actually, but you've probably heard them before. (If you were listening.) From almost every woman you know, and more than a few men, and definitely anybody in between.

I know how to steal. I also know when and where it will work, and who is not fair game. I don't do it any more, or generally recommend it, but the whole system is built on have and have not. Charity often comes tied up with strings; paychecks never have enough stretch; hunger is food but also beauty.

I know how to give. Half of my lunch, a shirt that will actually fit you, my seat on the bus, a piece of rose quartz, rolled between many working hands. My whole day off. Job leads, plant cuttings, my fifth copy of The Ethical Slut. A place in my heart. My full attention and a direct gaze.

On the rare occasion that all of the below is true:

a. I eat out

b. I have leftovers

c. I can't eat or take the leftovers

I leave them on top of a newspaper stand, or a bus bench. Someone nearby is absolutely hungry enough to be glad of them. I have been.

I know how to change a tire, brush the corrosion off a battery that won't spark, and check the fluids. I have only ever owned one vehicle, but in a pinch I refuse to rely purely on the kindness of strangers.

I was bulimic for awhile in high school. What stopped me was the knowledge of how many hours my mother had to work to provide the food I had just wasted. Better to learn to love being fat.

I know that if you pull the side wires out of a under-wire bra 2 sizes too small, you can still fake that it fits. This is especially helpful for people who buy their bras second hand because $80 is also a (good) weeks worth of food.

I know that weevils don't make something inedible. If it's flour, you sift it through a fine screen, if it's rice or pasta, you skim the top of the water. If it's bread, you don't usually have to worry about weevils, and mold is easy to peel or pinch away. Even more so off of cheese. If you can't imagine doing these things, I think maybe you haven't really experienced hunger yet.

I know how to make sure I can always run, if I need to. I don't like to run, but the same boots that are good for running are also good for kicking and stomping, so I'm ready regardless.

I know how to turn one potato into two extra servings, two potatoes into a meal, and three potatoes into a feast. i know that potatoes aren't on the 'clean diet' lists, and I also know that food is not simple, and clean is another way of saying 'expensive' or 'good'. i know that food that warms your belly and keeps it away from your backbone is worth any number of varieties of kale.

I know you're not supposed to wear different shades of black together, or white shoes after Labor Day, or horizontal stripes if you're fat. I know those rules were made by rich people looking to get richer by selling us shame. I know to ignore them.

I know that masculinity isn't always about dominance, violence or sexism. I also know there are reasons we have to specify that, and that they are mostly spelled out on the skin of femininity. I know we can do better.

Hand Job Monologue

Tina Horn

So I've been doing sex work for about 7 years now, mostly as a dominatrix. My approach to sex work has always been this: You come into My world. My world is a campy flamboyant place. I'm always gonna be Me and you're always gonna love it.

Of course I've taken a lot of pride in learning how to do things I didn't know how to do before, like attach garter belts to stockings and how to apply a perfect cat eye in a cab rushing from school to an outcall. There are sex worky things I'm very happy to do, like talking in my woozy Laura Palmer voice, and giggling, and making concessions to people with different politics than me, and walking in stilettos. Sex work actually really taught me how to face my internalized misogyny and unleash my femme side. But because my femme side is about my agency, there are some things I'm not willing to do just because I'm being femme for pay. I'm not willing to watch what I eat, and I'm not willing to say no to getting the tattoos I want, and I'm not willing to grow my hair out or shave my legs.

And that has been extremely lucrative and successful and fun for a very long time.

Recently I finished graduate school and turned 31 (which in sex worker years is, like, basically geriatric) and I'm trying to focus on my writing career, so I needed something to pay off my student loans that I wasn't going to pour my heart and soul into the way I do with BDSM.

So, last Fall, a friend of mine invited me to work at a massage salon in midtown Manhattan. I figured, what the hell, I'll try my Hand at that. I imagined it would be similar to being a dominatrix and in some ways it is. We advertise online, and men bring us several hundred dollars for an hour of erotic entertainment.

I know you have all walked around midtown looking up at all the apartments above the crummy bodegas and sports bars and bourgie bistros and thought to yourself: who the fuck lives here? I'm here to tell you, the answer is: nobody lives there. They are all handjob parlors.

Every last apartment in midtown is a handjob parlor.

Every parlor has their own unique style. At the place I worked, let's call it Slumberpartyville, the pretense is something like this: We are a bunch of girlie girls hanging out in an apartment all day watching Buffy and doing each other's hair. If you wanna come over and hang with us you just need to bring a liiiiiittle donation that keeps it possible for us to afford spending our youth laying around being hot. We'll probably make out with each other if we're bored but what we really like is cock so if you'll just bring yours over, along with your tribute, we would like nothing more in the entire world than to play with it, laugh at your fucking jokes, and pamper the muscles and skin and lymphatic system that you don't take very good care of.

The point of a handjob parlor, I've learned, is: adult cisgender male nap time. If you think I'm exaggerating, let me tell you: one client actually looked at me blissfully right after getting off in my hand and said, apropos of nothing; "I just met my newborn nephew the other day. I looked into his eyes when his mom was holding him, he just looked so pure you know, so happy and completely innocent and alive with no responsibility. And I was like; That baby has got it made."

Now I want us all to contemplate something: right now, all over midtown Manhattan, a place where a lot of things get done in international media, finance, and politics, hundreds of men are taking their self-care into their own hands. Or rather, into the hands of sex workers.

Each man enters a space in which a woman he find attractive has showered, moisturized, exfoliated, done her hair, nails, and makeup, and dressed in provocative lingerie. She puts on a burned Portishead cd, feigns enthusiasm about his job and hobbies, sidesteps everything he says that offends her, indulges him with touch, pretends to be really turned on by having her nipples violently sucked, moreover pretends that the way she expresses arousal is by taking gasping! squeaking! breaths, gets super physical but doesn't sweat or in any case sweats sweet vanilla pheromones, then teases and touches him to orgasm. She then gives him a full body scrub with warm water and Dr Bronners peppermint soap and some of those loofah glove thingies. She smiles demurely while he puts his clothes on, and tells him she hopes she sees him again real soon, pretends not to acknowledge the wad of bills he puts next to the ipod stereo and waits until he is out the door to count his bills and find out if he tipped her or stiffed her.

After doing this work, I suspect that handjobs are what keeps the patriarchy robust. All these men have a chance to relax in the middle of the day, and I don't know about you, but after I rub one out during an afternoon siesta, I'm in a great fucking mood, I'm having my best ideas, I'm nice to everyone I see, I feel like I could work until 11:30pm!

Now as for my career in Handies, maybe this is news to you, but there is such a thing as online sex worker client message boards. The managers of Slumberpartyville the girlie salon, pay close attention to these message boards, and after a few months, the clients started posting that I was "too alternative" for Slumberpartyville.

Just in case you didn't know, "alternative" is code for three things: 1. Too fat 2. Too many tattoos I don't understand. and 3. Too obviously fucking gay no matter how masterfully she jerks me off. So this basically means men have decided en masse that I am not alluring enough to offer the service of a professional hand job, which is probably the most demoralizing thing a whore can hear. So eventually the women of Slumberpartyville fired me because they decided I was tarnishing their reputations with my irrepressible alternativeness.

Let me just tell you: I know what a satisfied customer looks like. I'm not gonna pretend I'm everyone's cup of tea, but what this message board thing means is that these men are getting off on me in their free time, and then going home and spending the rest of their free time sitting on a computer warning other men not to come see me.

This also means that the women who manage these places are constructing their business based on what men say on the message boards. Now, this is exactly like structuring a child's life based on the demands he makes when he's having a temper tantrum. Children need boundaries and so do johns.

The sad part is, I have always been really proud of my femme superhero drag. But I guess I just don't have the realness I thought I did anymore.

What I'm really obsessing on is the image in my mind of 24 year old me, the babyho with a swifter metabolism and longer hair and more of that probably that like elusive flush of youth and less laugh lines and fewer tattoos that reference 70s science fiction. I can see her, biking home with two grand hidden in her sneakers and the adrenaline rush of power coursing through her, feeling strong and smart and knowing she could keep doing this forever. I really wanted to still be that girl.

So I am considering retiring for the first time. It makes me sad, because there's always been a part of me that thought I could pull off this racket forever. But I've realized that this was just as much a fantasy as the fantasy men have had of me for years: a perfect object that never gets sick and is always in a good mood, a blank page for them to write their stories on. The glamour of sex work affects sex workers just as much as it affects clients.

When I was 24 it was easy to pretend to be someone I wasn't. I was young: I pretended to be someone I wasn't all the time: And maybe what my short career in midtown handjobs taught me is that I'm not all that good at pretending to be something I'm not anymore.

'utting Your Face On with Heels on Wheels

Photo by Mée Rose, Toronto 2014. L to R: Damien Luxe, Shomi Noise, Sabina Ibarrola, Angel Nafis, Alvis Parsley, Heather María Ács.

It's Complicated

Krista Smith, aka Kentucky Fried Woman

I believe that each one of us has a story. A way of weaving our personal narrative into the folds of our memories and brain matter so that we can live with ourselves. So that we can learn from ourselves. So that we can be our own hero or our own villain. So that we can learn how to work from hate to anger to vulnerability to forgiveness. So that we can survive. Whatever our reasons are, we all have a story. I want to give you mine. I think that somewhere deep inside all our stories live grains of truth, kernels of knowledge seeping from generation to generation, potions and lotions manifested to heal the deepest wounds of the heart. Most important to me, the tendrils of shared experiences our stories yield allow us to see the humanity in ourselves and each other. My story revolves around trying to find myself and my home amidst a lot of complications.

I have a real complicated relationship with my blood family. I can't stop loving them. And despite the fact that we can't find anything to say to one another the few hours each year we are together in person, I know they love me. I feel it. That love courses through me. That love has given me strength when I couldn't find it anywhere else. Yet I never felt safe to be my authentic self with my family. After 24 years of weekly family gatherings it was clear that my job was to be a wife to a man and have children we raised in the church and that anything deviating from this path was downright shameful. Shameful! Shame! I love my family and I hate spending time with them and that feels real complicated.

Part of the reason I left Kentucky was because I didn't feel safe to be me there. And I had bought into a certain common narrative which said that Racism, Sexism, and Homophobia clung to the South like nowhere else, a layer of filth Southerners would never be rid of. I moved to California ignorantly thinking I was leaving that filth behind and leaving my filth behind with it. I was shocked when I encountered racism in California. It looked different than how I experienced it at home but its realness could not be ignored. I went through similar struggles encountering sexism and homophobia out here. I get angry when people who live here, in this bubble, talk about the South, or the MidWest, or rural America...pointing their fingers and haughtily calling out how shit like that would never happen in the big city, on the West Coast, in San Francisco, in their own communities, in their own families, in their own homes. Bullshit I say. That shit is happening everywhere. That shit is in our own hearts. We are doing nobody any favors when we try to neatly package up this shit and say it is elsewhere. So yeah, talking about the South to y'all feels real complicated to me.

Talking about gentrification with y'all feels real complicated to me. The gentrification that is happening in Oakland and San Francisco is happening across the entire nation. All across the U.S. there is a migration of the rich, and folks of color and artists and queers and immigrants from all over the world, as some are ousting and some are being ousted and right before our eyes our cities become playgrounds that many of us will never be able to afford to play in. We know it is wrong. We know it is awful. Some of us hate on the techies and some of us hate on the hipsters and some of us stake our claim into this land because we've been here before this boom started and while any amongst us might say we belong here more than the newest set of others few of us talk about giving the land back to its original inhabitants. And many of us who participate in this migration are queers and many of us queers are white and for those of us who are we must wrestle with what it means to be white and leave our homes, even if it is seeking safety, to further claim and colonize a land in a nation that has institutionalized racism. I left home seeking safety. I am part of the gentrification of Oakland. That gentrification is directly strengthening a police state that is unsafe for many of us especially People of Color, gender nonconforming people, people with physical and mental illness and disabilities, people who lack wealth, the homeless, and sex workers. I can be intentional about how I live, but I can't escape my queerness, my whiteness, my own migration and participation in the gentrification process. So yeah....talking about gentrification is real complicated for me.

So then I think about going home. I want to stop celebrating my story, the story of queers who migrate to seek safety. We should be celebrating all the queers who stayed. All the folks living in the south and rural America fighting back against the filth of racism, misogyny, and homophobia. The folks who couldn't leave. The folks who wouldn't leave. The artists living and loving in the South and rural America every day. The Southerners who are fighting back and organizing and putting their lives on the line to create change with so few resources.

But then I think about the first twenty four years of my life. About the desperation to find community...the need to see myself reflected...the fear, self-hatred, and shame I constantly lived with. And I think about leaving this queer bubble that is the San Francisco Bay Area and I feel stuck. I don't know that I would survive going back home. It is all so complicated. So this is the story of my Home. Home means the best food I can think of. Home means family. Home means love. Home is filled with hurt. Home means being invisible. Home means failure. But home means love. I want home to be love. I want to love home. I want to be home. I want to find my home. I want to know a home. I want to know where my home is supposed to be. I want it to be simple. But you probably know by now. It's just real real complicated.

Photo by Amanda Harris, 2015. L to R: Vagina Jenkins, Kentucky Fried Woman.

DISMANTLE, CHANGE, BUILD.

The Faggot in the Pink House

Alejandro Rodríguez

FAGGOT: The house on 802 Silvestre Road was purchased by my parents in 1982. A four bedroom duplex in the Lower Valley of El Paso, Texas. My parents, Javier and Patricia, have been the sole proprietors of this duplex, in fact my mother tells the story that she choosed our house because it had the biggest lot out of all the other four bedroom duplexes on the block.

At one point my mother, father, oldest brother Javier, middle brother Paulo, my Tia, Lupe, her husband Paco, my Tia Sylvia, my cousins Xotchil and Alonzo, and my Tia Susana shared the four bedrooms and two bathrooms.

From the time I was 4 until after I left for college my mother decided that she wanted the house to be, "Un color melon." Cantelope my mother called it.

It was straight up P-I-N-K.

I hated it. As a child and through adolensese I felt it was a signifier of my sissiness, my homosexuality.

One day during 3rd grade, as I made my way out of the bus, one boy yelled to his friend, "Mira, ese es el pinchi joto de la casa rosa." As I exited the bus, I remember those words and the laughter from the other children cut down my spine.

The most painful part of this memory was that my cousin Oscar was right behind me, and I remember feeling so much shame.

In the years after I left El Paso, Texas my father decided that he would renovate the entire house and paint the facade of the house.

In the fall of 2012 I had to move from my first apartment in Greenpoint, Brooklyn. The stars aligned and the Goddess blessed me because Heather Acs reached out to saying she was looking for a roommate.

I agreed to stop by and take a look at the place. As I got off the G-train in Clinton-Washignton, I surveyed the brownstone neigborhood and thought to myself, alright, okay.

As I turned onto Grand Avenue, Heather waited for me a top the stoop steps to her parlor level apartment.

A Hot Temper Is Its Own Good Romance (Excerpt)

Alex Alvina Chamberlain

Tenderness deep like the ocean wrapped up softly in barbed wire. I am set free in this world of my own words, without turning in an entirely different direction, thankfully connection's aren't always those careerist things that some people get through their parents and others get through opportunism while other others don't get them at all. May my expressed emotions extend beyond the constraint of whether or not the dictionary contains words for them. I will not allow you or anyone to interrupt me with your hangovers, cynicism, drunkedness, tiredness, jadedness or made in America and honed in New York short attention span. Let's make a deal, let's not be those people without the guts to say what is real inside and instead speak to each other as if the whole world was going up in flames and remember that this is not far from the truth. And after I've told you everything, you can tell me everything and than maybe we can get through all the pissandshitandliesthatKILL other people and proceed to tear down ALL the advertisements in the subway.

"What fever: Will I one day be able to stop living? I who die so often as I follow the crooked path where the roots blast through the earth, I who have the gift of passion, when the dry tree trunk burns I cast myself into the flames. And I am not afraid of failing. May my failure annihilate me, I wish for the honour of falling. You probably wonder why I take care of the world? It is because I was born with a mission. When I was a child I once took care of an ant path. There is a whole world inside each little ant that I would miss if I wasn't paying attention."

Claric-eeeee changed my perspectives amidst accusations of gender essentialism from coherent mutilators of imagination who's view of disorder is missing a shot at the tennis court. Clarice and I prefer the smell of manure to the smell of newly painted pharmacies. I find that it is okay to lay there in that pile of poop and it is not because it is SUBVERSIVE for feminine people to talk about EXCREMENTS. Man, Woman, nonsense, I am nothing but a lioness splintered with arrows, foolish humans who think penetration kills oh believe me you've tried, by the time your 10 hour work day is finished I have multiplied and disappeared from your sensory field. HA! What a dirty trick I have played on you, I am water dirt blood and dead skin cells crammed down the drain on a journey to the sewer presenting a present to the rats scurrying away from the cats attempt to present death as a gift for the killer in you and the killer in me. When I die my blood will be scared shitless by the six feet of dirt overhead, clueless to the fact that it is too late for an infection. Bonjour Violette Leduc! It is impossible to be friends with her, everybody knows that.

The diamond needs the sun in order to shine bright. The fog is lending a shape to the air. I do not wish to be a slave to the senses of my eyes. I see a watermelon on a table and it is tears making space for solitary in solidarity. Covet my internal world I much prefer it to the actual loneliness in the company of club kids who are just like the popular kids in high school only with better outfits. I am standing completely still and it is not a waste of time. What did I do to not belong? Nothing, darling. Thank you, Thank you – that nothing was the best thing you have said or done all day. Are you beginning to understand now? If not well, then I guess I will stop doing nothing (for now, I'm longing for the next time already!), and start digging deeper.

Everything is moving slowly. It used to go faster. When I was 20 I thought I knew almost everything. The truth was that the only reason I thought that preposterous thing, was because I hardly knew anything at all. I could read a book about a subject and believe I knew everything about that subject. Nowadays I can write a book about a subject and still feel uncertain. It will take me at least 4-5 years to finish this book and by then some quick and trendy person has probably finished a book on a similar subject and gotten credit. My mother took two weeks to pack for a trip and chewed her food 32 times. I refuse to speed up. Exhausting forward-success-striving mode our world will not survive for long at this pace just ask the marathon runner who knows she can not run as fast as a sprinter.

You came and heightened a keen capacity of physical sensation in me. "I cut you out because I couldn't stand being a passing fancy. Before I give my body, I must give my thoughts, my mind, my dreams. And you weren't having any of those." Sylvia Plath IsOnRepeatAgainAgainAgain a siren cry from us alpha femmes. The warmth of his mouth moulds me into molten lava delivering me from the very center of the earth where I have burned with a Y and another heat than the sunlight for so long. Yes, this hot temper is it's own good romance. The death of reason is not blackness but another kind of light with emotions that follow no logic and desires that are like farewells. I know the fiction of the fix and shall go as I came. Intact. Burdened by flaws that torture me, passionate for the impossible and inflamed by solitude pressed against my lips removing all lies and masks. He kisses me hard exposing a bleeding open wound, but I'm used to residing in the rooms of the heart where there is blood everywhere. You see a bike ride around the block. I see an enthralling adventure around the world. Volatile and Vulnerable. I stopped and I watched you. You were so beautiful. The moment – perfect. I must never forget it. It means the world to me and than tears it to shreds so Now that I've met you, would you object to never seeing me again?

My first love 7 years ago, I tried to save him from killing himself, but had I continued the noose would have only grown big enough for both of us. A dear friend later also took his life and I was too busy with my own problems. Oh, Claric-eee, you know what I know and so much more that I one day hope to learn. Can I call you up in the middle of the night and tell you that the panther doesn't frighten me one bit, we look into each other's eyes and we transmit ourselves into each other, but I can not sleep because I've lusted for and loved so many men with blank expressions on their faces hard as rock as they move forward, they move on, and they hurt me so much more than the guys who catcall, punch my face, pinch my ass. Clarice and I took valium to put a pillow over our screams, but we are still screaming, you just can't hear it. Alas, I have spread myself out wide again, maybe I should get back to the point, although I believe there is always more than one question to be asked like: Are you afraid of being alone? Why? And if the answer to the first question is no. Then, are you afraid of being together? Why? When Fiona Apple wrote the lyrics "If you don't have a date, celebrate, Go out and sit on the lawn and do nothing, cuz it's just what you must do and nobody does it anymore?" it was in a time before social media and smart phones. I wonder if Fiona Apple is just like me and doesn't have a smart phone and doesn't like social media? And I wonder if she is just like me, big on stage and in writing, smaller in life and though she has many friends and fans on facebook the only person who has called her in the last week is the doctor confirming that she doesn't have strep throat. If she also feels that our shared experience of being raped may have led to more sensitivity and vulnerability, but that this is an asset not a defect. We met by waterfalls and in bingo halls and created arenas for ulterior realities with windows vanished into thin air exposed to the four winds giantesses far from loneliness. Care to join us or would you prefer to stay in your neat clean house sitting atop the point of a needle?

How can I find the language to explain to you how this means nothing and very much at the same time, bidi-bidi-bom-bom, insywinsyteenyweeny, as I am simultaneously wide open yet still missing pieces and the subway leads to coney island and the sunrise and the waves. Stillness. I love this. But we don't even see them in all their glorious detail and we don't even know three living beings under that surface yet we claim to know shit. I always attempt to venture under the surface too quickly but the waves this season are seemingly cool and I am warm with intensity and brightly colored broken glass scattered all over the ocean floor lighting up the dark. You may never understand, But these are my anchors. The ground is not quick sand. Allow your running to come to a halt. I fucking dare you to stay with me for a minute in these words because I smell of you and for a secon that's the kind of thing that makes us forget that we have created a pile of garbage the size of Texas smack in the middle of the beauty that we haven't proven (BUT I HOPE) that (ONE DAY) we (WILL) deserve.

Wolf pack in the Tenderloin at midnight

Celeste Chan

Walking up Hyde Street, wrappers litter the ground, wet from rain. "Hey Sweetheart," comes a low, gravelly whisper, the disembodied voice from a car to the left. The four women keep walking, past the locked children's playground, past the Gangway, past the New Century Theater with its promise of sparkling lights and dancing women, and then past rows of closed shops that look like dank confession booths.

They stumble into line at Grubstake, waiting on the sidewalk until they are called in. API and queer, butch and femme and in-between. Hong Kong immigrant and Filipina mestiza, Bangladeshi and Chinese/Malaysian. They swill beer and swish their legs, clad in a swirl of black jeans and leather jackets, magenta velvet dress, teal rhinestones and a crusty polyester gown. Finally, they are eating. They talk over turkey dinner and mashed potatoes. It is pride month in the city, this place of queer mythology. A buttery smell wafts from the kitchen. Onions curling up like sweet question marks. Sausages frying in a steel pan, flames fanning out blue halos. And then they are done.

Outside Grubstake, there is a glint of broken glass, lying silver in the ground. Brush against a beefy arm. Beer breath. She doesn't remember the words spoken, only the sights and sounds. Tense arm gripping a corona bottle. Her friend, full of Butch swagger, doesn't move. She sees the man's tight jaw. His head, a giant pink Cabbage-patch doll, bald, pursed lips, atop a beefy body. He reaches past her, puts a gleaming bottle between her friend's legs. "Are you a man or a woman!" he says. Laughs. His two faceless friends laugh next to him. Her friend doesn't flinch. Grabs the bottle tightly. Holds it. If she needs a weapon.

He looks. She and her friends stand unmoving, in the doorway of Grubstake. She takes off her high heel, readies it with her hand. She remembers reading somewhere, that you could pierce a human heart with a heel. Used with force, the spiked stiletto could cut through flesh, through muscle. So she gets ready. Cabbage-patch moves first, pushes past them. "Go back to Concord!" her friend yells. They are luckier than the New Jersey 4. Cabbage-patch and friends are a beige blur, pushing past the women and into the restaurant.

She needs to be in motion. Pulls her friends with her, to embrace the Tenderloin streets at midnight. Drunken heart, crushed. For what almost happened. For what didn't happen. They are morphing. From female to feral, swallowing the night sky. Deviant and defiant.

Previously published in the Lambda Literary Fellows anthology, 2014.

Note: this non-fiction story respects gender self-identification

Exorcize (Excerpt)

Damien Luxe

Photos on this page by Najva Sol, 201.

Enter jogging in heels & clothes with coverage for workout gear, excited,

SAY -- Do you ever have .... Feelings?

DO -- Drop to pushups x5, pause

SAY -- Like weird feelings in your body?

DO -- Deep breathing x3

SAY -- What about feeling? Angry, Hungry-Angry, Feminist Rage Angry, Confused, Shut Down, Like You Can't Surpass Your Childood, Like Capitalism Is Out To Break You, Scared, Tired, Wired, Jealous, Guarded, Frazzled, Over-Socialized, Anxious, Disembodied, Hurt, Frantic!!?

DO -- stop moving, point

SAY -- Well you and I have some things in common!! I -- Damien Luxe, motivational speaker and aerobics instructor – have felt many feelings ...
    ... but I got away from them – using dissociation.

Say it with me: DIS-SO-CI-A-TION:

Photo by Sophie Spinelle, of Damien Luxe, 2013

Divorce, disunite, disjoint, separate, part, split up, split, break, break up.

Kicked to the corner of abnormal psych, yet 64% of people report it. The latin root is dealingismus structuralbullshitiminus. Can't pronounce it, can't feel it.

The third-person singular simple present is dissociates, present participle dissociating, simple past and past participle dissociated. BUT ITS NOT SIMPLE! ... or is it?

DO -- Separate hands along 'line.'

Wikipedia tells us that dissociation is an act of disuniting or separating a complex object into parts. You and I are certainly complex objects capable of great acts of safety creation for our parts.

DO -- Stretch up to side.

SAY -- But, these definitions are theoretical. I am here for the actual, the real, the grounded. I'm here to introduce TO YOU selections from my forthcoming motivational / aerobics DVD: SPANDEX EXPANSION!!!! a toolkit for dealing with Dissociation -- And, in this methodology, unlike in capitalism, you have options.

Vagina Jenkins, 2013

The Lady Ms. Vagina Jenkins uses dance, movement, and performance drawing from traditional burlesque techniques to explore herstories of her working class, femme, sexworker ancestors, while interrogating the exotification of feminine bodies, race, and of exotic dance itself.

Photos by Sophie Spinelle of Vagina Jenkins at El Rio, 2013.

4

The Show Must Go Wrong

Shut Up and Take Off Your Clothes

Heather María Ács

• •

"Wait...they expected STRIPPERS?" The glares from the audience confirm that whatever they expected, this North Carolina lesbian bar audience is not happy with our fully-clothed arts. In the middle of touring the first annual Heels on Wheels Glitter Roadshow in 2010...we got an education in the social expectations applied to queer people who display femininity: just shut up and take off your clothes... We couldn't figure out why the venue and audience at this one gig was acting so strangely to us, until we spotted the poster we'd sent them a few weeks earlier taped up on the front door...

So begins our introduction to this book, as an example of the ways sexism and femmephobia fueled us to create Heels on Wheels. But, my sweet femmes and allies, there is much more to this story than a simple cautionary tale. It was an epic catastrophe.

We booked our first actualized tour in about 2 weeks flat. Originally, we had visions of a short, cross-country tour that focused on a performance/workshop model tailored for high-paying college gigs, that would allow us to do sliding-scale community shows in each city. We felt excited and proud to embark on a project where we'd be making art AND money! We had promised superstars Leah Lakshmi Piepzna-Samarasinha and Silas Howard that we would do all of the work if they would join us on this sure-to-be lucrative adventure. After months of work and hundreds of emails, we'd solidified one university booking. In Texas.

We couldn't ask these rockstar, experienced artists to leave their lives and jobs to join a tour where they were guaranteed to make no money, so we decided to fly them to Texas for the one college gig. That left the issue: how are Damien and Heather getting to Texas... There was no way Damien and I were going to let capitalism win and give up when we had already put in so many hours of organizing and hard work. Fuck it, we said, we'll drive through the south and just get by on community shows. The real goal was to have a blast doing that anyway. I'm sure we can find some way to get the money to get this thing started... Now that we had to reconfigure everything, we had to ask ourselves the questions, "Who do we want to bring along and how do we want to frame this tour?"

Damien knew right away. We should do a femme tour! We need more space for femme-inine voices. We need to cultivate an expansive femme visibility that includes all genders and many versions of what surviving and thriving as femme folks can be. Heather wasn't as attached to the idea of focusing on femme. She had been out as femme for years, and was less interested in including certain types of identity politics in performance, but it was true that, in almost every performance situation, people assumed she was going to do burlesque because of the way she presents. Burlesque is an incredible art form with a working-class history, but no one likes to have assumptions made about them again and again. Plus, Damien had the van and knew how to make the website, so she went with it.

"Failure" can be an incredible gift. If we hadn't "failed" and been given the chance to start over from scratch, Heels on Wheels would have never been born. Making space for queer femmes and femme-ininities was to become a gender justice mission that would change our lives.

We booked our musician friend Chicago, a tender, goth-y creature beyond gender, who was performing as Princess Tiny and the Meats, at the time, and Sequinette Jaynesfield, a femme to femme drag queen of epic proportions, who is most likely visiting us from a future planet that is ruled by felines. They, like us, were still new to touring, in it for the adventure, and did not understand the reality of how little money we would make (i.e., none, because after driving across the country in the van, we would have to fly ourselves home from Texas, while Damien stayed in Austin for a few months).

Damien made a gorgeous tour poster and after writing many emails to venues and community spaces, which received no response, we realized that you have to CALL people in the south. ON THE PHONE. As New York organizers, our minds were blown. But we started calling and got to talk to so many incredible people who were excited to book our show. We organized through friends of friends, targeting community spaces, lgbt centers, and gay bars. We found an adorable bar in Asheville, NC on the internets, or, at least, their website was cute, with a fifties beehive, beauty salon theme and swirly writing. The perfect place for a femme show! We cold-contacted the bar and got in touch with the booker, who also played in a band. Our musician friends, and lovely hosts, Humble Tripe, from Raleigh-Durham would join us. Asheville has tons of cool weirdos, so we should have a good audience. This is going to be fantastic!

Our colorful tour poster on the front door was the first thing we saw as we walked up to the venue. It looked amazing! "What's written on it," someone asks, "Something's scratched out." "I dunno, let's just get all this shit inside," another responded. Sequinette is dressed as Dolly Parton, which everyone loves. (Getting into drag in a moving van as the sun fades is a feat of epic proportions, but necessary when you are driving hours each day and only have so much time at a venue.) This seemed to be the only thing that could make the older dyke bartender happy. She kept taking pictures, and we were just happy that she was happy about something. The booker greeted us and showed us to the dressing room. A dressing room, how exciting! And the stage looked great! A handful of young m.o.c. folks were scattered throughout the space. "Yeah, we're drag kings in a boy band," the booker explained, "We're really excited to perform with you." None of them helped us with our bags. (Later, it would be revealed that though there was, in fact, a drag king boy band, the lounging masculines were not a part of it. They were just... hanging out. Not helping. Cool.)

We set up for the show, waiting for the audience to arrive. They didn't. There were a handful of dykes loudly playing pool who had no intention of watching the show, about three friends of the band from Raleigh, and that was it. We'll win over the pool dykes, don't worry! And homos are always late. Let's just get started. Sequinette opens the show to get the "audience" riled up with her glorious drag performance. Then, we bring on Damien for the "Hot Pink Mass" (included in this anthology), a farcical church service for perverts, freaks, and weirdos, where she wears a hot pink dress with abundant side boob, sings "Father Figure" in church voice, and leads us through a blasphemous journey of her experience as a christian teen.

At this point, the handsomely dressed owner of the bar has shown up with a couple of femmes. They pull a table into the middle of the room in front of the stage. This is so great, they're gonna watch the show, they're gonna love us! Heather begins sharing, "what the brain forgets and the heart denies, the body remembers..." (included in this anthology), a serious, heartbreaking piece about trauma, grief, and the death of her mother. As her painfully vulnerable performance unfolds, it becomes clear that the owner and her friends are wasted, and getting more shitfaced by the minute. They are talking and laughing loudly, sloshing their drinks around, paying no attention whatsoever to what's happening on stage. At the same time, the drag kings start darting back and forth across the stage behind Heather while she's performing in order to get to the dressing room.

Heather goes into crisis mode, performing harder than she ever has in her life to drown out the chaos, choosing instead to focus all her energy on one of the only people listening, a friend of Humble Tripe, who is sitting in the front row with tears streaming down her cheeks. Finally, Damien manages to snatch one of the drag kings off the stage, hissing, "Do NOT go up there again while she's performing," and the owner's table still doesn't give a shit about anyone.

Mercifully, the piece finally ends and we convene in the dressing room. "What the fuck is going on here??? This place is a shitshow!!!" Heather is experiencing a new and specific combination of rage and ptsd, she can barely get the words out. Sequinette shares that one of the only locals in the room, a curvy babe we'd clocked earlier in heels and cut-off jean shorts, is pissed because she's a christian and she thought we were strippers. "She's pissed because she thinks we're strippers?" "No. She's pissed about Damien's piece because she's a christian. And she's also pissed because she expected to see strippers, and she wants to know how long it's gonna take before we take off our clothes."

Pin. Drop.

Wow.

The drag king band starts their ... set, air playing their instruments and lip synching to one of those millenial bands that were influenced by Stone Temple Pilot, like Creed. Reality is beginning to fully rupture...

Why would they think that? "I specifically told them we were performing

music, theatre, and drag," Heather retraces her steps. Let's get a drink at the bar and away from this atrocious music, someone suggests.

Damien returns from smoking a cigarette with an announcement, "Femmes, there's something I think you should see." She leads us out of the venue to face the front door and points a manicured nail, "Look. Look what's scratched out." We peered in closer to see that someone had written "Lesbian Strippers" on our tour poster. And that "Strippers" had then been crossed out and "Drag" written over the top of it. Well, at least that is more... accurate? If we were stripping, we'd at least be making some money.

"Well," Chicago said, "let's give them what they want."

Chicago was into wearing these hockey player shoulder pads and tight little football pants at the time. He looked amazing and faggoty. After the awful drag king band, he went out on that stage and performed the hell out of his pulsing dance tracks like a true queen. He even changed the words to one of his songs, "I've got a Crush on You, " to "I've got a Crunch on You," in honor of all the close proximity snacking we were doing in the van. We sang along, cheering, screaming, and dancing our asses off! He shimmied out of his football leggings and danced around in his underwear. We laughed so hard to keep from crying. Chicago totally saved the day! That is what femme solidarity looks like!

We finally escaped the bar and headed off to stay with an old friend of Damien's and their tender pit bull. They lived in a "rural apartment," which was really a house in the woods down an unlit, scary ass, winding road. Tragically, their girlfriend had just left them that week...and taken all the bedding, so we slept shivering on randomly arranged couch cushions under our drag for warmth. In the morning, we discovered the dog had burrowed into Sequinette's suitcase and eaten one of her wigs because it seemed the dog was sad and experiencing abandonment issues.

And that, my darling femmes and allies, is the story of our, thus far, only show in Asheville, North Carolina.

Photo of Sequinette in "the bar" and Chicago performing, 2010.

WHAT'S HAPPENING (2013)

Damien Luxe

Trigger warning: car accident & trauma

In Olympia, four Heels on Wheels touring folks were present during the tragic, though thankfully not fatal, accident that happened to our friend, host, and co-organizer femme badass extraordinaire Siobhan.

She was hit by a speeding drunk/high driver that appeared and accelerated out of nowhere as we were crossing the street together. She is alive and going to survive, but she is in the ICU w multiple serious injuries, some of which have changed her physical reality forever. She needs/will need an incredible about of financial and many other types of support.

Immediately, community skills as street medics, space-makers, crisis interventionists, and caretakers materialized from the Olympia, Bay Area, and NYC folks present. We are so grateful for each person's presence; it was also extremely upsetting. Being so close to the physical harm of our old friend [and for some, a person they'd just met] was and continues to be traumatic for all who were there.

As folks work together to help and support Siobhan, it's with love that we request support for all of those in her networks, including the folks not present who are organizing for her, the folks who were there, and folks who love and care about Siobhan across the country. Because of the ripple effects of trauma, each of us will need various kinds of care and healing, even as we continue to give each other and Siobhan care and support.

Heels on Wheels canceled what was to be our Olympia show for Siobhan's community to gather, collect donations for her long-term needs, and write her notes, and we are not doing our scheduled show on Friday in Seattle.

We are rescheduling our show in Seattle to Tuesday April 2 and keeping our other tour dates, after taking some healing time and discussing among ourselves.

ART, RESILIENCE, and TRAUMA

We are continuing to tour because the work we individually do and collectively create is about healing and communities, and we want to continue to share this art as we strive for healing among our group.

The Heels on Wheels Glitter Roadshow is deeply about resiliency — our performances, our transformative organizing, the magic that we femme-ifest for ourselves and the people around us. Our working-class-led tour harvests resilience to make art and to share it in the first place. As a group we honor and experience a wide range of oppressions, marginalizations, traumas AND creativity, prevailing, survival, community, and general badassery in all forms. So, we know about healing.

And we know that art heals hearts.

It has healed each of us, and as performing artists for many years we've seen it heal rooms of people. We know that many permutations of folks immediately affected by this specific tragedy need healing, and also that each of us, including those not touched at all, moves through the world affected by trauma, harm, and the pains of living; and it's for that and for each of us and for the many communities we are part of that we tour in the first place.

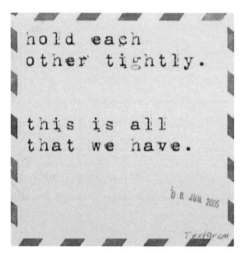

We need each other in many ways, and one way is to inspire resilience. This is one way to, in Heather's words from her piece, "hold each other tightly." This tour is one small healing gift.

WHAT YOU CAN DO & SHOULD KNOW

Heels on Wheels touring folks are physically ok, but we are collectively and individually in various states of shock, PTSD, and just fucking sad for our friend. We are also individual humans who are full of many kinds of feelings — you'll also see us cracking jokes and aiming for some fun. We might not all be excited to talk about our experiences.

At our remaining shows we will be collecting donation$ for Siobhan. We are also open to accepting healing items for ourselves, including: essential oils, crystals, jewelry, snacks, and/or talismans/gifts from whatever your practice may be.

As a tour, we look forward to sharing dialogue and our witchy and powerful selves with folks on the west coast.

xo, Damien Luxe, with Heather Acs, Shomi Noise, Lizxnn Disaster and Vagina Jenkins

Ed. note: This piece was originally published March 29 2013 on our blog.

I Really Miss Heels

Siobhan Katherine Flood

I still really miss wearing heels.

But I have recently decided that I like being alive more than I miss wearing heels.

I had organized a show for the Heels on Wheels babes in Seattle and they had just gotten to town that night. We were partying, catching up, singing epic karaoke. New friends and dear old friends. I'm sure that now we will never forget one another.

On March 27, 2013, I was run into by a car going 45 miles per hour by a drunk asshole who didn't and doesn't give a shit about ruining my life, almost killing me, maiming me, leaving me for dead, and not having insurance to reimburse me for my extensive hospital bills. I was already walking with a crutch at the time. It was a month after I had surgery to reconstruct my knee, as I was doored three days after I moved to Olympia.

I never thought I would be able to sit down and write about it. I couldn't even let myself talk about it for the first year and a half. I knew what I wanted to say. I saw the words form in my head. I knew that it would be therapy and I'm really appreciative to Heather for pushing me.

I don't have much regret in life. I know that if I really wanted to I could try to find someone to help me ride a horse (which I have never done). It hurts really bad that I can't hike up a mountain (maybe someday) and I know that the fear that I feel when I leave the house or cross a street will hopefully diminish someday. I know that If I didn't have my massive queer family I would be dead. It was so hard to continue living after that son of a bitch stole my leg. I had to do it for my friends, who were pouring so much love into me, and for my dog Buttercup.

Everything that hurts my heart seems to be losing its grip on me, the sadness, the anger. I feel like it's getting easier to imagine a future. Two years ago I couldn't plan for one.

Walking is getting less painful. There are always beautiful people around me lifting me up psychically, emotionally and literally. I'm so privileged to be given strength by my queer family.

I have been a community events planner and party promoter for years. The community I live in cares that I continued to throw parties after I lost my leg. It will always feel amazing to witness people having fun and looking like their freaky selves in a space that they feel safe.

Heels always made me feel like a Tower of Strength. But now that the option is gone, I'm still just a badass who survived being run into by a car and I can wear flats and sneakers and it doesn't fucking matter.

Photo by Rachel Robinson

Never Left Canada

Alvis Choi aka Alvis Parsley

. . . .

PRELUDE

"The passion for truth is silenced by answers which
have the weight of undisputed authority."

-- Paul Tillich

By sitting where you are sitting

you are representing an area

of the temporal lobe of my brain,

which is involved in the retention of visual memories,

processing sensory input,

comprehending language,

storing new memories, emotion,

and deriving meaning.

You will dictate the specifics of this performance –

how I move, where I look, in what tone I speak.

You are the trigger for my feelings -

subconsciousness that calls for my attention;

like a flashback that is out of control.

Sometimes when I go on and on on my own,

a memory flashes through my brain

all of a sudden.

"Oh! There is this thing that I remember."

"Ahhhhhhhh I need to talk about that."

"Um.

I am totally distracted."

Like,

right now.

INTERROGATION

I went on a performance tour for the first ever time.

The group was supposed to travel to Toronto, Montreal, and eight other cities in the United States.

After being at the customs for two and a half hours, I was denied entry.

My body was searched.

Two days of performing in Toronto and Montreal made me feel like I had traveled.

"I went on a tour!"

But as a matter of fact,

I never left Canada.

Put your hands here.

Spread your legs.

Wider.

To the back.

Look up.

Look here.

What is your citizenship?

What is your purpose of visit?

Who are you visiting?

Tell me the truth.

Stop playing games!

You are supposed to tell us the truth the moment you walked in.

I AM HERE

Many of you have heard of this story of mine -
a romantic story of mine that explains
why I am here in Canada.

When the story was still fresh,
I would give all the details to the listener
whether it's a group of audience or
a new friend.

I enjoyed recalling those memories.

As time passes by,
I began telling the story briefly
with less specifics each time.

It has been four years since the story began.
I grew up from a 25-year-old teenager
to a 29-year-old "adult".

I decided that this
is the briefest version of the story:
I
AM
HERE.

No one forced me. I had the privilege to displace myself.
It was a conscious decision.

Although when love is involved,
nothing is too conscious.

I am here because I can be someone else.

Here I can be free.

Here I am queer.

Here I grow fast.

Here I am an "artist".

But

here I have less money.

Here I am less.

Here I am a "person of colour".

Here I am queer and only queer.

Here I struggle.

Here I barely survive.

I was taught to give the "right" answer, not the true answer.

I was taught to lie because nobody in power wants to hear the truth.

My brain split into two at the customs.

"What is your citizenship?"

I wanted to say Canada.

I'm not even 1% Canadian.

And when I said

"I am a temporary resident,"

they said,

"you mean you are a visitor."

SUBMISSION

I stepped out of the van.

I wasn't sure if I would be coming back

even though I did say

"see you on the other side."

My intuition is always right.
But I don't always listen to it.
Sometimes I wonder what happens
if I only live by intuition.

No fear. Just follow.

Like leaves blown off the tree
into the air,
to the other side of the world;
or paper clips dragged by a piece of magnet.

No way to resist and don't want to resist
but submit.
What happens when I submit to my guts?
Drop your weapons.
It's time
to surrender.

DUAL

You are my doctor. I am your patient.
You are poking my brain.
The thing about memory is that
we don't only remember the event.
The exact feeling that we had
when the event happened is also stored.

The event and the feeling are locked together.
When we are triggered, we first relive the past.
It is not a recall.

And what we feel
is not just re-interpretation,
but is exactly the same
as how we experienced it in the first place.

I find myself a part of a specific situation
that progresses and evolves
just as the original situation did.

I am dual
in that I am at the same time
in the experience
and outside of it

observing it.
I am both the actor
and the audience.

And so are you.

ISOLATION
In response to the conditions,
I am a forager.
A city forager.
I am a traveling artist
going from neighbourhood to neighbourhood.
I am a visitor.
I am not a nomad
But I am uprooted.
I am here.
I live a fantasy life that no one at the border can comprehend.

What have you been doing in Canada?

Research.

What kind of research?

I research on neighbourhood engagement in art institutions in ethnic neighbourhoods.

Which institution do you work for?

I am an independent researcher. I work with different institutions.

Do you get paid?

No.

How do you support yourself?

I have savings. My family supports me.

Do you pay rent?

Yah.

***

A PLUS (+) times (x) a MINUS (-) equals a MINUS (-).

It doesn't matter how big the plus (+) was,

or how little the minus (-) was.

The result

is always a minus (-).

AS AN ARTIST

I ask you to be gentle with me

and my lived experience.

But do not use it as an excuse

to be gentle with my art.

Don't be gentle with my art.

But be reasonable.

You don't need to be professional.

But show me

how you connect.

You are the one whom I want to talk to.

I don't want to talk in the way that you do.

But I want to show you

my care for you.

True that I don't need your permission.

But I wanna please you.

I wanna please you so much whenever I go stage.

I wanna please you too.

I wanna please you so much whenever I go stage.

I wanna please you.

I wanna please you so much whenever I go stage.

HOLD ME

Someone has to die.

We seem to care for each other when something happens.

And for queer people of colour,

there is always something going on.

We are always responding to the systemic problems that affect us on a daily basis.

A close friend moves away

Getting sick

No food in the fridge

"There are only 28 days this month and I gotta pay rent soon."

Someone's hurt

Someone dies

We are always triggered.

I cannot answer the question

"How have you been?"

without only considering how I am doing

on that particular day

that particular period of the day

that particular moment.

What if we assume that we are not well

most of the time?

that we all have frequent moments of not being able to take care of ourselves

that our instinct is to be held and be taken care of?

What if instead of investing time on ourselves

we are supposed to spend more time on one another?

And in order to be able to take care of others

we must be able to first receive

to feel well.

What if we really are interdependent like that?

Please Put Your Oxygen Mask on Before Assisting Others.

Why?

Why is it that as adults

we need to breathe more
than the children
or seniors next to us?

Babies who don't get enough stroking
in their early years
will literally die
if not physically
then psychologically.

My mother used to have these stay-home factory jobs
where she assembled parts
of plastic flowers,
toys and electronic products.
It was when factories still existed in Hong Kong
before they all moved to mainland China.

I was a toddler.

When she worked with her back facing me,
I would ask her if she could play with me
just for a moment.
I would beg her to play with me.
She would hold me for a couple minutes
and quickly put me down again
so she could get back to work.

I believe that is where
my fundamental loneliness came from.

Please.
Please play with me.

MOTHER

When I trace the root of my humour,

I give credit to my father.

I give credit to him

for all the good things that I am.

I give credit to my mother

for all the destructive personality that I have.

She drove me nuts

until I stopped living with her.

True that I grew up in British Hong Kong

but I was disciplined in communist style by my mother.

Her strategies centered around three things:

Shame

Pain

and Apology.

None of it was verbal.

When she made me apologize,

she made me sit down at the desk

to write a repentant letter while she did her chores in the kitchen.

My introvertness was considered as lack of proper manners.

One time I didn't greet someone she knew on the street.

She was so mad.

But she waited

until we got home.

She made me stand on a stool

holding my ears with my small fingers

for four hours in the afternoon

to reflect on what I "did".

Four hours.

I suspect that was where I got my training as a durational performance artist.

I survived in my own thoughts -
in my own imagination.
Kindness is my norm.
And when shitty things happen,
it just seems ridiculous.

I guess I have no way to justify the existence of cruelty
unless it's a joke.

I was born kind.
And you can't make me evil.

FIT IN
Where does my body belong?
Where is the gutter?

The idea of getting to another country
by just crossing a short tunnel
is bizarre to me.
How is it a different place if it is this close?
Where do I fit without changing my shape?
How do I fit in without feeling suffocated?

Border is fantasy.
Border is fantasy.
Border is fantasy.
Border is fantasy.

Before teleportation becomes a real thing,
I would like to be able to Fedex myself to places.
Human packages become legal.
They are for people
who have low social status
or limited mobility.
They are affordable.
The only down side is that
you don't get much air –
you might die on your way to the destination.
It is risky.
But it is worthwhile.

You write an invoice,
declare my value
and place of origin.
Have someone pick me up.
48 hours later,
I'll be there
or I'll be dead.
No questions asked.

While humans are supposed to be more human than things,
Humans are more threatening than things.

Because things don't speak.
Things don't act.
Things don't move.
Things don't smile.

And I am capable
of all of those things.

The Show Must Go Wrong: Smokebomb edition

Heather María Ács

"Sure, you can work with us, just come volunteer at the next Peepshow!"

Sabina's first event was at one of our monthly Opentoe Peepshow salons in 2013.

At this point, I was still grasping to the belief that if I organized every single tiny detail and was EXTREMELY PREPARED that things would go exactly as planned.

AHAHAHAHAHA!!!

Reality Check: The Show Must Go Wrong

Photo by Nicole Myles of Sabina, Damien, Heather. Not from the Peepshow described.

We weren't in our regular venue because it was a day that a lot of people watch football in bars and our loving bar needs to make money to continue to host us, so we tried out a new space called Gureje run by Jimi, a super cool dude.

We had an awesome line-up. Silas Howard, Cristy Road, Merrie Cherry, and a performer who will remain nameless due to reasons that will be revealed later.

Cristy Road presented an unforgettable, never-before-seen slideshow of an illustrated tv talk show she created with her sister as a kid, hosted by Joan Rivers and a rabbit woman named Prudence the Pig.

Silas Howard presented an incredible slideshow and performance piece on the 1989 earthquake in San Francisco, queercore, and Freddie Mercury.

Merrie Cherry straight up didn't show. She's a drag queen.

Pro Tip:
Make sure you have enough people in the line-up in case one person bails.

Our final, nameless performer took the stage in a painstakingly handmade fishnet costume and began singing along to a thumping dance track. It's loud for an early Sunday evening, but the audience is in. We had announced to the audience that the performer would be using a fog machine. However, what they failed to mention was that they were going to set off a smoke bomb.

That's right.
THEY DID NOT TELL US THEY WERE GOING TO SET OFF A SMOKE BOMB IN AN ENCLOSED SPACE.

I don't know what kind of venues host queer art events where you live, but in Brooklyn they're not that big. And I don't know how many of you have ever been trapped in a room with a smoke bomb, but it's not cute. The air immediately fills with smoke, people start coughing, you can barely see. Luckily there were two side doors that opened onto a patio, which two HOW members ran to and flung open. Over the sound of people coughing and chairs scraping as the audience exited the premises, said performer repeated into the microphone, "Hey can you turn it up? Can you turn it up? It's not loud enough. I need the music turned up." Now the thumping of house music and smoke are pouring into the Brooklyn night on a quiet Sunday evening in a venue below notoriously cranky gay upstairs neighbors. The sound person has fled the room because she was having an asthma attack. The performer set off ANOTHER SMOKE BOMB, at which point I stepped onto the stage and blocked them from the already obscured audience, and said, "You're done. You have to stop. That's it. You're done." The performer was indignant, but I did not have time to deal with their attitude. I started circling the space while wildly waving the smoke towards the open doors and apologizing to the audience members, including my PREGNANT friend who attended the show because it should have been a lovely evening of queer art and community rather than a hotbox of faggotry.

I was full of rage, but trying to keep it together. How could someone be so irresponsible??? What if someone had an asthma attack? A panic attack?

Wait, someone is having an asthma attack. Am I having a panic attack? How could I be so irresponsible? Surely there must have been something I could have done to stop this or fix this. I was a complete failure. In one of my rage-xiety induced circlings I passed Sabina. We locked eyes. THIS is what we've invited her to be a part of? "Is there anything I can do to help?" she asked, in what I would learn is her consistently loving and solid way. "Uhhh, no, yeah, no, it's fine, I mean, it's not fine. I'm sorry, it's just, it's not...usually...like... this..."

So, the show didn't end there, oh no! The show must go on even if the show has gone tremendously wrong. Queers are, sometimes, forgiving, and so the audience members who were able to return came back inside once the smoke had literally cleared. Jimi, the owner, took photos of the final performer and the audience with a big smile on his face. Like I said, he's a pretty cool dude. Damien was dissociating. I was in a rage. Sabina was smil-ing the pain away. Nicole stewed with hatred as she tried to breathe. The final performer did something interesting, I'm sure. I can't remember. What I do remember is that at the end of the final performance seven firefighters rushed into the venue and froze when they saw the audience.

Pro Tip:
If firefighters ever enter your event, make sure someone yells "Take it off!"

Or at least in the stories you tell after, say that someone did.

So, a huge batch of hunky Brooklyn firefighters walked in, a gay porn fantasy. The room fell silent for a moment, then someone yelled, "Take it off!" The firefighters dropped their packs, threw off their jackets, and started sliding suspenders down their muscle-y shoulders. The crowd went wild!!!

Not really. It was, of course, awkward to the point of hilarity, but I was still wound so tightly, all I could feel was utter embarrassment and certainty that I was gonna blow a gasket. Something unfolded where a room full of queer adults had to explain to professional city workers that there was in fact, no fire, just a performance artist letting off smoke bombs to house mu-sic. Cool.

Even smoke bombs and firefighters can't deter a queer goodbye, so lots of folks were still lingering when the cops showed up. Fmfl. I was sure this would be the final straw. Jimi would be furious and ban us from the space forever. Fuck. But he handled them calmly and explained that everything was under control. He was actually quite happy with the event and invited us back anytime.

Sabina joined Heels on Wheels.

My friend had an adorable baby.

We included an addendum to our call for performers:

"If your performance involves body fluids, liquids, gasses, breaking skin, etc, please provide more details below and know that we will need to check in about this. NO SMOKE allowed."

Performers often asked about this request and all we would have the energy to say was, "Trust us. It's necessary."

Pro Tip: Trust us. It's necessary.

I received a voicemail from the performer who will remain nameless a couple months later. It said something to the following effect:

"Uhm, hey, I'm applying for a grant that requires video and I think you all took video of the show that night, so if you could send that to me sooner than later, that would be really great, because I really need to make this grant deadline."

Institutional Funding: Friend or Foe?

anonymous Heels on Wheels collective members

We don't have the energy to write this essay because we've spent so many hours writing grants we didn't get.[1]

---

1   Special thanks to the folks at Brooklyn Arts Council who have consistently supported us over the years and to Great Small Works for fiscal sponsorship. Thanks to NYSCA who hooked it up one time before their application process got so complicated we just couldn't.

Art and lettering by the Dandy Vagabonds. Photo: Damien Luxe, 2012.

5
Coming into our Own

Sisters

By Zachary Wager Scholl

We knew each others bedrooms like we knew each others secrets: messy, but there was bound to be something good hiding around here somewhere. Full of dust and stained polaroid heirlooms of our youth shoved into shoe-boxes; clothes that meant the world to us piled on the floor or falling out of the closet; drawers full of loose change, mix cd's and high school notes folded up neatly amidst the paper clips, gum wrappers, old condoms and weed; walls covered in scotch tape cut-out tributes to our pop star punk rock idols. We knew where the creeks in the floorboards were, and we knew who the different footsteps belonged to. We knew 7-11 nachos. We knew survival.

Out of control was your favorite saying, you'd use it for everything: my grandpa is out of control today; this bacon cheeseburger is out of control; Britney's new single is out of control. "Zachary, you are out of control!" Out of control, you'd tell me, when I came up with some plan for us to do that night. "Well what do you wanna do instead?" I'd say. This was summer, this was the suburbs, there's never anything to do. I mean, we could do anything we wanted. I mean, let's walk. Come on.

This is where we'd get dressed up, go out and roam the streets looking for M&M's: mischief and men, aka dick. You would come over to my house with your drag bag and get ready in my bathroom because my parents didn't care and your grandparents didn't know, and you had already gotten kicked out of your moms' house when your step dad found out and threw your dresses and heels in the front yard. My drunk dad looking up at you from the bottom of the stairs: "you look real pretty tonight." I'd put on my tightest tank top and jersey jacket while you contoured your face and brushed out your long, wavy lace-front hair. You were five different kinds of pretty: pretty like the soft edges of the glossy pictures you could take at the mall, like the way a sunset strikes fire across the sky, like the twinkle of new press-on nails, or like the blur of neon lights from Bailey's Crossroads. Pretty like a slap in the face. You ready?

There was a lightness when we walked, like as if there was air under our feet and we could walk for hours and hours and never get tired, nothing was too far. There was a closeness, like you could feel the heart beat of each baby boomer house; small, brick or clap board, all designed the same. Sagging porches, low voices, drooping eyebrows; small lights that would glimmer like the flick of a lighter. The heat radiated from every surface, expelling outward, pushing us forward while holding us back: the heat held everything. Gotta get outta this house, get outta these clothes, get outta this night all the Virginia haze had to offer. We would sway and swish along with the Oak trees; there was silence and crickets, the snap of a finger or the roar of an engine.

This was our ritual, our evening prayers put into action. We walked the scripture, working it out, talking and laughing and shouting between us the good word. When you're young and broke, a faggot and a drag queen without a car, everywhere you walk feels like an epic destination and testament of determination. Here we are, so small so brave, we made it out of the house and into the world: our presence is our defiance. We were like sisters. You'd tell me about your new crush at work, and I'd tell you about how some daddy gave me a blowjob under the stall in Barnes & Noble, and you'd tell me I was out of control. We talked about moving away, but where would we go? You wanted to stay here forever; I was counting down the days 'til New York. You'd say that you wished you had a boyfriend, and I'd go on about how we're resisting the patriarchal and heteronormative notions of intimacy by cruising, but I think you just wanted to talk about being lonely and afraid, except you never said you were afraid. You said you never knew what to say to a guy, and I said just be yourself, and you said but that's the problem. You said don't move away.

The plan was that if anyone asked, I was your cousin Christopher. We always had some plan, but I was never sure how much that mattered. I was your wingman, your defenseless body guard look-out girl, as we circled the blocks and squares of Kingsley Commons. There were always guys hangin out, walking around; guys with swagger who'd make eyes at you and then me and then us, not sure what to make of this weirdo duo. We'd circle and circle, talking in hushed whispers; our eyes peeled and ready, scanning the small two-story condos for any sign of movement. "When we're done, can we go and get some McDonalds??" I'd say. "Jesus, Zachary; you are out of control; yes, but just a little longer..." Eventually we saw him: somewhat short, stocky with greasy hair in his face, wearing cargo shorts and chucks. You went over to talk to him, twirling your hair around your index finger, leaning onto one hip, your done-up eyes sparkled with mystery and fun under the lamppost. I hung back a little, giving you some space, but watching for visual cues of what's about to happen. Your head nodded to the side and you took one step towards a grove of trees on a little hill by a playground: he followed you over as I kept up my sisterhood lookout. Afterwards, once we were far enough away, you said he came too soon and the fucker got cum on my shoes. I said that was sweet of him, a take-away of the moment, but you weren't having it.

When we crossed route 50 and walked into the McDonalds I laughed and said "I know that man" gesturing to the cashier. We made eyes at each other as I ate my nuggets and fries, and he glanced over to the restroom. He had sweet looking, sad eyes. I looked at the restroom one more time, and then back at you and said "I know that man. He followed me home on Halloween last year" and then I got up to walk to the men's room, licking off the honey mustard sauce from my fingers. You sighed and said "you are out of control, but don't take too long, okay?" as I sauntered off. I waited by the sink, washing my hands and looking at myself in the mirror. I was wearing a red & and white jersey jacket that said "BROOKLYN" across the chest. After a couple minutes he came in. Slightly shorter, he looked up and had a nervous smirk on his face. Hi, I said. Hi. He gestured towards the stall with his head, and I followed in behind him. There was this heaviness, pulling us down; closeness as he paused before kissing me. Everything smelled like piss and the air was thick with happy meals as we pressed against the metal stall. Down he went, fumbling with my baby gay zipper on my baby gay jeans that wouldn't baby gay budge. Swaying and swishing, I fell into him, and then back out. This was out of control, this was awesome. When he tried to turn me around and press his dick against the crack of my ass, I said I have to go; my friend, she's waiting. His eyes pleaded, as if to say please don't go, please don't move away.

"What the hell, Zachary?" you said as we walked back out into the night. You lit up another cigarette as we walked along the side of an empty route 50, kicking pebbles, wading through patches of grass and weeds, looking out into the distance. A slight breeze catches us, blowing a few strands of hair across your face, as you took a big drag causing little embers to fly out into the wind. You were always five different kinds of pretty. As we crossed the highway, near where the church is by that big hill of boulders with the huge cross on top, we stood in the middle, looking out in our bored defiance. "Oh god," you said, "there's just so much traffic."

Oh Bae & In the Summer of Erica

Shira Erlichman

OH BAE

Oh bae, all I want is a faux fur coat and to be surrounded by evergreens.

Oh bae, all I want is to live inside a drum you bang & bang, ya know?

Oh bae, don't you want to grow under the porch with me?

Oh bae, I made a garden up & everyone called it language.

Oh bae, did you know in French water is gendered? Yes, of course it's male.

Oh bae, they, yes They, don't know anything about anything tender.

Oh bae, I saw a flower give its whole purple cunt to a bee once.

Oh bae, all I want is a backside like a peacock's.

Oh bae, you say my backporch is like, perfect.

Oh bae, your library of kisses keeps me wellversed in drool.

Oh bae, did you know laughter is darkness clearing its throat?

Oh bae, badabing my cherry while time whistles by.

Oh bae, I killed the guy that said love is the platter, not the meal.

Oh bae, I fed him till he cried snotwhiskey.

Oh bae, I threw God my questions & the boomerang stuck.

Oh bae, who are we gonna be when we die? I wanna see it.

Oh bae, tear my shoulders apart like orange slices.

Oh bae, I covet my neighbor's hot chocolate.

Oh bae, run the bath until it's out of breath.

Oh bae, dreaming is a type of math.

Oh bae, who put the sun where it's at?

Oh bae, I put the sun where it's at every time I see it!

Oh bae, if I ever cared about anything, it's how anteater the anteater.

Oh bae, did you know feckless is a word? But feck isn't! What the feck?

Oh bae, keep my deck of cards warm while I go swimming.

Oh bae, the night has enough arms for everyone.

Oh bae, open the door. It's me.

In the summer of Erica, she said things to me. Things like "If you don't come visit me, I'm going to skin a cat and stick it in the mail." But then, she'd send me envelopes so thick they'd qualify as packages. There were pencil drawings in there: of her cat taking a shit, or the cute boy who worked alongside her at the post office. Quick sketches of a bird in a nest, the eggs voluptuous and offkilter. Her handwriting was like a thirteen year old boy's, but sweeter, ragged, violent and loopy. The pencil would smudge off on my hands.

That summer I lived at home and would fling open the top stair's harsh gate, run down my parents' stairway, to at least two letters a week. This week she went on a date with the cashier from the Mexican restaurant. This week she was thinking about the year her dad died and how the doctor had told her brother he was "the man of the house now." This week she was doodling elaborate animated shits with flies licking it up like drunk groupies.

This week she filled the entire envelope with glitter and wrote in criminally huge bubble letters HI SHTINKY BUTT and this week was going to be the one where I finally told her how I felt, which was: When I moved into your dorm in December, and you painted my nails, you held my fingers like sushi and I wanted to die. Which was: When you would get changed halfinfrontofme, flinging vintage finds off your body like tossaway prayers, I was breaking up with my girlfriend in my head, I was holding a pillow against my chest like a door on top of a door. Which was: When I first saw you, my tongue became a rock and I swallowed it and now what I want to say lives at the bottom of my stomach, collecting moss, and your sexiness is a canopener I swallowed which is of no use to the rock. Instead I said: OK, I'll visit.

It was summer and I decided to break my longterm girlfriend into seventy very visible sharp pieces in order to figure out the wilderness between us, which I was sure you were aware of, which I was sure, once I pointed to the fire with a wildly lit branch you would nod, and maybe take off your pants, and maybe take me.

When you picked me up at the bus stop you shrieked like a disappearing witch, but there you were: blonde, frizzy curls swept up in a manic hello. Oo la la silliness curving to greet me without a hug, but with affection. Me, I was rediscovering high heels that summer. Cherryred pencil skirt up past my bellybutton, little white tank top, bloodied lips, careful cat eyes, newly cropped pixie cut: I was a spell.

The sky was stuffed with clouds. You opened the car door for me, because I had a suitcase, and we spilled inside into our usual electric cacklings.

That night, at the foot of your bed, I told you. You laughed. You bounced on the bed, like a child. You asked me how I felt, still laughing, then apologized, "Oh my god, I'm sorry, I just don't know what to say, how good for you, how great!" and then because we didn't know what to do I left to sleep on three thin blankets on the floor in the other room.

There is the moment when the envelope is not fully open yet, where the finger is snagged on something what the most jagged, toughest piece of the paper, or maybe the art trapped inside is lifting its voice and its voice is so raw it clings to a nail.

There is a poet from my birthland who once wrote "You gave me a letter opener made of silver. Real letters aren't opened that way. They're torn open, torn, torn."

When I woke the next morning, you were gone. I sat at your kitchen table writing affirmations in my red spiralbound notebook. I am happy. I am loved. I have everything I need. It was a "practice," as I liked to call it, but truer eyes would dub it a disease. The worm of positive thinking was squirming its way through my skull, into my gut, through my hands and poof, making me a believer. Everything would be okay, love was all and all was love, or something.

The mirror told a different story. The mirror showed a fading girl. A girl who was missing meals and reading too much into tea leaves and gambling with hope. Hope is a kind of terror. The mirror showed a girl who'd paid a psychic $60 to tell her what she needed to hear, which was:

Erica.

Late afternoon you walked into the kitchen. Sunlight was everywhere, especially your curls. I put the pen down. You pulled up a chair. "I can't," you began, against what the psychic had said; you talked and kept talking until my blood turned a cool tequila, clear with fermented hope. You riddled the air with strange facts: "I even called my exboyfriend to talk about it; Theo would know what to do," you said, for seemingly no reason.

Maybe I was a letter. Maybe God was made entirely of hands. Maybe tears are a form of letteropening.

When you suggested without suggesting that I should go home early, that worm dug the dark soil behind my eyes: Everything is okay. I am loved. I am happy. With the phone to my ear, I bought the next available bus ticket, while you chased a fly, slapped a wall, and gave up. "We cool?" You asked, picking up my suitcase, putting it down, leaping around the bright room, not knowing where to put your nervousness. "Sure," I slurred. The word took forever, as if it didn't believe my mouth.

I question my muscle memory

niknaz

I question my muscle memory that wants to start writing from the right to left. And then I question myself for questioning. But it's true. It can't be muscle memory but a never created memory. Unfutured. My desire is perhaps so strong to will it true. But not today. I don't have those right-starting words today.

If only I could draw...

Last night I wanted to laser-etch the moon behind the 7 cranes as I was on the overpass riding home. Sandwiched between 135th & Amsterdam & the men in the van playing poker by Grant's Memorial. Riverside Drive. Even the name evokes hidden magic potions of the Hudson and Harlem.

It arm-wrestled gravity so effortlessly. It? Me on my bike, the moon in the sky, big, rich, round. Very round.

Magnetized to me.

For 100 blocks. Suspended to my left. Cityscape foreground. Unblurred.

First woman

Bekezela Mguni

Call me eve

I'll split a pomegranate with you

Share worlds unknown

Only selfish gods would hide

Insecure about their place in the sky

I really want to know you

Beyond dusk

Before dawn

Close and quiet

Loud if you like

I'll have you oceans wide and bottoms of seas deep

As vast as you are

An endless horizon

A new constellation

A thousand time reincarnation

A Song of Solomon chanted by his most devoted lover

I will write you new gospels

A universe of possibilities

Salvation living on the tips of my fingers

This body is holy

My name, a hymn

Call me

My walk, a prayer

Watch me

Liberation, in my embrace

Come

I will hold you

I can

Constellation

Sassafras Lowrey

· ·

Star watched as the blood and black ink mixed at the tender skin over the place on her wrist she used to slash when she was little. The dude, cigarette hanging from his lip, pulled the gun away and wrapped it in a plastic bandage.

"No charge," he said arm encircling her shoulder. "Come have a drink with me."

Star snarled a smile and said she needed to go freshen up in the bathroom. There was piss on the floor and sharpie graffiti on the walls of the little room. She thought about the last time she saw Dean, how hy had fucked her hard and fast in a rest stop bathroom, cock sticking through the button fly of hys faded jeans, her stockings torn to let him in, panties pushed aside. The throbbing on her wrist was for hym.

Every time a butch left or broke her heart she added another star.

She rumbled through her purse, pushing aside band-aids, candy, quarter machine toys, and keys, while chewing on the bleach-fried ends of her pink hair. After touching up her sticky bubblegum lip-gloss, Star slowly weighed her options. She could throw $40 on the counter and run. Walking into the shop she'd planned to pay, but it wouldn't leave her with anything for food or gas. The alternative was to let him grope her in a bar for a while. Then, Star noticed the little window above the toilet.

She turned the water in the sink on full blast. The drain was clogged, and the sink started filling. She had to hurry. There was no lid on the toilet, so she balanced as best she could on the piss slick seat and cracked open the window. Just as she'd hoped, the back parking lot was empty. Star pushed her purse out first onto the concrete and then, careful to not scrape her wrist, pulled herself up. Normally, she loved her thick hips but cursed them now, as they stuck against the frame of the little window. As she worked to wedge them free, she could hear tattoo dude cursing and asking if she was ready yet.

Star spilled onto the sun-baked concrete, pulled her skirt down, and raced for her car. The drivers side door was beat in so badly it no longer opened, since that night a couple months ago when a coworker saw Dean waiting in the parking lot to pick her up after the shift was over. She quickly crawled in over the passenger seat, tossing fast food wrappers and wigs into piles in the back, and shoved her key in the ignition. The dirty My Little Pony keychains dangled to the spiderweb of stockings that stretched in tatters over her knee. She sped out of the strip mall, wrist pulsing in time to the old motor. As Star hit the highway she reached below her seat, grabbed the first cassette, and smashed it into the player.

"That girl thinks she's the queen of the neighborhood....."

Star knew she shouldn't waste the gas, but all she wanted to do was drive. She let the mix-tape hy'd made turn over and gunned it into Georgia. By now, it was getting dark. She was supposed to be at the Winn Dixie. That was the newest gig, deli girl. She worked ever-rotating part-time jobs, three at a time, to cover the rent on her little garage apartment and to keep its roach-filled cabinets stocked with Wal Mart groceries. She started adding as she drove, the cash rolled into the toe of her leopard print heels, the bills pressed under the shelf paper in the kitchen, and now the $40. She could still make rent and eat, for another week. Winn Dixie would have fired her for getting another tattoo anyway.

Star pulled off the highway and turned on a back road. She hadn't planned on going to the bar tonight. She hadn't planned anything since hy left. In the Charlotte parking lot, she tugged her hair into ratty pigtails and added more lipgloss. She pulled the bandage off the new tattoo and rubbed melting ice from her pre-tattoo soda over the oozing mess to clean it up a little.

Star hadn't been out since hy left. As she walked in, she saw a group of femmes in the corner staring. She knew them, but wouldn't call them friends. Star'd never had many friends, mostly just whichever butch she was tucking into bed with her. She walked past the bar, heading to the bathroom. There, she splashed cool water onto her face and dabbed her wrist dry with some wadded toilet paper before heading back out.

She hadn't expected to see Dean, had heard hy lost hys mind, fagging and shacked up with some baby butch at hys mamma's house, eating her food and leaving Star to pay all the rent on the place that had been theirs. Star hadn't had parents in along time. Back in high school, she was the sort of girl the teachers talked about, all tight jeans and tissue tits spilling out of babydoll t-shirts. Only Star was the worst, never sneaking off with rodeo boys.

She ran away with the first butch she ever met. Mel lived in a trailer just outside town and would pick her up from school in her rusted truck when she got off the construction site. Star would climb in, scoot along the torn bench seat and run her short chipped nails up Mel's denim thigh while they peeled out of the parking lot and past the football field. One day she never went back.

A year later she got her first star.

Star hadn't expected to see Dean, but there hy was, sitting on a stool behind the pool table. Star froze but then hy smiled. Hy motioned her over and she went, as though nothing had happened. There was no sign of the baby butch. Star didn't trust herself if that little shit were to show hir face. She pushed the thoughts of stomping baby into the ground with her pink combat boots out of her mind and concentrated on Dean. Hy asked how she'd been. She lied that things were fine. She didn't ask how he was. Star reached to run a finger down hys thigh, right above the knee but hy grimaced and pulled back.

Hy'd seen the star.

Dean asked if the tattoo meant it was over. Star thought about the ring she kept in the glove compartment, the one hy had shoplifted from Wal Mart all cut glass and fake gold. She'd said yes to being hys wife, something she never thought she'd be to anyone, and a month later hy left. She wanted to drink, to allow herself to forget the bills stacked next to crusted dishes on her counter. She wanted to forget the weeks she spent sobbing on the cracked linoleum of her living room floor, flat and faded like the inflatable unicorn she'd begged hym to buy her at the county fair, television blaring evangelical telethons because she couldn't peel herself up long enough to move the antenna.

"It doesn't have to be," she said.

Tonight, hy looked as good as she remembered: slicked back hair, tight jeans and crisp white t-shirt pulled taught over the ace bandage that held his chest down as tightly as she let hym hold onto her heart, cock stretching hys left thigh.

Dean saw her eyes flicker down just for an instant, and knew Star was still hys.

Dean grabbed her hand, and Star followed hym back into the bathroom. Hy pressed against her. "I've missed you," hy moaned into her neck. Star's head fell back against the wall sticky with piss and posters for shows. Dean wished he hadn't drunk so much. Hys mind drifted to that time they went to the mall, how Star had been trying on dresses that wouldn't zip over her curves.

In the food court, hy'd lost his cock. Back then, hy packed with a cup like baseball players wore. There was a group of teenagers, the sort hy was most scared of, with cowboy hat shaded cold eyes. There were more of them than hy could fight. The boys were laughing. Dean froze but Star bent and grabbed hys dick from the floor shoved it tenderly into her purse. She grabbed hys hand and walked them past the giant bible store and out of the mall into the parking garage. Hy never admitted it out loud, but hy felt safer with her. Dean knew Star never ran away from a fight. Dean opened her door first, then climbed in on the driver's side. This was before her car got beaten in. Hys hands were greasy from the fries they'd shared at the food court, but she opened for hym anyway. She couldn't have been comfortable door handle pressed into her back, but hy needed this, needed her. Dean opened hys eyes as hy trailed beer-fed kisses across her celestial collarbone and realized hy couldn't afford to lose her.

When they left the bathroom, Dean felt dizzy, drunk on Star's cherry lipgloss. Hy saw the femmes, mostly exes, in the corner. They tried to catch hys eye, but hy looked away. Star said she had to get going, that she worked the early shift at the gas station. Dean did the math and realized by the time she made it back to town she was only going to get a couple hours of sleep. It wasn't until hy unlocked and opened the door of her car that hy realized hy still carried the key on the thick clip that rocked against hys hips as hy walked. She crawled into the dark car, skirt riding up her ass. Hy wanted to crawl in next to her, let her drive him home, head resting on the torn fishnets of her thigh, sink into the sticky warmth of their sheets. Even if she'd let hym, hy couldn't. That baby butch was curled up in Dean's childhood bed, hys mamma asleep in the next room. Mamma would be waking soon for her shift at the hospital and needing her car.

Dean sat on the curb watching until the twinkling of Star's taillights were lost behind the curve of the road. Hy thought of going back into the bar but there was no point. She was gone. Dean was alone on the damp concrete, staring into the crisp sky lit with stars.

from Fuck You Dad, A Cabaret to End Patriarchy

Sassafrass Lowrey reading / Photo by Damien Luxe

Mette LouLou von Kohl & Sabina Ibarrola / Photo by Damien Luxe

Photo of Heels on Wheels member & anthology curator
Andrea Glik by Damien Luxe

How I Learned to Wear a Dress to the Gay Bar

by Bevin Branlandingham

There was a period of time when I lived in Philadelphia and had only recently found the identities queer, fat and femme and was happily exploring what it felt like to have words and meaning to how I felt inside.

I would get ready for queer dance parties and bar nights and constantly second guess my outfits. I'd eschew a dress as "too much" or "too fancy" and opt instead for cropped pants and Torrid tee shirts. This was not how I wanted to look but how I thought I should look. By that point I was comfortable wearing make-up and outwardly expressing my girly tendencies, but couldn't quite cross the threshold to dresses unless it was a fancy occasion. In my perception, it seemed like everyone else was wearing cargo shorts, ribbed white tanks and visors.

After the insecurity won out and I dressed down for the bar, I'd see a girl in a dress. And I would seethe with feelings. I wished I was wearing one and here she was, brave enough to do what she wanted. And she looked good.

I never felt hostile towards the femme who wore a dress to the bar. I just felt envy that she was the only one and was confident enough to do it anyway. This was before I developed a nuanced understanding of femme competition and understood it was a byproduct of misogyny. That just because she looks good doesn't mean I can't look good, and, frankly, when there are a bunch of femmes, especially fat femmes, looking killer, it amplifies all of us. My friend Naima said on my erstwhile podcast FemmeCast, "When other queer fat femmes are looking fabulous around me it makes me feel more fabulous."

This cycle of underperforming my style and feeling butt hurt when I saw other femmes performing their gender was simply a new version of what I had been taught growing up as a fat person. Years of conditioning to not take up too much space, not call attention to myself and not offend people stifled me. This conditioning made it a reflex to deny what I liked—sparkle, shimmer, bold patterns, color. This conditioning was also impossible to achieve, as not taking up too much space is impossible when the world is not made for your size.

I hid myself in men's clothing, swimming in garments too big for me. I remember my favorite piece from college was a shimmering men's button up pink shirt with a dragon pattern on it in a bright pink. It was ridiculous and I never wore it because it was always "too much." Oh but I loved staring at it in my closet!

When I was 21 I found a pair of shiny flared jeans that I wore as often as possible. I felt so killer in those jeans, even though in hindsight I shudder at how poorly they fit me. It was my first attempt at wearing sparkle as a neutral and I wore them as often as possible. Even on first dates, paired with a sensible v neck sweater two sizes too big. I believed the bigger clothes camouflaged my fat and toned down my femininity

I experimented with more feminine silhouettes when I got a part time job at Lane Bryant, a US plus size chain store found in malls, while I was in law school. With deep employee discounts it was very little risk to try new things. In my newly acquired Plunge bra, the first push-up bra I had ever seen for a fat person, I was able to show off cleavage for the first time. I found it really empowering. My new friends in the drag king troupe we founded in Philadelphia recognized me as femme and taught me it was a good thing.

But even with my friends cheering me on, I didn't feel brave enough to try being the only person in the bar in a dress. I still felt the need to fit in and tone it down.

I also didn't believe in my sex appeal. Friends would tell me how hot I was and I thought they were just being nice. So wearing a dress when I went to the bar said something about how I wanted to be seen and I wasn't ready to go there yet.

Certainly I had lust in my heart and I thought I had it all figured out, but the longer I continue on the journey to self-empowerment and authenticity, the more I realize it's a slow process. My hesitation to be the only femme in the dress at the bar was a version of hiding in those giant sweaters to camouflage my fat. I was camouflaging my sex appeal by not performing my gender to the level I really wanted.

Self-confidence is a muscle that takes practice building up. It's not a switch you just turn on. It's a daily act of bravery, leaving the house in a body different than what society deems appropriate. It's wearing something that scares you for the first time around your supportive friends. It's dumping friends that don't support you. It's taking the risk to learn who you are and then taking tiny steps to learn how to be true to yourself. It's faking it till you make it. It's borrowing other people's confidence in you until you believe it yourself. It's filling your head up with positive messages about your body and going on mind diets to eliminate the lies that other people tell you about your body, your ability, your gender presentation, your sexuality, your sex appeal, your age.

Quentin Crisp was an Englishman living in New York (Sting wrote that song about him) who was famously queer and flamboyant. He was gender non-conforming long before that was a buzz word, and frankly he would have hated that term. Quentin was a genius and said that, "Style is being yourself on purpose."

Developing the confidence and bravery to stick out enabled me to find my own sense of style. Doing that work helped me finally feel at home in my body and my skin after a lifetime of disembodiment, self-hatred and hiding in plain sight.

It was performing with that drag troupe, with those supportive friends, that taught me how far my gender went. Being in male drag was never right for me. Many of my FTM friends found their first outlet in drag and for me it was the opposite. Wearing facial hair and binding felt false, but changing into a push-up bra, fake eyelashes and a feather boa was exactly right.

The thing is, my gender, as soon as I started really exploring it, goes way beyond wearing a dress to a gay bar. My gender is Dolly Parton meets Miss Piggy meets Ginger Spice. It's over the top, flamboyant and a bit scandalous. It will never, ever fit in. It's suited for the stage because it calls attention. It's the opposite of what I was taught growing up fat.

I have employed a lot of methods to feel comfortable presenting my authentic self at queer bars and in queer spaces over the years. Surrounding myself with other queer fat femmes helped for a long time; with that posse I was never alone wearing a slutty dress and showing fat skin. I dressed in layers to give myself options for how weird I would get. I got a lot of performance gigs so it didn't seem out of place that I was dressed differently.

Once I realized who I was, how I wanted to present myself and was able to build up my self-confidence, I never questioned wearing exactly what I wanted to a bar. Now I am actually surprised when I'm not the most over-dressed person in queer spaces. But I also know by going out in public, being myself on purpose, I'm giving other people who are developing their own self-confidence, the knowledge that they are not alone.

Panda Pong

Anti-capitalist robot performance from the Heels on Wheels 2011 Midwest tour.

Photos of Panda Pong, Bloomington, 2011.

Excerpt from OVERHEARD

Kirya Traber

• •

Characters (in order of appearance)

TRAIN CONDUCTOR: Voice-over. Black female. Late 40's. New York

AUTOMATED TRAIN ANNOUNCEMENTS: Voice-over. Male. "Neutral American" dialect.

BUSHWICK ART GIRL: White, CIS Early 20's, West Coast

THE POET: Black male. CIS. Late 20's, New York

"Q": Black. AFAB. Masculine presenting. Early 20's. SF Bay Area

YVONNE: light skinned, POC. Gender unknown Feminine presenting. Early 20's, New York

CHORUS OF HARASSMENT: Voice-over. Various masculine & feminine, a range of dialects.

KIRYA: Mixed race, AFAB, gender-queer. 20's.

Note: All characters and voices are performed by Kirya Traber with the exception of the AUTOMATED TRAIN ANNOUNCEMENTS, which are modeled after the voice of the NYC Subway.

Time and Place: Now, Kirya's memory; The Subway.

[LIGHTS UP. We hear the sounds of the NYC subway as if we are on a platform waiting for a train. We see five chairs set in the formation of a NYC subway car.

Enter KIRYA. She takes a moment of pause at the edge of the stage, in full view of the audience, as if waiting for her train to arrive. She wears jean shorts and a tank top. We clearly see her legs and under arms are unshaven. Her hair is pulled back to give full view of her face.

A sharp, mocking laugh is heard. KIRYA is startled, but does not move from where she stands.]

TRAIN CONDUCTOR

HEY! You gonna get on?

I gotta close these doors!

[Startled back into motion, KIRYA, comes center stage, looks about, and takes a seat on the subway.]

AUTOMATED TRAIN ANNOUNCEMENT 1

"Stand clear of the closing doors, please."

[The actor stands to perform the following characters. They speak directly to the character KIRYA (represented by an empty chair with her bag beside it) and never one another.]

BUSHWICK ART GIRL

[Stands a few feet away from KIRYA's chair, gazing a moment before she speaks. To KIRYA]

I love your Afro.

And your... your beard?

It's so badass.

THE POET

[A few steps back from, BUSHWICK ART GIRL, leaning on a subway pole. To KIRYA.]

You real natural type, ain't you?

I feel that

You don't really see that out here

nobody is really real, ya know?

BUSHWICK ART GIRL

You're an artist, right?

Like a poet?

I think maybe I've seen you perform before.

THE POET

Everybody got a mask on.

Feel like everybody frontin all the time

But you're...

real unique.

BUSHWICK ART GIRL

I really like your poetry.

And it's so badass that you don't shave.

I wish I didn't have to

I mean

I just do it for work.

THE POET
You don't see a lot of females who do that--
stay all natural--like 100%
Says a lot about you--about your state of mind.

BUSHWICK ART GIRL
Patriarchy. Ya, know what I mean?
Of course you do.
Beauty standards are so geared towards this...
heteronormative Euro-centric "ideal"that just prioritizes a colonized body
ya know what I mean?

THE POET
I just need someone I can talk to
on my level.
I had to cut everybody out. I can't trust these fools.
Can't even have a conversation.
BUSHWICK ART GIRL
"The personal is political."
I really believe that...
It's just... at work...
    [Approaching KIRYA now to speak more closely]
Ya, it's pretty conservative.

I wish I could just make it disappear
during the week --my hair--
and then get to have it all back on the weekends.
I don't know...

But you!
You totally resist normative beauty.
You're so badass.

THE POET
You're different.
I need that in my life.

Tryna make changes-- tryna change my whole life
I need to to be inspired.

BUSHWICK ART GIRL
You remind me of my friend, actually.
He throws these totally rad warehouse parties
in Bushwick.
It's kind of an open mic.
He's trying to make this
anti-oppressive art space that de-centers institutionally validated artistry.
Anyone can perform.
THE POET
Ey, you like poetry?
I thought so.
I write... a little.

You mind if I share something with you real quick?
It's something I wrote...

BUSHWICK ART GIRL
It's a lot of underground artists
a lot of queer folks.
From mostly Bushwick and Williamsburg I think?
You could do your poetry
if you want.

THE POET
[Recited as a poem. He performs this in a "spoken word" style, with skill and sincerity.]
Wanna set the record straight
Yeah it's true I got a record
got caught up in the game
ain't proud of my mistakes
young and alone
now out on parole
been lost in the jaws of the system
listen

I'm wishing
for one more chance
to prove i'm on a mission
I wrote this you listenin?
if you look through my eyes
and see what I seen
a brother on lockdown
a father at 16
Ain't askin I'm reaching
not schemin I'm dreaming
motivated by the blood
that runs through my veins
to my child, my son
my hope for a brand new day
never claimed to be the best
though I'm nicer than the rest
take my place on the stage
I ain't here to entertain
I'm here to educate
got my eyes on the prize
no I won't back down
gotta keep my head up
so you can see my crown

BUSHWICK ART GIRL
It's gonna be so badass.
I'd love to hang out, actually--
And I really think you'll totally be into it.
I hope you can come.
[The actor becomes, Q, placing fliers in the frames of subway posters.]

AUTOMATED TRAIN ANNOUNCEMENT 6
"Ladies and gentlemen, backpacks and other large containers are subject to
random search by the police."

"Q"

Hey I know you?

SFState, right?

You were friends with Alicia, right?

Yeah, I go by "Q" now

I'm just out here promoting for this party I help out with.

You should check it out

It's gonna be hella dope.

Last time ALL the baddest bitches were there.

Fat booties for days.

No fat chicks tho.

Just skinny chicks with BODY--light skinned and Latin girls--dressed nice.

It's a real classy type event.

You gotta have a tie and jacket just to get in,

you feel me?

or studs do...

If you a femme...

then it's like high heels and shit...

I mean, you more...

femme... I guess... right?

Anyway, yeah

I do this party promoter thing now

It's cool

meet hella girls

Actually that's how I met my girl

Yeah, I got a girl now.

She a bad bitch.

She don't even look gay neither.

She used to fuck with the D, but now she's on me.

Likes how I get it

cause I can buy my own shape and size!

[holds up hands and gestures crudely]

I mean... I don't know if you're into femmes or ...

studs... or... whatever

I mean

it's whatever. Do you!

Man... I haven't talked to Alicia in a min!

How she doin?

[sits]

Thas whats up.

I miss that kid...

We used to be TIGHT, back in the day

Stay posted up at the Queer center ALL day.

That was the SPOT back in the day.

Yeah, you remember!

All the fine honeys would come through.

We was jus a couple of scrawny little baby studs

thought we ruled that school.

But we didn't know nothing--

Didn't know how to act or dress or nothing...

Yeah, I mean, it's all love tho

we was straight outta high school, I mean,

we didn't really have any like

role models or nothin.

Like nobody teaches you how to be gay, right?

It was just me and Alicia against the world.

My mom wasn't exactly supportive

I mean, she was OK with me being gay

but she hated me dressin in boy's clothes, ya know?

She just has this one idea

about what her baby girl should be like

and I'm not that...

In high school when we used kick it at LYRIC in the Castro

Yeah, you remember LYRIC?

That was the spot too!

I'd have to borrow Alicia's jeans and change into them after school

--like at a McDonalds or something--

and then change back before I got home

My mom caught me this one time
got my ass beat so bad...

She is always breathin down my neck
chasin after me with dresses and shit, to this day!
Even tho I'm grown.
Dressin like that
Makes me feel like a clown or something
This ridiculous outfit on, makeup, ridiculous shoes.
Like a clown...
Anyway I gotta put up the rest of these fliers
but you should come through
I'll buy you a drink
And tell Alicia I say what's up
if you see her
[Q goes to "EXIT", glancing near the door, where the actor becomes, YVONNE.]

AUTOMATED TRAIN ANNOUNCEMENT 7

"Ladies and gentlemen, for your safety please do not block or hold the car doors open while the train is in the station, and please, do not lean against the doors."

YVONNE
Do you mind if I--

[gestures to the seat]
THANK YOU
My feet are KILLING me
These shoes are so fucking hot, but jesus
I feel like my ankles are literally gonna break off
The price you pay, ya know?
I mean, shit.

You don't ever wear high heels? girl don't be shy!
Don't act like you ain't pretty just cause you different looking.
I see that smile under your hairy lip
Girl, you are hairy.

[laughs]
But at the end of the day, it's not how you look.
It's about HOW you wear your shoes. Straight.

You wanna know the secret to walking in high heels?
You've got to walk like you LOVE your shoes. Straight.
That's it!

I bet you would look great in some...
open toed stilettos. Red.
I think you could rock em.

You know, I didn't buy my first pair of pumps till I was like, 17
for a Halloween costume.
Straight.
I was kind of a... ugly duck type in high school...
Anyway
This one Halloween I got in my head that I wanted to be
Tina Turner.
Way ahead of my time.
I had this red sequin dress that I got at a Goodwill.
Cut it off, just below the ass. Picked out my hair
--kinda like yours--
bought dollar store red lipstick,
and $20, black pleather stilettos I could barely squeeze my size....
ten
feet into.

I was just gonna go to my homegirls house down the block
and out of nowhere
I saw these grown women walking by
all in black,
tight pants, full-face, long straight weaves,
and these Via Spiga pumps
they knew how to walk in.
Beautiful.

I tried not to make eye contact,

rushed across the street as fast as I could,

but knew they saw me.

Heard them whisper.

Then they called out to me from across the street.

"Hey Tina!"

Ooh!

"HEEEEY!"

I wanted to wear those shoes every day after.

And I pretty much do.

I wanna be famous.

That's why I wear these fucked up shoes.

Gotta sacrifice to make it to the top.

I mean sure,

sometimes I wanna just kick back

let my hair out like you

I guess it would be easier

But I want it ALL.

I'm talking tour bus, paparazzi, selling out stadiums

I want TEN high healed back up dancers--

men and women.

I want queens and butch daddies backing ME up!

Diana ross, chaka khan,

Tina

Even The Bey

ain't got NOTHIN on me.

When I make it

people will cry and shake,

and pass out

just seeing me in the street.

Everyone will love me.

Remember my name:

Yvonne.

[YVONNE performs choreographed dance to "Yoncé" by Beyoncé. Sounds of an cheering stadium crowd underscore. She blows KIRYA a kiss, and "EXITS," becoming KIRYA, who sits in her chair.]

Photo of Kirya Traber by Nicole Myles, 2013.

AUTOMATED TRAIN ANNOUNCEMENT

"Ladies and gentlemen, a crowded train is no defense for unlawful sexual conduct. If you believe you have been the victim of a crime, or a witness to a crime, notify an MTA employee or police officer."

Chorus of Harassment

(KIRYA sits in a subway seat facing the audience and is still as the sounds assault her.)

Hey girl. You look so good. I like that. I like all that hair. You look mad good. I could take care of you. I know how to take care of a women.

You got mad side burns. Why don't you shave your face?

Hey! You are hairy as fuck!

Oh my god! Look! What a freak! She ain't never heard of no razor before?

She mad nasty.

Hey girl! Where you walking so fast?! Hey! Hey! Let me shave you. Let me shave all that nasty hair of your body. Hey! I'm gonna keep sweatin you all down this block. Hey!

You're so incredibly beautiful.

You see her? That's what you'll look like when you grow up, if you're lucky.

LIGHTS shift on KIRYA. The subway sounds go out. Quiet. She is alone in the theater with the audience.

[BLACKOUT]

The B in Ballyhoo

Hana Malia

Linguistic origins of Ballyhoo:

"Publicity, hype," from circus slang, "a short sample of a side-show." There is a village of Ballyhooly in County Cork, Ireland. In nautical lingo, ballahou or ballahoo meant "an ungainly vessel."

Jolly Dolly. Ella Mills. Alice from Dallas.
Mary J. Powers. Ada Briggs. Rosannah Richardson.
Marie. Baby Betty. Diamond Kitty.
Minnie the Mighty Midget. Jill. Lady Teresina.
Anna. Ida Williams. Gertrude Barker.
Princess LaLa. Annie Morrison. Marie Lill.
Miss Collassa. Mickie Smith. Baby Ruth.

She has lured you under the pretense
of control top panties. Once
she has slithered her serpent woman's way
into your bed, you will undress her
and the miles of uncontained flesh will roll out—
scrolls onto your well-fitted sheets.
You will know the secrets beneath
a fat girl's skirt.

And all the nameless Fat Ladies,
Ringling Brothers gold. These days
morbid spectacle is headless fatties
from behind—evening news props

amateur girls we only see bent over,

fetish tags: Fat Teen Fat Mature Fattest of the Fat.

But you were grinning, measurements-as-signatures,

skirts hiked up, postcards—

no one even bothered with an envelope.

My trick is not nylon. My trick

is to be huge. To be more thunder

between my legs than any summer storm

or fat joke you ever smirked at. It is

to teach you how to want the ones

you were warned against, make you hear

the everything I mean, when I say, only something.

Making a joke of you cost them three rings and

three-hundred dollars a great-depression-week.

Tabloids spoke your torrid love affairs

with Midgets, elephants, your fat sisters.

But I speak both your glory

and daemons because baby

you put the B in Ballyhoo

and they killed you all the same.

My trick is to excavate the fridge often

enough. Capers like kidney stones, food

forgotten when the party is over.

There is nothing like a fat girl eating

alone and Mom, the rotten smell reminds me of you—

head on the toilet bowl all guts and grinning.

There are some safe things, some air-tight things.

Peanut butter, mustard, apple sauce.
Everything else will just have to go.

Okay fellas, this is how it works.
The Fat Lady is going to go
behind the curtain and any of you
who wanna give me a dollar
can follow right behind.
She's gonna sit on down, she's gonna
lift up her dress, she's gonna spread
her legs, and she's gonna show you
her pussy.

The fat lady sat in a rusted folding chair
 and spread her mighty thighs as far
as she could. Then she lifted her dress
 just above the knee, and with her finger
she pointed to a tiny black cat
tattooed on the inside of her thigh
and said " Look at my pussy boys,
look all you want!"

Somewhere deep down, you know my trick.
That these snapshots of a thin woman's ribs
are not mine, not worth pay-by-the-hour
when the phone lines betray the sweet roar
of my three-hundred-pound tongue.
Somewhere you know what your money's worth,
how hungry I am, how my holes go on forever,
how it's just like the cartoons—like feeding

a tic-tac to a whale. You have no
idea I am a whale,

a thunder storm, a massacre, a side-
show.

The trick is that sometimes you
have to sit

right on someone's lungs

to be truly breathtaking.

Sometimes you have to massacre
your own flesh

before they can.

Have to overcharge them.

Bat your lashes.

Curse your pretty face.

Make them pay for your pretty face.

Until they give in

And cough up

For every unfurled

inch of you.

Ready the Pry

Some mornings you wake

Knowing night will bring the wolf

And there is nothing to do

But gather armor

And agree to wait

With three extra arms

For sunset and the embrace,

To sit still near the window,

Limbs excessive,

Knowing it will hurt.

To breathe against luck against

Your rubber band waist

Your trembling toes curling

And clutching the thinning
sheets,

One arm poised at the window

To ready the jump

One stiff between your thighs

To ready the welcome,

Praying wolves don't hunger

For what is given without a fight

The next clutching the match-
book

The fourth gripping a photograph

Of the fancy lady wolf he calls
home,

Positioned for the threat

Of strike and cinder

The last clutching the hinges

Of your sticky sweet jaw

Readying the pry, in case

You fall howl-less

My Hairstory

By Foxy Squire

· ·

Performed at Dark. Nude. Storytellers: Hair

My hairstory begins with tears.

In walks my father to a room full of tears. My mother is crying because of the hardship of trying "do" her babies hair. Or tame up them naps. (Naps are the ugly descriptor of the very tightly curled hair that can sometimes grown into a circular ball due to the curly nature of the hair.) My sister and I are crying from the pain. My parents come to the conclusion that the peaceful solution is to start our perming journey, which they believe is a permanent solution.

My mother is a smart, college educated bougie black lady of elegance and good tastes with the belief that perming will help her young ladies get ahead in life and be easier on her when styling their hair for the day to go to a pre-dominately white school

This chemical treatment referred to as a relaxer because it "relaxes the curls in your hair to straighten them". It is sometimes referred to as the creamy crack because it becomes an addicted habit that must be satisfied. If you take all the money spent on relaxers you could by a house or support a very steady crack habit

So the perms start around 5/6 yrs old. When I say that I hated getting my hair permed I do not use that word lightly. I HATED IT. I would sit in the chair and have this thick heavy vaseline smeared around the edge of my hair line and along my ears. Then this white chemical stenched goo was glopped in my hair with a paintbrush type instrument until the stylist see the napps straighten trying to beat the substance before it burns your scalp. After a washing this stuff from my head, I would have a wet back from water that seeped in during the rinse. My head is throbbing and heavy from the water it's time to dry completely before styling and you were put under the salon dryer, which seemed to consume my very soul from the inside out and burn my shoulders. I did my best to escape by turning the dial to shorten the time or put on cooler air.

When I was around my senior year of high school, after years of complaining about relaxers my mom was finally ready to take me seriously. She said that I could put my hair in braids for the next few months and that i would have to show her how I was going to take care of this nappy hair that I was de-termined to have. Thank goodness, I was always an excellent researcher and found websites and recipes to follow of how to wash this new strange hair ant then lots of pictures of other fashionable black women with natural hair. After 3 mos I presented my finding in the most concise manner possible and fielding every possible question my mom throw at me. It worked! I was going natural but to my dismay my mother stipulation was that our stylist had to cut my hair into my new afro.

Our stylist had given me the impression that she did not want a natural head in her chair. Aside from being less revenue in her pocket, she had no formal training with my hair and used a pair of hairstyling scissors. My first afro was awful. She cut so many dips and valleys that my hair looked like the rocky mountains and my dad had to go back and fix for my prom night. But in the end I stayed natural

I left for college with my afro intact and would hear my mothers complains about my afro on many phone calls home. So, it was time from something drastic. It was the week of easter. I scrambled around and found a ride home and back for easter weekend. That friday, I handed my roommate's boyfriend a pair of clippers and stated, "Nope you don't need a guard." I wore a hat the whole car ride determined to not reveal my new style until after my folks saw it. When we were a few miles from my house, I changed into my long black skirt and a black/white boatneck top. Using my house key, I opened to door and stated, "I am home". My dad rounded the corner with his patented "hey hey" and mom followed. She caught one glance at me and fell to her knees. With her head hung low she asked with all the genuine concern, "I just have one question. Do you still love Jesus?"
With a respectful matter of fact tone, "Yes, mom. Cutting my hair did not change my religion."

Finally I have graduated college with my BS in Chemistry and moved to NJ to start my new life. My mom and I are talking on the phone about my upcoming plans because I moved to tri-state with $1000, 2 suitcases and no job. In a motherly tone she asked, "So, what are you going to do?"
"I am going to find a job Mama, " I replied.

She says, " Oh, I know you are an intelligent young woman, I mean what are you going to do about your hair. No one will hire you with an afro."

There was a moment of silence.

After all that I had accomplished my own mother still did not see that my afro was not going to stop me from doing what I wanted. I told her, "Mom they won't care about that. I am smart with a degree from an ACS accredited college I will find a job." Two weeks later, I was starting work at LorealUSA with an afro and lab coat.

It is astonishing to believe that we as people of color do not love and cherish this crown of curls we have been gifted with. We have the privilege and right to wear our hair in whatever style we wanted and be taken seriously as human beings. My hope is that though my hair story began with tears, it will not end with tears.

saccharin

annah anti-palindrome

my gender is

someone's unfinished attempt

at cleverly defacing

a misogynistic bill board advertisement

it's a tampon applicator full of pop rocks

the mace you thought was breath spray

the tattoo you most regret:

a parable of faded but legible mistakes

my gender is

your high school english teacher's eyebrows

plucked thin and painted back on

into a perpetual state of concern

it's the place in your throat that stays dry no matter how many times
    you swallow

the sticky-hot flush of finally achieving literacy at age 14

the sound of a twelve step trauma story that aches the roots of your teeth

for days after it's told

my gender is

the bullet we engraved your stepdad's name into

and left in the liquor cabinet for him to find:

a proper and fair warning

it's the state of agitation you feel

when you squeeze into a pair of boots way too small for your feet

and choose to wear them anyway

because they are the only ones you own with steel toes

my gender is the repurposed scrap fabric:

window dressing/ tablecloth/ porch blanket/ nightgown/ miniskirt/
	DIY cotton menstrual pad

you now use

for the purpose of flagging

it's the unwashed hands of a lover grasping at your most hollow parts

the note between notes that bellows from your throat

when you've finally found the language

to tell someone How you wanna be fucked

my gender is

the water bottle filled with bleach

sprayed into the eyes of a trucker

who picked you up hitchhiking

and refused to let you out at your exit

its the lipstick on your teeth

the gum you fell asleep with in your mouth

your mom's secret renegade romance

with her femme dyke hairdresser

my gender

is the laxative you finally slipped into your bosses coke

after he harassed you at work

for the last time

its an ally's learning curve:

the tender throbbing in your chest

when you tell someone you're sorry

and you actually mean it

my gender is that stray eyelash

the one stuck to your left cheekbone

that you were hoping someone you love

would get close enough to notice

Mama Rock is Dead Manifesto

Ashley Young

Here in lies mama rock;
she is dead
gone, buried amongst dirt and gravel
earth opened, body in, closed shut.

Here in lies mama rock;
invisible woman,
mammi, big breast ready, half human
full, thick and nothing but emptied
rock face, grey aged thing, mindless
memory-less bundled bits of dead earth.

Mama rock was a nurturer,
belly warm for huggin, pillow crafted body
sold over and over and over,
hands on her hips
"do you know what time it is?"
grumpy old women with a rock for a face
alone, lonely, always alone, waiting,
living for her children to come home
flat feet, bare foot, always in the kitchen preparing,
ready, waiting and willing
always willing and her body
was a sexless thing

cause mama had had all the children she was ever gonna have
and sex, sex is for young skinny things
for those not fully lived their life yet things
sex is something other people do
so mama hid her body
behind layers of clothing, behind closed doors,
behind herself for nobody to see
cause she was never a body
she was just mama.

Mama rock died of young age;
she died because she wasn't as old as she thought she was,
she died because she realized that she had never really given herself
    that name,
she died in the house fire of herself,
she died slow until nothing was left
but what she always was,
nothing left but her own self
and the name that own mama gave her

because her mama
has everything to do with mama rock,
bed bond, tied to her mind mama,
pill after pill after pill mama,
that rock trying to rescue her,
years of a little girl falling into quicksand,
waiting, hoping, wanting for her health,
now knowing she save her own mama
she can only save herself.

So now that mama rock is dead,
now that she is gone,
now that she is buried in the deep, deep solid ground
here's what she, what I will no longer do:
No I will not make you pancakes after your long nights
of fucking escapades while you lick your syrupy stained lips
only to bury your head in my chest for comfort and talking and crying
then walk away when you are done just to come back for breakfast
    the next day.
My chest is mine.

No I will not untie my red bandana from my untamed head
to wipe your tears and let your snot cover my sleeves,
"Baby you just let it out. You tell mama all about it."

Fuck that.
No I will not be your twisted face of sleep, a rock,
a core unturned, unbroken, solid heavy weight for you
to stand upon when the ground has come out from underneath you.

There are more surfaces for you to stand on, and honey, it ain't me.

No I will not kiss your boo-boos, mend your torn clothing,
be your late night phone call, your ass better call Tyron.

I will not be your butt wigglin' hugger, one way lover
breakin' my back to please you mama.
That shit is done, it's finished, it's cut

cause I am tired of fulfilling everybody's expectations,
of people thinking this body is just a house,

walkin' in, haven't even taken your shoes off,
all up on my couch, kickin and screamin,
eating the marrow from off my bones to purely nourish yourself
and you didn't even ring the damn doorbell.

Well I have neighborhood watch now
and they know if and when you are coming
and only I can open the door to my own house
cause I will no longer sacrifice who I am, what I am or how I am.

My body is a pleasant, soft, curvy mine;
she screams, yearns, breathes,
opens, fills with laughter, fills with self
and is sick and tired of digesting your poison,
you can't feed that shit to her any longer.

My body is capable of receiving love,
real love, sweaty, tense, sticky, urgent love,
harsh, real, endless honest love

and I am not a rock.
I am a human being, capable of breaking,
ready for the constant hurt of change,
ready for those ready to listen

and this skin changes shape
but never changes color,

defines and redefines but is never defined.

So now I honor mama rock by returning her to the earth,
no tombstone, no funeral, no nothing,
just a simple gathering, a few words,
she would have wanted it that way.

I know, I was her once,
suffocating under her weight
under the way I thought I owed it to the world
but now, I owe it to myself.

Don't cry for her cause she was dying all along,
she was just waiting,
waiting for her fat sparrow wings to spread and fly free.

Here in lies mama rock
and what's left is me.

6

Fisting
With A Full Set

Constant Cravings

Caitin Rose Swee

Constant Cravings is a multi media installation consisting of a hot pink soft sculpture with two orifices ejaculating a stream of slip cast ceramic unicorns, an ecology of queer feminine beings such as ceramic fingers with long nails and mystical crystal formations, and projected video of a mouth drooling gold glitter.

This is a part of an on-going series of installations called pleasure land-scapes; these hand-crafted spaces interrupt the heteronormative construct that the queer life is a life of disappointment, pain, and alienation. My work explores the affect of queer collectivity and world making. The world is a constructed space with heteronormativity as the axis where queer desire, love and bodies are not supposed to exist and thrive.

Our movement through the world is constricted, blocked, and regulated by heteronormativity that denies us access to our own feelings, bodies, and the bodies of other queers. Yet we keep popping up all over the world and through out time with sticky fingers and thunder in our hearts.

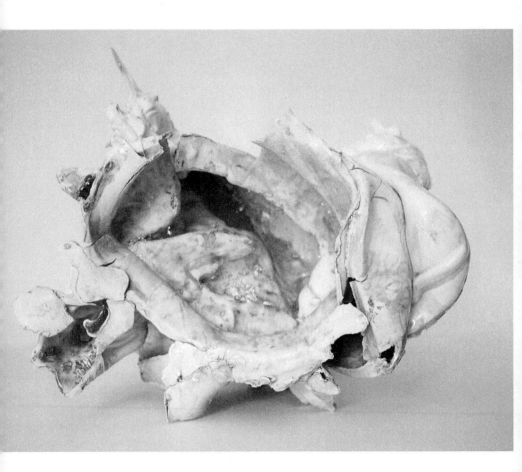

Constant Cravings is my love letter to my radical queer communities and the way we collapse the structured mold of heteronormativity and form new bodies, pleasures, and intimacies. Our collective persistent desire is unstoppable. We are hungry holes that will consume the world; the secret passages to a landscape of self-determination and riots of pleasures.

F***

Meliza Bañales aka Missy Fuego

You were hoping she would say, "Will you fuck me?" But she asks you to go inside her. You know in order to do this some part of you already is. You use what you always fall back on, your hands. And this time it is a fist. The truth is, you never go in that way. You're never sure she'll let you and sometimes doubt your ability to push in the right ways. But she asks you to. You know your bodies fit when the woman under you doesn't even have to ask you to go slow, to take it easy. You like to

think this is the secret language of women. It's not reserved for anyone in particular just the ones willing to hear it. You know there is a type of magic hidden inside her and she wants you to find it. Then, one hand slides itself into her hair and grabs it just enough to tilt her head back and let a small moan escape from that beautiful mouth where so many words live. Then you take your other hand. Your good hand. The hand you can't live without because you use it for everything. The hand you take for

granted until right now when you feel the muscles in your body tighten and your heart beat against your bones you wonder if she can hear it. You take that hand, and you go to work. It makes its way inside and her face changes and she opens for you like

pages and water. And she allows more of you to enter her and you can't help for a split second think of all the ways and all the people and all the whispers that have been right where you are right now. You take her archaeology and try to read the writing on the wall, try to find the culture and the history so that you,

you can be different. You won't take it and put someplace else

for everyone to see. No. You will let it stay put and just be

thankful you got to see it at all and thankful her eyes are closed so she can't see the dumb look on your face because to you, this is not discovery. It's not fine-tuning an instrument, it's not trying to hit the right notes. It's just a moment. And you want to make it last as long as possible. So you keep going and maybe now you're thrusting your good hand deeper and deeper while your other hand gently holds her throat or cups around her

head like a baby bird. You hear the sounds she makes, feel her nails dig into your arms and back and her body is in flight and you move together.

Then, it starts to happen. The good hand takes the form of a fist and though it pushes into her it doesn't

fight its way in. And the pushing is a punching, faster and faster. And once again you can't help but think where you're fist has been. How many protests its cut through the air, how many times its defended the country of your body against those who would hurt it, how its punched walls and doors and windows and could never find a way out of its own pain or into its own sanity is somehow right now completely holding this woman up and if it moves a certain way it has the ability to ruin her or set her free. This is no dick. No cock. It takes time to enter.

You have to forget yourself so that you can practice the lost art of listening, not to her breath but to her want. Patience is

not a virtue here it is a requirement and there is a strong chance you might not make it all the way in sometimes but a sure chance that you are forever changed when you come out. And her

mouth that is usually so full of words only manages to let one of

them out, "Fuck...Fuck." And when her sounds have turned to high-

pitched moans, then screaming, then crying, then more screaming

and the length of her has become one wide-open geometry— then.

Then you really give her what she wants, what she's asked for. You go. Inside. And to say that she cums doesn't quite cut it because really, both of you arrive. Together. And your hands, these tiny wonders that you criticize for being too small or too rough or not fast enough to keep you fed or housed turn out to be everything that one woman needed right then. And you exit the same way you went in but never the same. And you let her breathe it all in, while you lie on top of her and kiss her and fall into her hair you let her feel it all and you hold it. That space.

That moment, now gone. It leaves you, but it lives somewhere else now.

The Revered Femme Bottom

Amber Dawn

. . . .

I love every loud mouthed hard assed fuck with you

skin soft like a loquat as they punch
your cunt into infinity femme

I love girls who will fuck you up for no

and every good reason

   -- *I Love Hard Girls*, Leah Lakshmi Piepzna-Samarashinha

The first woman (besides your mother) to slap your face
painted her bedroom floor red a few days before your date
and your knees sank into gummy coats of enamel while she
made you wait. Her window was wide open, undraped, and August
heat bulldozed in and all your sounds blow horned out.
She said relax your jaw and you wondered what made her choose
leather and if your cheeks smarted as handsome bright
as the floorboards. Afterwards her pupils
were lust-drug dilated. I love a dirty fuck she cooed
I love every loud-mouthed hard-assed fuck. With you—

being so spring chicken—you hardly knew
what you loved but you bought yourself
a harness and cock at the womyn's sex shop
and joined the other dykes in the phallus procession.
The dog collar and wrist cuffs acquired for fashion

or foreshadowing. Lip piercings damned your smile.
Your scalp confessed to a bic razor. You made anger your order.
When you pronounced your cunt a warrior the daddies
trained their mad eyes on you. Suited denim rough, but bare
skin soft like a loquat as they punched your cunt into infinity. Femme,

you never considered yourself femme
until a lover hailed you, femme slut pretty pretty
Honorific. Femme meant worship,
this lover, devoted, Please, femme-gasm
for me, soak the sheets with your femme
If memory serves, this may have been
the first time you were proud of your body.
Only a fire-gut can ejaculate like you.
A sparkplug sweet thing. A true
lover of girls who will fuck you up. For no

one could have told you
the dearest souls roll rough trade.
This bit of brilliance showed itself bit by bit.
Fuck by loud-mouthed hard-assed fuck you learned
to receive adoration just as well as you took a beating.
No one could have told you adoration
would trial and thrill you more than welts
on your young skin. Reverence's markings
are permanent, and so reverence you were given
and for every good reason

Ring of Fire

The Miracle Whips

The Miracle Whips is a queer femme performance troupe that works to promote models of progressive femininity, create radical erotic possibilities, and disrupt conventional notions of sexiness. We are a feminist collective that provides a healthy dollop of sass with your social commentary.

Our piece Slut Revival is a testimonial showdown against the shame of sexually transmitted infections (STIs) in our dyke communities. It includes the classic Johnny Cash song Ring of Fire, re-written/re-imagined by the Whips for this piece. These are our lyrics.

I want to disclose something

And it makes a fiery ring

Bound by stigma and shame

No need to follow that game

I have something like a burning ring of fire

I went down, down, down on her

And spread the herpes virus

And it burns, burns, burns

The herpes virus

The herpes virus

I too have a germ that is dire

We rubbed, rubbed, rubbed

And warts, I acquired
And they sprout, sprout, sprout
Like cauliflower
Like cauliflower

The taste of dyke is sweet
But the research is so weak
Since dykes have STDs
Let's have discussion please

We swapped cocks in the moment of desire
We shared shared shared
And trich she acquired
And it foams foams foams
A trip to Kaiser
A pill from Pfizer

I hooked up with the butch at Goodyear Tire
We fucked fucked fucked
In her truck we retired
And I scratched scratched scratched
Crab infestation
Those damn crustaceans

And it burns burns burns, the ring of fire, the ring of fire

Bruises

Leah Horlick

. . . .

This was not an original practice,/but thinking for a time, that it
was/felt like being able to choose/when spring would arrive
   - Sara Peters, "The Last Time I Slept In This Bed"

The new rule was that if it hurt
    and I wanted it,

I had to ask someone to do it for me.
    And so I never asked. The first time

it's an accident—I am perpetually
    drunk, full of adrenaline and she is a professional

athlete. You like pain, she marvels
    at me, astounded by my threshhold

for spring. For a week I can't sleep
    on my front, wear a push-up bra,

hug tight. Frozen peas, frozen
    corn, one defrosted bottle of gin.

I have a thirty-second panic
    in the shower, think I wanted this, one acceptable

rock in my pocket. The new
    rule. The next time, it's a surprise

for us both, for such gentle
    creatures. This time, I show friends

like jewelry—pointed out under sleeves or
    backless, in warm weather, like magnolias.

This time, look—how my skin
    comes back darker, like I've been out

in the sun. Look how much you
    love me. Little maps. Look,

you tell me,
    we match, all spring.

Lewiston, Idaho

Kit Yan

. . . .

It's been two nights,
Twenty conversations,
A Grindr profile, and a Craigslist Ad,
I notice one post a week in the men for men section,
I notice five active people on Grindr,
And even fewer with profile pictures.

Every person I talk to not "out,"
Every person in a self-described closet,
In this mill town, I meet-
Married and straight,
On the DL,
Full of secrets.

I know I am lucky,
Big city, prides, play parties,
Full-faced sex, dungeons, and queers,
And I ask myself to remember that-
Identity is a luxury.

My surfer boy tells me he cannot send a face pic,
He needs to be discreet,
We meet in my motel,
The room is dark,
The sheets are stained- patches of oxidized blood,
Reds and browns,
The bed is unmade,
The walls are worn with anonymous sex.

We do not meet for drinks,
No dinner, no date,
No one in this town can see us,
No one can know.

We do not take lightly the safety of
these four walls,
This creaky bed, the lumpy pillows,
The internet, the wireless,
The shelter of the cigarette smoke
soaked curtains.

We are headless horsemen,
We are faceless ghosts,
We are brilliant, beautiful nobodys
tonight.

I ask him what it's like to be gay
here,
He doesn't know.

I fuck him slow,
My mouth on his belly,
My mouth on his thighs,
My hands on his calves, his ankles,
My breath on his desire.

He fucks me hard,
Urgent, full weight, all the way,
Hungry.
His hands on my ass,
His hands around my neck,
His gut against mine.

We take pleasure in this hour,
Never taking for granted this warm
feeling of skin against skin,
Condom on hard cock,
Hot cum inside latex inside our bodies.

We praise the nasty,
We praise the dirty,
We praise forbidden, and
Let the threadbare sheets wash over
our sins.

More Than Yes

Gigi Frost

· ·

Hi, how're you doing? I have a story for you tonight.

(take out cock, put purse down, look at it, pause, look at audience)

(putting it on) A femme in a harness and a mini skirt is cool, subversive, powerful. She is a trendy glittered manicured hand with smooth round nails, the snap of a black latex glove, an icon.

But that was never me.
This is the kind of femme cock we get to see:
In drag, a-shirt and a mustache
as a femme top with latex and a whip
because you are a gender bending, binary-busting badass

This is the femme cock we don't see:
quiet
naked
because she asked me to
because I want to fuck close to her
to make her come

I am a bottom, and a femme. But before I used those words, I fucked my girlfriend.

My first girlfriend was butch, maybe. She was not stone. She loved girls, but she wasn't sure a girl could satisfy her they way boys had. Well. She told me that the way I fucked her, letting her swallow me, bracing my right elbow in my left hand for better leverage, the way I fucked her convinced her that girls could satisfy her. And I was so proud, coming up for air, flexing my muscles, leaning over for a kiss.

But she said she was worried that I was missing out on something and that something was a penis. She wanted to buy a cock and fuck me with it.

OK, sure. why not?

She said the woman-owned sex store was too expensive, so we went to a chain, you know, the one with the purple polo shirts. She chose a taupe colored monster that came in a box illustrated with silicone-titted babes in high heels and we went on our merry way. I wondered why we couldn't get something less creepy, like a nice, tasteful iridescent blue swirl. But whatever, it was her idea, it was her toy, she was going to fuck me with it.

Except it turned out that all of this was a front, that what she really wanted was for me to fuck her. She was missing something, and that something was me, with a cock, inside her.

She had been afraid to say so. But ok, sure. Why not?

All that pride I felt in fucking her went out the window when I put that thing on, the harness cut into my flesh and highlighted every body part I hated. And it gave me the worst wedgie I had ever experienced. I know, they make the other kind, with the straps around the legs, but then you look like you're going rock climbing. And we were cheaping out, remember?

Why didn't I just put a shirt on? Why didn't I put on boxer briefs? Because I am a girl, and girls have sex naked. Because we had turned up the heat. Because I thought I had to give her everything at once, a cock in her cunt and the sight of my naked body.

There was no one I could turn to, no way for me to figure out how to give her what she needed and still feel sexy myself.

(start taking harness off)

It was a butch-femme love story, a kinky love story, a story I've told you before. But with that harness, tangled up in a mess of blankets, a seed was planted.

A seed of shame, of inadequacy that I carried with me and let my partners water, *(drop harness)* let them give it sunshine and fertilizer every time they rolled over, every time they struggled and lied and evaded rather than admit what they wanted, every time they lay silent and still on their backs while I fucked them.

Misogyny taught the butches I've fucked, or not fucked, to distance themselves from their bodies, to stay stoic even when experiencing pleasure they've asked for and sought out.

They wanted it, they said they yes, but I somehow got the sense that to be a good femme you had to be careful not to enjoy it too much.

A good femme asks. A good femme never, never, ever wants her partner to feel obligated. A good femme doesn't ask unless she already knows the answer. But a good femme does ask, because if she doesn't she's lazy and ungrateful.

What bothers me is that femmes are all too often not asked. Butches start at zero - nothing is assumed. Femmes don't have the luxury of a blank slate. We are assumed to want, to need, to be empty holes. It is taken for granted that we will say yes, talk dirty, ask for more.

For a long time, I carried them all with me. The ones who said no. The ones who said yes. The ones who were offended at the very idea.

After a while, I figured I was just plain lousy at fucking. Maybe it wasn't for me. I learned not to trust my self or my partners. I didn't trust them to show me what they liked and didn't like. I didn't trust myself to listen to their bodies. I wasn't sure how much pleasure I was allowed to have from all this.

Maybe, I thought, I would be a stone femme. I would date stone butches who kept their clothes on and fucked me with their cocks, with their hands. My pleasure would be the center, the beating heart of our lovemaking.

But why does stone femme mean a femme who gets fucked by stone butches when stone butch means a butch who doesn't get fucked? Is femme just a hole in the ground, an empty void? Can I ask for something, anything more than silence and still honor how brave my partner is for saying yes?

"This femme fights back." said the hot pink signs we made for the pride parade. and "this femme fucks back." I wanted to carry that sign, but was it true? Not always. What about a sign that says "this femme fucks back with consent" or "this femme fucks back, but only if you want it bad." Or, better still, "this femme fucks back if you promise to moan and wriggle, move your hips, gasp and say thank you."

How do femme bottoms who fuck back claim our power? By asking for help, by naming our desire but also our needs, by soaking in their words when they say yes, when they say thank you, when they say please. By refusing to give it up to people who won't give us the satisfaction we give them - of responsiveness, of enthusiastic consent.

I want to give them the release they give me, i want them to be in their bodies, feel pleasure, let it spread.

why don't femmes fuck back? maybe it's because we've been met with so much silence. Maybe because yes is great, but yes please, please, please, is even better.

(pick up harness, throw over shoulder, blow kiss, exit)

Spelling of my name

Sossity Chiricuzio

I've been told I sometimes look
like I would eat you up
like I would suck your bones
clean
and hollow
leave you flying
high and rune marked

it's true
I love the meat of you
miles of magic
woven just under the skin
I love my teeth
swirling across your landscape
lightning and flash floods

four pearled inches
held in check
around soft slow licks
that take all three breaths
you'll forget to breathe
to get from collarbone
to jugular

like just now
when you gulped
oxygen, trying hard for subtle
as if you weren't trying
to get my sharp attention
as if you hadn't flapped
your signal flag like a flare

the tang of pheromones
sweat gathered
into the small of your back
thin skin stretched taut
fluttering with your pulse
morse of ache to read with my tongue
tip butterfly soft and merciless

if it is 10 minutes
I will make it feel like an hour
if it is an hour
I will make it feel like a freight train
if it is a freight train
your cells will know I love you
and the spelling of my name

Photo series

Mée Rose & Leanne Powers

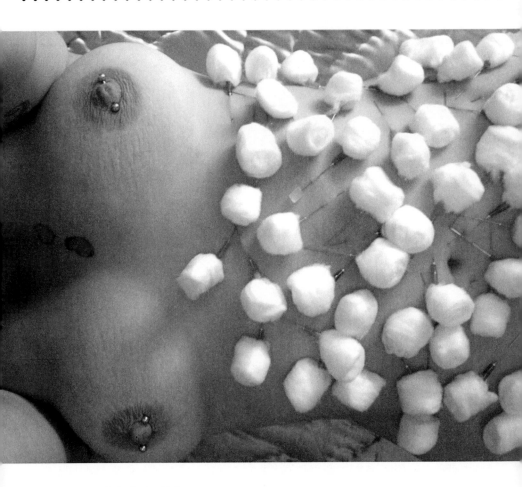

Mée Rose (Underbelly)

Underbelly is a still from 'fluff film', a video I made in 2013. The work is an experiment in self-love. BDSM and sex as a solo venture towards healing, growth, and transformation. Facing insecurity, welcoming loneliness, building strength to continue on living and loving myself.

Mée Rose & Leanne Powers (FEMMEDADDYLITTLEGIRL)

FEMMEDADDYLITTLEGIRL is a collaborative piece that reflects roles and dynamic in a femme//femme bdsm relationship. The language is playful and shameless in its exploration of values, consent, and perversion. This work was made on canvas using cosmetics.

Following page,

Mée Rose (Inner Child)

Inner Child explores the theme of femme//femme age play, and femme worship. I use my own body to mirror the young girl who peeks up the skirt, and also, my body as a literal extension of the larger than life femme being gazed upon.

Blood Love

Alex Cafarelli

there was sand up our cunts but our needles were sterile
back and forth tearing open sealed scars
my broken hand sliced your heart
pierced my femme
cut your boy
til one raw mess of salty dyke princess Sir
lay bleeding
wide open pulsing time
with the ocean's steady breath

i threw you hard on those tiny quartz crystals by the waves
threw myself on top,
legs pinning you and giggling cuz you didn't feel me coming
knocked your breath into the ground
knocked your throat into my bicep
my hard thigh jammed up your ass against my muscles brackish wet
i held you down as you struggled
for your heart back in one piece this time

our formula was water plus blood plus cunt
sometimes there were witnesses
sometimes we were safe
we cut grief out of our bones against the iron in our blood
the 2 of us with 6 genders each all tangled up in 3 years of scalpels
bleeding offerings to black dirt and golden sand

Winter at the river you carved a triangle

pointing to my ass

3 sharp slices line by line on my sacrum

i never wanted you to stop and that's all i remember next to clean true
pain that underneath felt like snow cold and pure cleansing ice melting red
cross my ass

thick with bloody lube and full of daddybutch cock

against the back of my shut tight pussy

our prayer was blood and water

tears and spit

sand and sweat

sometimes we took handfuls of cum out of our pockets

we always left something behind

Fall at the bayside I strung fishing line just outside the scars

where your tits used to be

drawing a map to the edges of your sewn back nipples

i sewed you up, fixed a knot and pulled tight til you shook

the blood made a pool at the top of your cock

mingled sweat of your junk and the blood from your chest

formed an altar for my hand to make a fist inside your aching

Summer at the lake we had no sharp edges aside from the chainmail at our
throats

so you took a chunk out of my left inner thigh with your fangs

between my screams and the thrashing

you drew all my dead souls into your mouth

and I came on my bit open thigh

it was Spring when I last took your blood into my veins

by the pool of rain that collected in the parking lot corner

i took my straight razor
to just above your right hip
sliced so deep it turned white
no blood at first
but at last my hand wrapped tight around your throat
holding lust and just a little bit of fear
until your blood came fast on cold cement

3 years, 12 seasons, 36 moons
of soaking in these symbols on my body that was yours
you say it's strange that your new lover has no scars

3 years, 12 seasons, 36 moons
of my ownership spread thick across the angles of your skin
you say it's strange that your new lover has no scars

no violent memories tucked away in her underwear drawer
no ashes of photos left to rot in the bottom of the well
no secrets
no terrors
no scars

you show me the dry scar on your hip
and your habit to brush your finger over it
when you're nervous or sad
or you miss my sharp way in
the scar is still whiter than your magenta sins
when your new lover wraps her arms around your waist
holds you up against her smooth unbroken skin

7

Real Talk:

Making queer art happen

Oh Snap! Pizza Slap!

Heather María Ács

We are Brooklyn queers. We. Love. Pizza. Pizza is always there for you, 24 hours a day. She will never leave you, break up with you via text message, or post some bullshit on FB that sends you into a downward spiral. She is always hot, ready, and waiting for YOU.

One day in the spring of 2013, Damien and I were enjoying some delicious slices and the idea came up: "Wouldn't it be amazing to slap someone with a slice of pizza?"

"Uhm, YES!"

And because we are femmes who get shit done, Pizza Slap was born.

At a following Opentoe Peepshow, folks from Brooklyn Transcore needed to raise money to get some queers a slot at a punk festival (yes, a punk festival that cost money). "Would it be cool if we made an announcement?" "Sure..." I said, glancing at Damien, "But I may have a better idea, hold on..."

"Is this the moment?" I hissed at Damien,

"Is it time for... Pizza Slap???"

What better way to inaugurate the first Pizza Slap than by slapping the shit out of a white trans-masculine punk dude?! "He's in!" "Quick we gotta get some pizza before the show starts!" The pizza procurer returns with... Sicilian slices? Frankly, I was disappointed. I was envisioning holding the crust while the cheesy triangle flew through the air, landing with a more "stingy" than "thuddy" effect. "Well, I guess we'll have to make do with what we have."

"So, if you wanna see some queers get to Punk Island and you wanna see this guy get slapped in the face with a slice of pizza, drop some money in the bucket that's goin around!" Dude unexpectedly takes off his shirt, which makes me wanna slap him even more. Was that really necessary? Someone geniusly thought to "mic" the sound of the slap. "Ok, everyone, we gotta do one last thing, on the count of 3 we're all gonna say:

OH SNAP! PIZZA SLAP!!!!!

Video still from May 2013: the very first pizza-slap contact ever made.

Right before the slap commences Dude decides to share, "You know, I don't even like pizza."

"Shut up Dude."

"3-2-1"

"OH SNAP PIZZA SLAP"

I came down hard with the slice.

Pizza Slap Pro Tip: A Sicilian slice, though it doesn't have the jaunty triangular shape of a classic slice, is much, much heavier.

I don't think he realized how serious I was.

And then he did.

Everyone did.

Sauce flew everywhere! The slap was SO LOUD! Everyone gasped! Heels on Wheels members laughed SO HARD. Success! I was no longer disappointed. Dude said he had pizza sauce in his ear for days. Dirty punk. (Luckily, this is all documented and available for online viewing at https://www.facebook.com/heelson-wheelsroadshow.)

And thus, Pizza Slap became a Heels on Wheels tradition. We pulled it out at Fuck You Dad, our annual event to end patriarchy that takes place on father's day and started in my backyard. Hiiii, neighbors! We will be talking shit about dads through queer performance art and slapping people with pizza - don't mind us! (Don't stress, my neighbors are bourgie white people). Pizza Slap expanded into different techniques with special flairs. The Double Slap sandwiches a person's face with a simultaneous Pizza Slap on each side. Down the Line offers a lucky individual the opportunity to Pizza Slap a whole row of people with one slice. We model consent before our slap fests. People get free pizza for getting slapped. It's pretty adorable.

In 2014 we decided to pay homage to performance art rock star Nao Bustamente's "Indigur-rito," a piece she performed in 1992 in San Francisco. That year marked 500 years of colonialism in the Americas and in order for artists of color to get funding, many felt they had to make work around this instead of what they wanted, which is racist and f-d (please refer to "Institutional Funding: Friend or Foe?"). Nao's response was to strap on a burrito with a harness and invite any white men (or, when no one came to the stage right away at one show, anyone with an "inner white man") to the stage to get on their knees and take a bite of her burrito in penance for 500 years of colonialism. If you want to watch the hilarity that ensued, the piece is documented on her website at www.naobustamante.com/art_indigurrito. html. I love this piece. Clearly, we knew we should follow in her footsteps.

"We can definitely get a slice of pizza into a strap-on. All we have to do is roll it up!"

Perfect.

At the following Peepshow, I came prepared with a flashy apron. (I'm not tryin to get messy pizza cock all over my look.) Sabina was not prepared, "I forgot to wear my cute underwear!" "Hurry up," Damien "calmed" her in the bathroom, as they struggled to quickly shove an extra large slice through a tiny o-ring during the break. As quickly as one can do such a thing.

"The next video we would like to present is Nao Bustamante's Indigur-rito..." We shared the quistory of the piece and Nao's work; the audience watched with reverence and laughter. "And now, in honor of Nao Busta-mante's important legacy, we would like to invite any self-identified men and masculine folx to the stage who would like to atone for a world of misogyny and femmephobia." We revealed our pizza cocks and announced our challenge with dignity, pizza cocks flapping. We held back huge grins of anticipation with faux serious, real threatening looks. And come to the stage, they did.

"What's your name," we ask our first volunteer, who kneeled patiently before Damien, hands politely clasped as Sabina shoved the microphone in his face.

"Guy."

*****

Pizza Slap continued to expand with flair. Annie Danger added the Heli-copter, where a few people form a small circle in the center of a larger circle and spin around while multiple slice holders on the outer circle slap each face in turn. (Re-read that sentence until you can truly visualize this wonder. It's worth it.) There's the Full Body Belly Slap, which we used to initiate Loulou at a Peepshow when she first joined Heels on Wheels. The list goes on.

Pro Tip: If a line-up is a little short, throw in a Pizza Slap!

Pizza Slap takes many forms. Gleeful retribution, a celebration, initiation, hunger management for feelings-heavy events, free food for broke artists and audience members. We invite you to create and femmifest your own Pizza Slaps! Remember, consent is sexy and document everything! #ohsnappiz-zaslap #howroadshow

All together, one last time, ***OH SNAP PIZZA SLAP!!!!!!!***

Excess & Vitality:
Thoughts from Critical Reperformance So Far

rosza daniel lang/levitsky

In 2013, I began a series of work called Critical Reperformance. In it, I present works in a range of performance forms, translated onto my own body[1]. The series is partly an intervention on the versions of "reperformance" that have been developed by Marina Abramovic' and other artists whose work has become part of the canon of performance art (and their peers in the dance world, like Yvonne Rainer). Like them, I believe in the importance of keeping body-based performance work present in the world as a living repertoire, rather than solely in its documentary traces. In contrast to their often hagiographical and archival approach, I work from a critical, and often antagonistic, relationship towards the pieces I present.

The critical perspective involved in this project is, to me, inseparable from my appreciation of the work I reperform, and the artists who have created it. In some cases, I'm dealing with work which has shaped my practice as a cultural worker; in others, my love for a piece has grown out of the experience of translating it onto my body. I see critique and antagonism as an important part of performance practice - as a hugely important form of intimate relationship[2] between performers and repertoires, and among performers. To me, performance as a form of analysis and critique of performance is hugely different from written analysis in terms of the kinds of knowledge it creates, the ways that it transmits understandings (both emotional and intellectual), and the effects it can have on the world. My understandings of this approach come out of Black, trans, and queer performance traditions, from Ethel Waters' radical rewrite of "Under the Harlem Moon" in Rufus Jones for President, to the Ball/House tradition's reinvention of the high fashion runway.

This piece is a short exploration of some of the territory the Critical Reperformance series has covered so far, as seen through a precursor project and a performance within the series.

The Critical Reperformance series began with The Artist Is Absent, a daylong event I instigated and co-curated which presented reperformances of 17 works by Marina Abramovic (many of them created in partnership with Ulay).

---

1   So far. Some pieces I plan to include in the series will involve other performers as well as, or instead of, myself.

2   I'm influenced in this understanding by Barbara Myerhoff's Number Our Days, and its attention to political disagreement and argument as a form of intimacy.

The event was sparked by the many ways that Abramovic's MoMA retrospective was a missed opportunity[3]. Not in the work of the performers at MoMA (several were friends and colleagues; all had deep commitment to the assignments they were given), but in the decisions made about how to present the works, and about what bodies to present them through.

I, and my co-curators Ariel Speedwagon Federow and Quito Ziegler, wanted to see Marina & Ulay's work treated as a live repertoire, as pieces that can sustain actual critical engagement rather than archival distancing. Pieces that can bear - and demand - the audience's attention, and discomfort, and powerful responses. Pieces that involve vulnerability, risk, and danger. And not the risks and dangers we saw at MoMA - a workplace full of underpaid performers who had to threaten a job action to even get Workers' Comp coverage[4] - but the risks and dangers of being bodies together in space and in action.

an excerpt from "body of knowledge", my pre-event curatorial statement:

the connection the performer builds with the audience is above all a bodily one, unmediated by language: a brush of skin; an extended examination of the specificity of the performer's physical presence; a scent of the sweat of exertion or emotion; attention to the sounds of breath, of impact, of screaming or the syllables of words uttered to remove them from memory. between performers, as well, the relationship is one of body to body, where what matters are the specifics, the concrete details – how long is the hair that will be tied to mine? will our heights while sitting be more or less different than when we stand? whose lungs drain more oxygen from the air we're sharing? whose cheek reddens first from a slap? what matters, then, for the vitality and flavor of a performance of an abramovi or abramovi /ulay piece, is the bodily knowledges that performers and audiences bring to the given or chosen space. these kinds of knowing are the compass and sextant that we navigate our lives with, the silent senses that give meaning to the words we try to map the changing territory with. like gossip, like rumor, like all the informal tactics of understanding, these bodily knowledges are consciously refined and articulated mainly by those who need them most – those used to being written out of official com-

---

3   I saw the MoMA retrospective with J Dellecave; our conversations at the show and afterwards were the base on which The Artist Is Absent rested.

4   For more on that, see MoMA reperformer Abigail Levine's writings on the experience.

prehension. and for the knowledge of bodily specificity, the more elaborated understandings come through the bodily practices of queers, trans and gender- deviant folks, those whose desires and bodies are called perverse, inexplicable, uncanny.

In The Artist Is Absent, it was largely the decisions we made about which bodies to place Marina & Ulay's work on that held the critical weight, and the power, of the reperformances.

A few examples:

"Nude With Skeleton" was reperformed by Tuesday Smillie. Abramovi's juxtaposition of her own Serbian Yugoslav body with a figure of death, or of the solid interior of the body, resonated with the violence that targeted Bosnian women with particular severity during the Balkan Wars of the 1990s (by which time she herself had been based elsewhere for decades). Smillie's body - the body of a trans woman - is far more directly exposed to violence (though with the equivocal protection of whiteness), and entangled in very different ways with questions of permanence and mutability.

"Balance Proof" was reperformed by Leah Rafaela Ceriello & Hana Malia. Replacing Marina & Ulay's thin, androgynous bodies holding a large mirror between them with two large women whose style marks them as femme shifts the impact of the piece. Fat femme naked bodies against a mirror trouble the meanings of reflection, of pairing, of mutual support, of visibility in ways that the original performance did not.

I reperformed Carolee Schneemann's "Interior Scroll" for the first time in 2014 as part of an evening of my new solo work at Dixon Place, which I called Hysterical Translations, and again a few weeks later as part of a mixed bill Heather Ács produced at the Wild Project.

When I initially conceived of a Critical Reperformance project, I had put "Interior Scroll" on my list as a semi-facetious gesture. After finding more information about the context of the piece, I decided that I had to actually place it on my trans dyke body, as soon as I had a chance.

selections from my program note for "Interior Scroll" reperformances:

this performance is part of my ongoing Critical Reperformance series, which began in november 2013 with "Blowjob [repeated]" at the MIX Queer Experimental Film & Video Festival.

Carolee Schneemann performed this piece twice: in 1975 at a women's art show in East Hampton, and in 1977 as an intervention at the Telluride Film Festival.

in 1988, Schneemann revealed that the "happy man / a structuralist film-maker" who she debates in her scroll text was in fact critical writer (and, at the time, occasional performer in avant-garde film) Annette Michelson. it does something to the piece to know that its sharp analysis of the gendered politics of form is wound around a feminist artist attacking a woman she disagrees with by portraying her as a man, within a highly biologized vision of essential sexual difference.

it does something else to remember that Michelson had fairly recently resigned as an editor of Artforum in protest of an art-show advertisement bought by Lynda Benglis, depicting herself wearing nothing by sunglasses and a rather large cock. an image which hovers between looking like a commercial porn version of a dyke with a double- headed dildo and like a commercial porn version of a trans woman.

In this performance, i replace a reading from Schneemann's Cezanne, She Was a Great Painter with words from two trans dyke writers. my scroll text is a remix of Schneemann's "Scroll 2" with my own writing, which takes a different approach to bringing debates among critics and cultural workers into performance, and refers to events of the summer of 2014.

The "words from two trans dyke writers" were Elena Rose / LittleLight's "The Seam of Skin and Scales" and excerpts of Susan Stryker's "My Words to Victor Frankenstein Above the Village of Chamounix: Performing Transgender Rage". Each is a classic piece of political poetics, firmly anchored within a feminist analysis and straining against the exterminationist impulses against trans women shared by liberal and most radical feminisms.

the scroll text i used in reperformances of "Interior Scroll":

i compose letters dream of my lover write a grocery list rummage in the trunk plan the drainage

this body is not your metaphor these bodies trans intersex

(do you ask the difference) are not for your dissection

inquisition abstraction these are not interchangeable currency

of monetizable faked failure

this body is particular these specific bodies do not respond to interrogations speaking into life a dead surgeon a dead inquisitor does nothing but use our blood to revive him as we gasp into silence dismembered under your sheets

how many feminists does it take to make a rape joke funny (but that was in another country / and in another country / and besides the wench is dead)

in another language

how many rape jokes does it take to make a senior fellow (if she wears yellowface, too)

your intentions do not matter while you hold a knife to our bodies while you name yourself expert

walk away we do not need you here or anywhere

what if i told you i met a happy man

what if i told you he said we are fond of you you are charming but don't ask us to listen to you

we cannot

there are certain words we cannot hear the personal the persistence the dense the primitive techniques

but i don't take the advice of men they only talk to themselves

what if i let you think i was talking about a man for eleven years

he protested you are unable to understand and appreciate the system he said we can be friends equally tho we are not artists equally

what if i told you the truth

what if i named names

it wasn't anthony mccall it was annette michelson

it wasn't jack halberstam it was diana taylor (jack too) it wasn't stephen lawson it was jesusa rodriguez (stephen too)

i said i said i said we cannot be friends, diana and we cannot be artists, jesusa i said i don't talk about men, jack, stephen i said we cannot be equally

your work has no meaning beyond the logic of its systems

grid tenure track visual set strictest implications it exists for and in and for only one gender

she told me it was a valuable opportunity for dialogue i asked does that make me a trans artist? oh no he said we think of you as a dancer

clutter feelings sensibility indulgence mess diet and digestion there is dye in it and death already buried alive

i have slithered out of the excesses and vitality i am the monster that spawned you

The "events of the summer of 2014" I referred to took place at the Hemispheric Institute for Performance & Politics' biennial Encuentro in Montréal. First, a performance by Jesusa Rodriguez and Liliana Felipe of a show that centered on the reenactment of legal and medical violence on the body of an intersex dyke portrayed in ways that framed her as a trans woman. Then, attempts by the Hemi leadership (Director Diana Taylor and Encuentro Producer Stephen Lawson) to evade addressing the effects of the piece on the trans folks present, to pre-empt our addressing those effects ourselves, and to refuse meaningful responsibility by publically repackaging the entire situation as an inherently positive "opportunity for dialogue". In my scroll text, I used passages from a piece of writing that I and other Encuentro participants had planned to present as a counter to Rodriguez and Felipe's show, before Taylor and Lawson made it clear that they would attempt to coopt any such intervention into a 'dialogue' designed to avoid accountability. The parallels of all this with the politics of form and emotion addressed in Schneemann's scroll text are remarkable.

Performing "Interior Scroll" was an incredibly powerful experience. Not because of the scroll's logistics, though figuring out how to effectively and reasonably comfortably anchor and unreel the infamous prop was its own adventure (FYTMI: soft cloth; a small obsidian heart; an NYC- issue condom; plenty of lube; packing not winding). But because the flow of the piece is so well constructed, moving from presentational and attentive to the audience (the robed entrance; the anointment with mud; the art-model poses and first reading) to the inward attention required by the dual focus on scroll-as-object and scroll-as-text as the words emerge from the body in two different forms.

Partly because of the intensity of the performance experience, I have less of a sense of how the reperformances functioned for the audience than I'd like. I do know that some folks who saw it were new enough to the work to be stunned when I produced the scroll, and that others were surprised at how much else was in the piece. But beyond that, I can't say.

Transcendence is Infinite, or Musings on the birth of Lilac Poussez

By Hannah Morrow

"To the ladies in the audience: I know you're jealous of this Queen! You know you're never going to look as good as her. Ahaha. Because of course, we all know the only one who can make a perfect woman – is a man."

Thus spoke Mado, Montreal's most influential Drag Queen, on a hot summer stage several years ago. I felt my body tense up and the word "MISOGYNY!" shoot up through my throat. Mado owns a lucrative white-centric drag bar in the village and her voice is heard beyond queer circles. Why does she want to promote competition amongst femmes, especially one that, according to her, only men can win? But an embittered sigh came out of meci instead, knowing that were I to attempt such a public call-out, she would rip me to shreds with casual cruelty. I, standing in my humble cotton dress and under-developed self-esteem, knew that I was no match for her. The two women standing in front of me whispered about how she was right; they were jealous. I felt the opportunity to turn that moment into an exchange of solidarity pass me by too. I was paralyzed with resentment.

That moment was emblematic of some of the main lessons I learned that year. That was the year I had become immersed, head to toe, in Drag and gay male culture – opened to universes of the most glamorous, politically engaged, passionate, community-minded, visionary, magical, loud, intelligent, prophetic and fun groups of people I could imagine. It was a revelatory time, and I was forever changed for the better. Being exposed to Drag Queens' views of reality helped explode decrepit boxes sitting around in my mind I didn't even know were there. For months, I felt like I had found artistic and social Paradise. But once I got deep into it, when the glitter settled and I could see more clearly, that familiar demon named patriarchy reared its ugly head again.

The magic of Drag began to fade for me, and all I could see in some performances were cis gay men using representations of women's bodies as an artistic, sexual and symbolic performative language for other men, without a requisite respect for women. I was fully aware that the act of adorning oneself in femme Drag is inherently an act of deep reverence for the Feminine Divine, whether subconscious or not (goodness knows this urge is commonly displaced in myriad ways under patriarchy), and that the defiant prowess of iconic women is a fundamental cornerstone of inspiration for almost all forms of femme Drag. It was mystifying when a Queen would stigmatize another for actually being sexually attracted to women, or touch and criticize our bodies freely, or look down on us as lesser beings, bolstering their egos at our expense. A sad awakening swept in. Drag, my magical getaway from hetero-patriarchy, could function as objectification, just as inhumanly as your average Dolce & Gabbana gang rape-esque fashion ad. Gay men, after all, can sometimes fulfill society's constructed image of "woman" far more easily than women can, and they don't even need drag to do it.

At drag shows, an insidious jealousy pierced my enjoyment. When I would watch a Queen who had barely rehearsed her number get up onstage and flail around with a piece of tulle, or throw glitter as a distraction from the fact that she clearly hadn't memorized the lyrics she was lipsynching, to a crowd of friends screaming "YAS! YAS! WERK, HUNTIE!" I would bitterly think to myself "Ugh. How come I can't just get up there and say 'look how feminine I am' and have everyone fall all over themselves to love me?" (This illustrates a painful ignorance of the work that goes into being a Queen – I had no clue.) Thankfully, this didn't go on for too long before a friend sent me a Wikipedia page describing "faux queens" – women who declared themselves as Drag Queens! Praise be to Venus! All the toxic resentments melted out of me as another previously invisible binary was torn down. Of course I could do it if I wanted. Of course no one was stopping me. I was already a highly feminine person and a performance artist, after all! Soon after, I knew I would always regret it if I didn't discover this realm of consciousness for myself. And OOH GRRRL, what sublime riches lay ahead!

Knowing that the mere act of becoming a Queen would be ample confrontation of misogyny all on its own, I relaxed into it completely, re-finding that reverence and respect for the craft. I find one can only really come at it with reverence and respect, because how else are you going to learn to, say, make hip and butt pads from scratch, spray paint your shoes, keep six layers of makeup flawless on your face, wear a few wigs at once, lug pounds of costumes and makeup across town, all in one day and without fucking up your nails, and then get onstage and hold yourself as though you feel perfectly natural looking at the audience through cakes of makeup & lashes, in a costume taped to your body with huge heels and a wig that limits & focuses your head movements? One truly must find it in oneself to become a super-being. Femme Drag is a decision to exalt yourself above the average human. Once I got there, I began to understand where some of that "holier-than-thou" attitude comes from; simply standing in Drag in public is already an accomplishment. For me, finding the courage to take up more space and the audacity to believe I'm the hottest bitch in the room was nothing short of revolutionary.

The Queen who was the closest thing I had to a Drag Mother, the illustrious Connie Lingua, only ever gave me one real tutorial: she made me practice saying the sentence "BITCH, I will CUT YOU" over and over again until I made her believe it. She offered me no explanation, just demanded I find that certain fierceness. For weeks afterward I turned the words over in my mind... Bitch, I will cut you. Why was that the one lesson? Eventually, something crystallized: Queens (and people of all genders who express femininity) are legitimately risking their lives by being in public, so the spirit of being willing to risk one's life for the sake of truly living endows femme Drag with a kind of sacred, defiant vitality that takes lots of guts to get in touch with. Of course, Connie may have also been preparing me for the fact that I may have to genuinely protect myself at some point, and ideally I could do it with grace. The word fierce has taken on a far richer meaning for me since then, and has continued to unfold over time.

This seems to be one of the reasons why every so often I get someone asking me why I don't see female-to-femme drag as appropriative of these traditions of survival and resistance. In these cases, I point to the fact that the very notion of a form of femininity created by men that women are barred from experiencing would obviously be a sexist paradigm, and subsequently would make it in itself disrespectfully appropriative. Further, I see that question imposing an unnecessary gender binary, since the categories "male-to-femme" and "female-to-femme" don't satisfy all "Drag Queens." There are many trans women who have played crucial roles in the shaping of what most understand as contemporary femme Drag, and to disregard their contributions as women in this art form would be highly disrespectful.

After all this, I'm utterly uninterested in feminisms that rejects male-to-female Drag completely; sure, one can allow misogyny to ruin things (although I know sometimes it's not a question of "allowing", it just ruins things on its own accord), but I am down to work through that with my queer sisters in symbiosis, learning from and challenging each other constantly. Mind you, I have received far less stigma from male-to-female Queens than I thought I would. Almost none, in fact. I wonder if that's partly because the process of inviting more and more of the Feminine Divine to channel through me, far from shooting me further into gay male culture as I thought it would, has actually led me towards new circles of feminist performance art, in a blatantly spiritual way. The desire to share these riches with other women, and to try to handle my personal empowerment as an invitation for other women to do the same, slowly overtook the appeal of the glamorous clubs and after-parties I once craved.

And so it goes that Lilac Poussez, my dear sweet alter ego, surprises me with truths latent inside me, leads me on adventures through unchartered realms of perception & inspiration, and femme-ifests brand new dimensions for myself and others to step into. Are we truly living at the cusp of an age of multiplicity, wherein the Feminine will reclaim its rightful place at the centre of our consciousness? I choose to believe it. Let us offer as much love for one another as we can muster, as we each search for the divine inside ourselves and become our own deities, however difficult this may sometimes be.

Photo by Sophie Spinelle, 2013. L to R: Shomi Noise, Vagina Jenkins, Celeste Chan, Damien Luxe, Heather María Ács.

Queering Burlesque

Melanie Keller (Ursula Unctuous)

imaginative

unexpected, no limits

queer & femme & free

I find myself in a constant state of questioning. I'm questioning personal issues like my convictions, my sexuality, my gender presentation; and questioning societal issues like the status quo, respectability and gender norms. Nowhere did I find the freedom to both explore answers to these questions of the human experience and flex my creative muscles as I did in burlesque. It is an art form with the performer at the helm of control, from music selection to costume creation to choreography. In 3 or 4 short minutes, the performer can have a captive audience questioning whatever they thought they knew about life. This stage is the spot I chose to publicly pose my own questions and agitate notions of normalcy.

Queering burlesque is more than a strip tease or shocking an audience for laughs; it's a personal reflection and a critique of society. The specific drag routine that I was lucky enough to perform with the Heels On Wheels Glitter Roadshow in 2012 was a product of internal ambiguity and a test of my own and burlesque's limitations. At the time I was working in an office setting, dressing high femme and experiencing lots of sexual harassment from men. Dressing femme at work meant spending my days listening to comment after comment on my body, my appearance, my "fuckability". I brought this all into my burlesque piece as I struggled to deal with seriously wanting to present more masculine. What did this mean for me? How does this fit with my femme identity and how I usually present myself? Within the confines of my office, I felt no contradiction in cutting off my hair, wearing suits and presenting more masculine from there on, while still identifying as femme. Could I do this every day when I'm not in the office? How femme could I make my more masculine presentation and where is the line between femme and butch drawn?

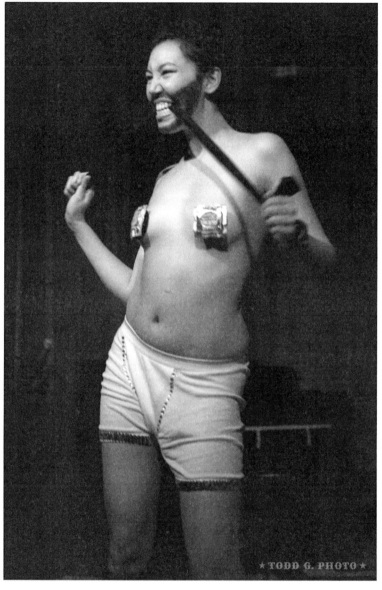

★ TODD G. PHOTO ★

In this act, I'd say that I'm a butchy-femme. I've asked myself before if that even exists, but the true question is: why shouldn't it?

Queering burlesque showcases the true fluidity of the human body, from its movements to the costumes it wears and what it can become throughout the course of one act. It can push the limits of what is not only possible, but acceptable. This performance in particular was me working out what is possible and acceptable for myself. Feeling free to do what is most comfortable for me and redefining "femme" on my own terms is the great value that I take from being a burlesque performer queering it up. I still question my convictions, my sexuality and my gender presentation, but I don't feel such conflict with it anymore. Queering burlesque on stage is my way of challenging the audience to do the same.

Femme2Femme Drag:
Queer Femininity, Performance, and World Envisioning (excerpt)

Andrea Gussie Glik

Femme2femme drag helps us as an audience imagine a queer feminine identity that cannot exist in this misogynistic/transphobic world. High femme drag is an extreme form of femininity in a world that does not have room, or even safe spaces, for that expression; Women's presence in drag culture is constantly disrupting the male dominated spaces of gay clubs and stages.

Heather Acs aka West Vargina is a femme2femme queen based in the Brooklyn drag and performance art scene. Her politically based performances blend glamour and politics in a way that inspires agency and community to the crowd instead of powerlessness. Her work disidentifies with a passive femininity that is apolitical. In his book Disidentifications, Josè Esteban Muñoz writes about Vagical Cream Davis' drag and how it embodies the practice of disidentification. This can be applied to drag in general: Disidentification is a performative mode of tactical recognition that various minoritarian subjects employ in an effort to resist the oppressive and normalizing discourse of dominant ideology. (97) Here, Muñoz is working through what it means to not play into the binary of identification and counteridentification. Performing disidentification means that the subject is working on and against, not just with or counter, to a cultural stereotype/trope. Drag does this with femininity by working on against ideal versions of womanhood. The queen that Muñoz writes about, Vaginal Cream Davis, takes her drag to this level by working against and complicating ideas of race and sexuality as well. What West Vargina is working on and against is the idea that femininity is a shallow, apolitical gender expression.

West Vargina's work not only pushes back against the gender binary, but it also fights this idea that working class people and queer people can't have "nice things". Her most glamorous and over the top piece, which is with Sequinette, is a double Dolly Parton piece, meaning that they are both in full Dolly Parton drag, wearing giant blonde wigs and gold dresses. The lip sync is to a cover of the song "Stairway to Heaven" by Led Zepplin that Dolly Parton did. The piece portrays an alternate universe of glitter, glamour, and magic. When West Vargina talked about the piece,

Photo L to R: Dusty Lynn Childers, Heather Acs, Sequinette, Shane Shane 2014.

she talked about it as her dream reality or world. It was the first drag piece that she said "I need to do this"; instead of being in someone else's piece, she needed to do it on her own. For her, this piece was her fighting against this idea that working class people and queer people can't have glitz and glamour. She got this big beautiful wig, and handmade costumes, and while her shoes were still from Rainbow, and the back up dancer's costumes were made out of scraps, for eight minutes she got to be a true queen. She was Dolly Parton (and didn't just have one Dolly on stage, but TWO), and transported her audience to a beautiful world that's away from this oppressive one we live in. She explains, "That piece was very much about the world being a fucked up place and me wanting to make something beautiful. I had really specific goals about that piece, I wanted to create something that was lavish, and opulent and magical and beautiful. That piece was directly in response to this world being awful and me wanting to create eight minutes of something beautiful that takes you somewhere else"(6).

When I saw the Double Dolly piece with Sequinette and West Vargina I couldn't help but feel like I was shown this glimpse into a queer future that Jose Esteban Muñoz writes about in his book Cruising Utopia. In this book, Muñoz explores the stage that queer performance is acted on as a portal. The stage shows the crowd/audience what a queer future, a queer utopia could look like. Many performances show audiences for a brief moment what a world where queerness is possible, and celebrated, is like. Muñoz writes on the stage being a place of queer future potentiality:

> I dwell on and in this stage because I understand that it is one brimming with utopian performativity that is linked to the ideality that is potentiality. This potentiality is always in the horizon and, like performance, never completely disappears but, instead, lingers and serves as a conduit for knowing and feeling other people. (113)

On stage is a place where queer people can look and see a future that may be possible. The feeling of "maybe this could last forever" is always there during a performance. When the lights go back up, a cold feeling washes over the crowd, because they are back in reality, and are quietly begging the universe to return to that moment that they just witnessed on stage.

Femme2femme drag creates a feeling of potentiality for queer utopia. Not only because it is glamorous and over-the-top, but because it carries a promise of another time or planet where everything can always be covered in glitter, and there can be more than one Dolly. Femme2femme drag shows us what a celebration of femininity that is otherwise deemed as "fake" or "too much" could look like. This kind of drag creates opportunities for people, specifically femmes, to see people on stage who look like them. Muñoz writes on utopia, "Utopia is an ideal, something that should mobilize us, push us forward. Utopia is not prescriptive; it renders potential blueprints for a world not quite here and the now is transcended by a then and a there that could be and indeed should be" (97). Femme2femme drag lays blueprints for a world where gender is what you make it, where everyone can have glitter and glamour, where it is safe and even respected to be high femme. It helps us picture a world where women's art is respected, seen as real, and is cheered on as much as men's work is. Femme2femme drag directly addresses misogyny within gay and queer culture and brings to light the violence against femme bodies. This kind of performance goes against everything women both cis and trans are told to be by both mainstream and gay cultures. It is loud, unapologetic, and serious. While many of these queens use humor or camp in their performances, that does not lessen the intensity of the work. Femme2femme drag is real drag, and it is also resistance to the hetero and homo patriarchy, and it is an unapologetic celebration of femininity.

An Open Letter from the 2012 FemmeCon Co-Chairs

jen valles and Krista Smith

Hi Dearest Community,

First off, we just want to send a lot of love out to all queer femmes, particularly to all femmes who have ever attended FemmeCon, to all femmes who have ever organized FemmeCon, and to the founders of FemmeCon. We are bearing witness to pain surrounding the organization of the 2014 Femme Conference and and our hearts and solidarity are with all femmes who are invested in creating a sustainable, inclusive Femme Conference that centers the needs of those most marginalized in our communities. Because we are invested in this conference and together spent years of our lives committed to building and creating this conference, although we are no longer involved with the organizing of it, we also just want to share our wishes and dreams for what Femme Con can be. What is abundantly clear to us is the investment that many femmes have in this conference and we see this as an opportunity for more community members to step up and invest the kind of commitment, time, intention, and resources that this conference will need if it is to not only continue, but to thrive and be a place that feels safer to those more marginalized within the queer Femme spectrum.

When we took on the responsibility of co-chairing the 2012 conference, it was with transparency that we were rolling off organizing the Femme Conference in any way, after the 2012 conference. The two of us had spent a collective 12 years organizing this conference and it took its toll on us mentally, in our personal relationships, and financially. We needed to pass the torch on while we still had love in our hearts for the conference and this meant saying goodbye to all official organizing responsibilities. While we have continuously been available to the 2014 Conference Chairs in an attempt to help them with anything that might need to logistically produce the conference, we had to draw a firm boundary around our organizing capacity and we appreciate this being respected.

We also want to take a moment to publicly state how disgusting we think it is that the "Gender Identify Watch" folks are using what is happening righ now as a platform for their vile hatred and trans-misogyny. This is a moment for the entire Femme Community to join hands and say NOT IN OUR NAMES. We stand in solidarity with Trans Femmes and Trans Women and say, "Oh hell no!" to the Gender Identity Watch agenda.

We believe in the importance of having a space like FemmeCon. FemmeCc is not perfect. It has never been perfect. There is so much work that we as a community and that the folks organizing the conference have to do to make the FemmeCon space a safer more accessible space for all femmes, particular femmes of color, trans femmes, femmes with limited or no financial resource and femmes with disabilities. As conference organizers and conference chair: we spent years actively trying to figure out how to better serve all femmes but there is still so much work to be done on that front. Our hope was that b rolling off we were creating space for folks with new energy, new ideas, and of identities that are specifically impacted by this conference's shortcomings We believe in queer femme communities with all of our hearts and know tha we can do better and must do better and are sorry that we could not get the conference to the place of our collective dreams but we know that this must and can happen if this conference is to continue.

Finally, as indicated above, we are tired. The years of organizing FemmeCc took its toll on us. Trying to create a space from a place of love for a margina ized community of folks, many of whom experience multiple forms of oppre sion on a daily basis, for as little money as possible, while trying to meet as many accessibility needs as possible, which unfortunately costs a lot of mone while under the constant public eye of a community that is rightfully investe in this, is unbelievably hard work. Doing this while also living at the intersec tion of multiple forms of oppression, with our own histories of trauma, and doing this as a volunteered labor of love that required our personal money, time, and necessarily required that we could not access the supports we put i place for other conference attendees (due to conflict of interest or any appea ance that we may be running the conference unethically) compounds that in ways we don't even know how to articulate. Both of us had to balance our ov mental health (with which, years later, we are still struggling), put our personal relationships on the line, and work with the constant worry of finding the money to make miracles happen, and the constant belief that we had to do better and must do better. It is painful to not be in a position to step up and help the conference in some kind of more meaningful way at present but we feel like truly the torch must be passed on and we hope that queer femmes can understand our own personal needs to live a more sustainable life.

We love you queer femmes. We want to see you shine as bright as possible and we hope that folks who have the capacity, desire, skills, commitment to organizing, courage and love for femmes that it takes to produce a national conference by femmes for femmes can come together to create a future Femme Conference. This probably also means that those of us with more privilege within this community step back and leave plenty of room for those of us with less privilege to claim space. But there are ways that every single one of us can contribute to creating queer femme space. Although we cannot be involved with organizing anymore, we are, as we have always been, here to provide historical knowledge, logistical information, love, and whatever support we have the capacity to provide.

We also want to once again thank the founders of FemmeCon and everybody who has ever organized this conference. Organizing and creating queer femme space has contained some of the most beautiful experiences of our lives and we are forever indebted to the folks who made that conference happen.

In solidarity,

jen valles and Krista Smith

Ed note: this letter was edited for this anthology, and originally posted on Facebook May 14, 2014.

This is not a test:
Sliding Scale, Accessibility & Self Care

Damien Luxe

My skill sets for making Heels on Wheels function come from my experiences of being poor, punk, and sharp. I know what it is to tell myself I Can't, and what it means to discover I Can. From the outset, we wanted all our shows to be as accessible as possible to anyone who wanted to participate or attend. This is about understanding marginality. That meant looking for venues that were all-ages and physically accessible, and keeping our door fees affordable, yet still committing to always pay artists.

We ended up using sliding scale admission most times. For us, being as happy to accept $2 as $20 from someone for their admission meant that people like us – that person who sometimes only has $2 – can still have access to art, community, and the possibility of seeing themselves reflected. It also means that the person who has $20 needs to be willing to throw in, too. This form of mutual aid is no small matter, and in the real-life practice of working with sliding scale door fees, we learned a lot.

Ultimately, we presented our door fee as a range, with our "ideal" (still-affordable) price in the middle. For example, a show we'd ideally get $10 for would be $5-$15 at the door. It was after the second tour that we realized that we needed to do this midrange scale-setting. Our door person, often the seasoned Lizxnn Disaster, noticed that we consistently received the average, or middle of whatever scale we set.

Because we also believe paying artists, even at honorarium levels, is crucial to our economic justice mission, we wanted to find ways from the stage to say "Hey if you have money to throw in, please do because this goes to artists! And, if you don't we're also stoked you came!" I think that one complexity of class is around entitlement: the swapping of "I can't" and "I can." I see this manifest as: people who don't have access to much money may just not see themselves as "being the worst off" and so not take a price break – and yet, people who do have access to money already have the experience of entitlement to options, and so take those lower-cost options. Finding the balance here never perfectly emerged. We did have a lot of sold-out, at-capacity shows!

Paradoxically, the reality of booking venues in cities we're not from and on a limited budget meant that sometimes we were in 21+ spaces or places that had stairs. Some cities have very few queer-positive stage spaces. Often, places that don't serve booze or are newer and ADA-compliant charge to use the space. This brought us a conundrum: we could use time to find a new space, money to rent the space, or use the space and know some people could not come. Paying for a space would mean charging more, spending more than our usual few hours space-hunting would harm us. This was a constant reminder of the ways that capitalism and class [e.g. assumed resource-access of "the arts"] work in tandem against ranges of ability: it costs more and takes more time to have access needs, and rarely are the financial access needs of audiences considered. Heels on Wheels worked on a small-scale and within our own access and wellness limitations, so there was a limit to our ability as well. We made the best and broadest venue decisions we could, knowing that we rarely got it perfect, though in 2014 we had an all-ages tour! In the service of artists we curated and communities we brought together, we chose to book a show over skip a town, and I think that was the right decision overall.

As the de facto CFO of Heels on Wheels [aka the troupe dad], I handled the bottomline financials. I love this stuff and it comes easily to me. In what ended up being my job running a small-scale multi-person arts organization of anticapitalist political queers who are trying to make art while operating under capitalism I was lead to another paradox: contentiously, I suspect that adding money past a certain level would have alienated the entire endeavor, even as making community-driven art without (much) funding is incredibly hard. What do I mean by that? If Heels on Wheels rolled up in a cushy tour bus and all our artists had riders and stipends, we would have been almost automatically out of touch with the people we wanted to connect with as collaborators, bookers, and audience. And, since we had basically the opposite – my dented van, a $10/day food allowance per person, and literal begging via crowdsourcing for sustainability funding – we were positioned to be among people who shared our disdain for exploitation, and we wore ourselves the hell out. There is no limit to heartfelt magic, but there is a limit to the hours in a day and the resources at hand. Those hours are even shorter if you happen to need dental work or a chiropractor you can't afford, which happened.

It's unacceptable to me to quantify all possibility in terms of money. Specifically because I have out of necessity and, later, wit operated underneath most resource systems, I enjoy refuting their limitations. However, there is a reason that most arts organizations that persist have staff. There is a limit to un/underpaid labor that important considerations like self-care bring into the equation.

It's also unacceptable to burn yourself out in the service of others, something that also happened at times. We learned about going hard -- and then we learned about pausing. Self-preservation is crucial: come it from archiving, witnessing, sharing, or resting. May we all in our sweet glory persist.

What You THINK Tour Will Be Like ...
and Then What it ACTUALLY is Like

Heels on Wheels Collective Wisdom

TOURING's GONNA BE LIKE THISSSS!!!

Oh, actually, this is happening:

And, this is happening:

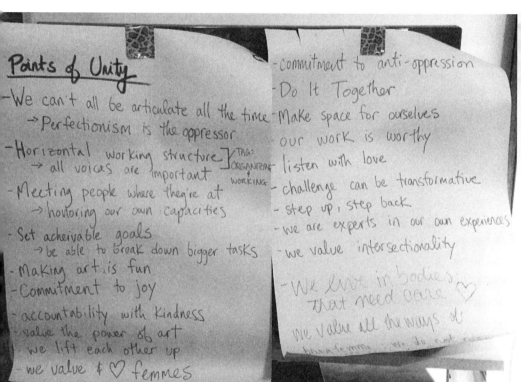

TOURING's GONNA BE LIKE THISSSS!!!

Oh, now this is happening:

TOURING's GONNA BE LIKE THISSSS!!!

The one time we made lotsa $$$! Detroit hooked us up!

All we see are signs... ONE dollar signs.

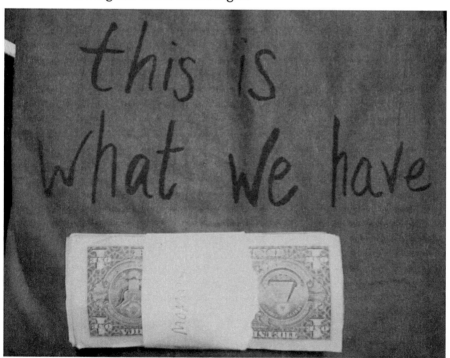

What You Need to Put on a Show (The Heels on Wheels Way)

Heels on Wheels collective wisdom

1. ***Artists***. This might seem obvious, but don't leave it to the end - start here. Partying with everyone is better than just partying with the same ol folks you know, don't you agree? This means showing up at other events, asking around; thinking ahead and booking ahead so you get a banging line up.

1.5 ***Content [of Artists]*** Ask your artists what they are going to perform. Care what they are going to perform. Notice if they say something that doesn't seem ok to you, ask more questions, and say no when you need to.

2. ***Venue[s]:*** this is paradoxically the bane of our existence in NYC, and the site of much friendship and adventure outside of the City. Collect venues that you enjoy and can work with like best friends, as they will make or break your live art practice. NYC suffers from a lack of all-ages wheelchair-accessible venues that are affordable. Thus, the interelationship between capitalism and ableism tightens.

3. ***Staff***: e.g. people who are NOT the performing artists who are pre-arranged to do things at the venue. These roles you'll need filled include:

- Femmecees to host,
- a door person to take $,
- a stage/house manager to wrangle the artists and femmcees
- a documentor to take photos/videos

4. ***Snacks***. Snacks. Snacks. DO NOT FORGET THE SNACKS. Ask your artists and staff what kind of snacks and don't starve the vegan/gluten-free/candida diet people around you. Hangry makes bad community art.

5. ***Promo***: Write a blurb, create an image, make a hand-drawn flyer, make a website. Now, send emails, put up posters, let your listservs know, tell the local papers and blogs. Find out who likes artists of the type you're presenting and tell them, give your venue & your artists the blurb. Who doesn't like cool art?

6. ***Lineup/Curation/Show Order:*** Some people go to graduate school to learn this, but here we are, in real life, taking care of business. Since you know who's performing and have a sense of what they're doing, put it in an order that will give the audience some high and lows in a roller-coaster. But not one of those death-drop roller coasters, and not one of those kiddie rides either.

BYOCL

Heels on Wheels collective wisdom

. . . .

There was one show where the venue owner told us there was absolutely no lighting, so instead of doing the show in semi-darkness where no one could see, we had to expose people to the harsh overhead lights the entire time....except....

When the venue owners' girlfriend came out on stage to play music with another performer, she produced clip lights outta nowhere with beautiful red and blue gels, creating the most gorgeous lighting. She and other people we had not seen yet materialized to reverntly hold the lights, perfectly highlighting the girlfriends' face.

We were jaw drop. Where the F did those lights come from??

THEN, she took them away as soon as the number was over and hid them from us.

W. T. F. But, that's okay because we got glitter ALL over a giant carpet square she had in the space and she was not pleased. "We usually have a rule against glitter," she had said earlier.

...

Protips:
. . . .

Bring Your Own Clip Lights [BYOCL]

Be willing to sweep

Bring sharpies & paper scraps for bios

Bring change for the door

Low stakes - high standards!

HOW IS...

a lot of work
power in femininity
doing things our own way
a little family
strength in vulnerability Intersecional
so many things
snacks
creating + destroying
femme 4 femme
glitter
a party
accessories
Challenging the status quo
Outfits! Looks!
adass punkrock feminism in action
ot just because we want to but because we have to

6. 5 *Intermission*: Take care of your audience so that people are not falling asleep or urgently needing a break because there are So Many Feelings.

7. *Money*: eeeh. Just kidding [kind of] - pay your artists! Try to book venues you feel good about paying! Pay yourself sometimes too, so you can get snacks for yourself [see #4].

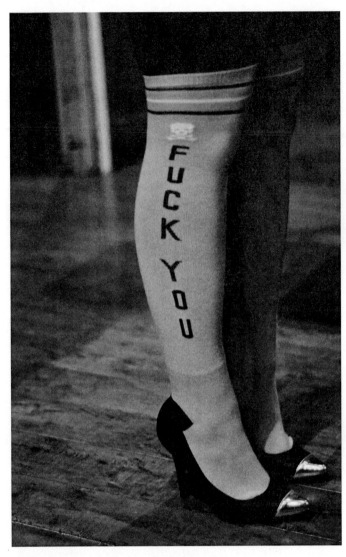

Photo of Amanda Harris by Sophie Spinelle, 2013.

Props to Sex Workers

Heels on Wheels Collective Wisdom

This one goes out to all the sex workers. Even if a piece isn't about sex work, that doesn't mean it's not about sex work. Even if people aren't writing about sex work explicitly, that doesn't mean there's not (many) sex workers included in these pages. We shouldn't have to write about/reveal each aspect of our identity for it to be noted, respected, and recognized as part of our whole.

8 *Ancestors* & Family

The revolution will not be cited.

Kama La Mackerel

The revolution will not be cited.
It will not have a bibliography, or a title page.
Neither will it have a supervisory committee.

I was the first in my family to attend university,
As a matter of fact, I was the first in my family to even finish school.
Eighteen,
a full-scholarship in hand,
I left my island,
I hopped onto a plane
and flew towards the Ivory Tower,
the one where I would finally realize my upward social mobility.

I remember the anticipation and the anxiety in my mum's voice,
as she would call me every Sunday to enquire about my health.

Long distance calls,
from this small country of mine,
were expensive;
the number of words we could exchange were
rationed, calculated, controlled and saved up,
much like when I was a child
food, water, electricity,
every single vegetable and fruit,
every single grain of rice
were all rationed, calculated, controlled and saved up.

Every Sunday, my mum called me for eleven minutes:

four allocated to my dad,

seven that she would claim for herself.

Her voice would shake with anxiety as she would ask me about my health...

But more than anything she wanted to know how I was dealing with school,

whether my assignment grades had moved from a B+ to an A-,

whether my Professors and TAs were fond of me,

whether I was actively participating in class,

whether I would keep my scholarship

and whether I would come back home in a few years,

as the honour of the family,

degree in hand.

"Stay strong," she said.

"Work hard, and it'll all be fine."

Throughout her seven rationed minutes every Sunday,

she repeated her mantra, religiously,

like a prayer for me.

In the meantime, she rationed her own eating habits,

fasting to please the Gods and Goddesses of the Hindu pantheon:

Tuesday prayer for Hanuman who will remove all obstacles from my path—

she had some rice pudding before sunrise and nothing until sunset;

Thursday prayer for Ganesha known as the most intelligent of Gods—

she was allowed only fruit throughout the day;

Friday prayer and fast for Kathigaï who would send me strength and perseverance—

again, she would have some rice pudding before sunrise and would eat or drink nothing but water until the sun had set.

Thus were her sacrifices,
thus were her weekly prayers,
thus were her days and days and days of fasting,
because my mum had a dream.
She had a dream.

From the depth of her guts,
in the folded layers of silk that softened her most cherished secrets,
my mother dreamt.
Her dreams were made of the sound of an engine,
the constant humming of a sugar cane factory
as it worked day and night
to produce more and more and more,
for one extra rupee,
for two extra rupees,
for three extra rupees,
for just a little bit more money,
just so that she could send her two kids to school.

Her dreams had the thick scent of molasses,
the kinds that impregnated our village day and night
as the sugar cane got crushed,
and the thick liquid would ooze out
and haunt our mornings and our evenings with its smell;

like an uninvited guest,
this smell did not knock on our door
and it entered the intimacy of our homes
and clung to our walls, our tables, our chairs,
our furniture, our clothes, our hair, our skin...

Her dreams tasted thick like coarse sugar
greased into a long-running engine
that controlled the rhythm and the beat of our hearts,
that disciplined the oxygen coming in and out of our lungs,
and governed our every word, our every thought, our every mind,
our every word, our every thought, our every mind,
our every thought, our every mind,
our every thought,
our every mind,
our every mind,

Our every mind, colonized
just as much as the bodies of our ancestors
that were dragged onto this ship,
ripped from their land, their family, their culture
to come down to the island where they would work
in fields in the unrelenting sun
from dawn to dusk, from day and night,
from the top of their burnt sweat-soaked heads
to the tip of their coarse fingers
where the only sensation knowledgable to their body was
pain.

My mum had a dream: she dreamt of a revolution.
She dreamt of a revolution located in the Ivory Tower.

I read the other day that Ben Harper,
the son of Stephen Harper, Prime Minister of Canada,
decided to go to Queen's University to study commerce.
I wanted to send the article to my mum,
but then she wouldn't quite get it.

She might just ask me:
"But Kama, why didn't YOU go to Queen's University."

I'm scared of failing my words.
I'm scared of not being able to tell her:

"Mother, I dropped out of university
and I dropped out of the Ivory Tower
because I believe in a revolution too!
I believe in a revolution where we'll rise into this world
and smash those patriarchal and colonial institutions
that are built on centuries of racist, sexist and classist legacy."

I want to say:
"Mother, James McGill founder of McGill University
made his fortune because
he had slaves that he bought and sold
and exploited and bled to death
just as much as this sugar factory
bled your father and your mother, to death,
and before them, bled their own mothers and their own fathers to death..."

I want to say:
"Mother, I refuse to be complicit in a system of domination
that perpetuates itself and upholds its colonial violence
and refuses to make space
for you,
for me,
for us,
for our communities,
for our histories,
for our ancestors,

our archives,

our legacies,

our beauty,

our past,

our present

and our future."

Because Mother, I believe in a revolution too.

I believe in a revolution will not be cited,

That will not have a bibliography, or a title page.

And will not have a supervisory committee.

Kama La Mackerel, about to inspire the first standing ovation at an Opentoe Peepshow. Photo: Damien Luxe, January 2015.

Photo by Damien Luxe, 2013. The making of tour t-shirts!

The Brown Queen

by Alejandro Rodríguez

• •

CHARACTER:

THE BROWN QUEEN
An effeminate 22 year old, Chicano, from West Texas

The set is minimal. The back wall has a scrim with an outline of El Paso, Texas then New York City. There is a projection screen: upstage center. There's a twin bed on the middle of the stage and a bed stand next to it. A body lies on the bed. It is morning. An alarm goes off and music starts playing. Character begins morning routine; brush teeth and get clothed.

Scene 1
• •

THE BROWN QUEEN:

My story begins in the basin of the Franklin Mountains, in El Paso, Texas; the city where I was born and spent the first 18 years of my life. The sunset in El Paso is like no other, it's full of pinks, blues and some orange. The sunset in El Paso is the most beautiful I have ever seen.

One of my earliest memories is with a man and a car; in the years to come I will have many encounters and memories with men and cars, but this one in particular is a special one.

I was about four years old, it was a Sunday afternoon, and I was doing what I now regard as one of my favorite pastimes-driving around aimlessly, in El Paso, also known as cruising.

On Sunday evenings, after church, we would visit my grandparents. My grandfather would drive me around in his 1963 Rebel Rambler. As we cruise the streets of Downtown El Paso the radio blares "oldies".

Mexican-American and Chicano culture have a strong relationship with Motown music. The nostalgia in the music must remind our grandparents about their youth, falling in love for the first time, or driving around aimlessly on Sunday evenings. It's the music they always played when my cousins and I would visit. There's something about Motown music that simply became part of our culture.

We're cruising down Alameda Street and from the busted speakers begins playing a song to which I can't help but to sway from left to right. (MUSIC CUE) I asked my grandfather whose voice was blaring from the busted speakers. He spoke two words: Diana Ross.

Diana Ross.

Who was Diana Ross? I wanted to sound just like she did!

Do you have a picture of Diana Ross? Can I see it?

After driving around for a while, my grandfather drove back to the house on Concepcion Street.

I quickly reminded my grandfather of the request I had made earlier. That man always delivered! He handed me the following picture.

(DIANA ROSS IMAGE ON SCRIM)

I...I didn't know what to say...she..she was FIERCE!

Ladies and gentlemen in that moment, on a Sunday afternoon, in 1991 I was introduced to Diana Ross, that brown beautiful queen and the word fierce, which has now become a part of my daily vernacular.

And that's how my memory works. With music. Now that my grandfather has passed this is how I remember him.

DIANA ROSS AND THE SUPREMES, "BABY LOVE" PLAYS. LIGHTS FADE OUT. IMAGES ON SCRIM.

Scene 2

THE BROWN QUEEN:

The memories that I have of my mother from my youth are far and few in between.

I remember watching a televised concert of Mexican artist Juan Gabriel. You must understand that the relationship between Juan Gabriel and a Mexican woman is a sacred one.

Juan Gabriel is a sixty year old music artist, who was raised in Ciudad Juarez--just like my mother. He has written over a thousand compositions, won countless awards and performed all over the world.

This is a picture of Juan Gabriel in the early 1970's. (IMAGE ON SCREEN). A picture of him in the 1980's. (IMAGE ON SCREEN).) A picture of him performing at El Palacio De Las Bellas Artes in Mexico City. (IMAGE ON SCREEN).)

Juan Gabriel has been called "El Divo de Juarez", "The Divo of Juarez". From a young age I knew about him, and what I found most intriguing was the spectacle of his performances. His costumes were always flamboyant. There was something about his gestures, his movements that simply fascinated me.

Although at the time I wasn't aware of the definition of feminine or femininity, I knew it was something that I should not do. I was reprimanded, yelled at, even beaten up by family members and schoolmates. I was constantly told to stop running like a girl - a statement that I never understood.

Juan Gabriel has never really "come out". A couple of years ago during an interview he was asked about his sexuality to which he replied, "Lo que se ve no se pregunta." Which loosely translates to: What you see you don't ask? Between you and me we both know that Juan Gabriel is one of us - a sister. I know this. You probably assume it. So does my mother.

When I first came out, my father, he told me that he didn't care. I'm his son and I can do no wrong, his love is unconditional. As for my mother, she wasn't fond of the idea at first. She sat across the dining table and as the words came out of my mouth, "Soy gay", her face went blank. It wasn't because she didn't know; it was the fact of having to deal with it.

Photo by Damien Luxe of Alejandro Rodriguez, 2015.

For years we didn't speak about my sexuality.

During my last trip to Texas my mother and I sat on the couch and on television was the Spanish version of Judge Judy, La Juez Laura. The case dealt with a homosexual couple who had been kicked out from an establishment because they had kissed.

Throughout the entire time my mother nodded her head to things that she agreed to.

The judge ruled in favor of the gay couple, as the credits rolled my mother said:

A mi me gusta mucho lo que la juez dice. Ella quiere mucho a los...gays, y siempre pelea por sus derechos.

God, I really wanted to start crying.

In the very indirect and reserved way that my mother has always been, she told me something that I never thought I would hear.

She understood me.

And that's all I needed.

LIGHTS FADE OUT. Music plays. PICTURES OF MOTHER AND THE BROWN QUEEN.

When your mother tells you

Sabina Ibarrola

When your mother tells you that it would be better if you weren't here, this is what you remind yourself:

That in dreams we get a whole 'nother life while the body is sleeping.

That making tea is a form of alchemy.

That my closet is full of femme hand-me-downs.

That there are many ways to be mama'd.

That they say Athena chopped her way out of her father's forehead
with a battle axe,

That she was born a grown woman.

That grit makes the pearl, not the other way 'round.

I Disown You Right Back,
with Mrs. Trixie Cane

T.L. Cowan

Hi, I'm Trixie Cane, and I want to talk to you today about an exciting new family values initiative that I am part of called Withdrawing Awesome Feminist Affection And Homosexual And Trans Assistance, Support, Love And Labor From Awful Religious Relatives. Or, WAFA AHATA SLAL FARR for short.

WAFA AHATA SLAL FARR has started the "I Disown You Right Back" campaign.

As part of the I Disown You Right Back campaign, we have designed 5 that postcards that you can send to your Awful Religious Relatives, notifying them that you are withdrawing your affective bonds and labour from their lives, effective immediately and continuously, until they stop supporting shitty religious organizations that trash women, trans people and homos.

Card #1 promises Awful Religious parents that if they continue to be assholes, that you, their Feminist, Homosexual or Trangender child, will not take care of them in their old age. This card saves you that uncomfortable phone call and all of that explaining and teaching. Instead just give up on your parents of yours and send the postcard that says: Dear Mom & Dad, I Love You But You Will Die Alone.

We also have cards for those two-faced siblings and cousins who support hate-mongering Religious Figures but still want to prove that they are cool by inviting homosexual,

Dear Mom & Dad,

I ♥ you,

but you will die alone.

xoxoxo

ransgender and unmarried female family members to their heterosexual
ifestyle celebrations.

Card #2 reads: Dear Mr. & Mrs. The Bride Will Be Taking Her Husband's
Name Blood Diamond Storage Solutions Rape Denier Promise Keepers
And Hymen Fakers, NO TOKEN GAY COUPLE/TRANS PEOPLE/HAIRY
FEMINIST ARMPITS IN THE WEDDING ALBUM FOR YOU!

Card #3 is for those relatives whose wedding albums you were already
suckered into. This card allows you to kindly, but firmly, respond to the next
stage of familial obligation, and reads: "No more baby shower gifts for you,
you over-breeding, gas-guzzling creationist weirdos."

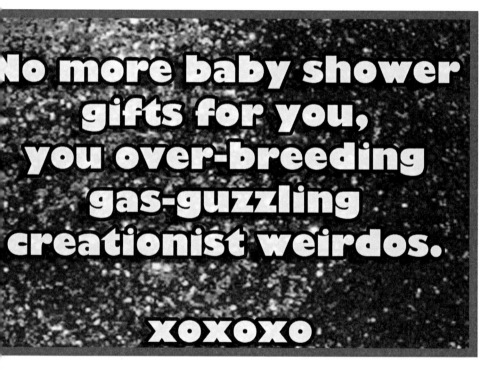

Card #4 carries a versatile "I Disown You Right Back" message, appropriate
or any Awful Religious family member.

It reads simply: "Need a Compatible Organ Donor? Don't Call Me."

We here at WAFA AHATA SLAL FARR acknowledge that, while it is out
of the question for some queers, trans people and feminists to truly abandon
their Awful Religious Relatives because of the ways that families of color,

Indigenous families, immigrant, migrant, poor families and families with disabilities are systemically and personally delegitimized and persecuted even worse sometimes than white homosexuals, trans people and feminists, and sometimes *by other homosexuals, trans people and feminists*, many of these individuals who feel that they cannot in good faith actually follow through on a threat to disown their Awful Religious Relatives, still want to send a stern warning.

For these friends we offer card #5, embossed with the following extra sparkly message: "Seriously?"

Friends,

Thanks so much for your time. On behalf of WAFA AHATA SLAL FARR and the "I Disown You Right Back" campaign, I'm Trixie Cane, with a message for all you neglected and abandoned females and homosexuals out there:

Give the gift that really says family values! Order your mix-and-match set of personalized maximum emotional pain payback postcards today!

Production Details: "I Disown You Right Back" was first work-shopped at the Opentoe Peepshow in November, 2012. Since then Mrs. Trixie Cane has performed this piece in many venues, and the video has gone basically viral.

Dear Mr. & Mrs. The-Bride-Will-Be-Taking-Her-Husband's-Name-Blood-Diamond-Storage-Solutions-Rape-Deniers-Promise-Keepers-and-Hymen-Fakers:

NO TOKEN GAY COUPLE, TRANS PEOPLE, or HAIRY FEMINIST ARMPITS IN THE WEDDING ALBUM FOR YOU!

xoxo

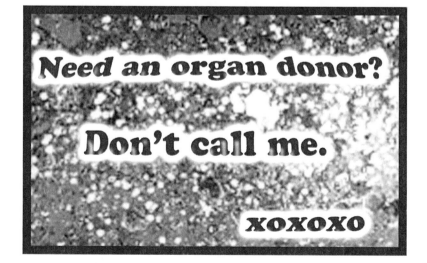

Need an organ donor?

Don't call me.

XOXOXO

Ode to an Old Queen Part 1

Glenn Marla

Part 1

It is because of you that I know who I am, It is because of you that I feel I matter, It is because of you that I can be who I am.

You are older than me, and I'm not as young as I used to be.

You my dear sweet love are a survivor

I want to sit on your couch and hold you so close

I want to look deeply into your eyes and ask you enthusiastic and earnest questions!

Were the bath houses really fun? Did you feel free? Did you ever see Bette Midler perform in one?

Tell me how New York used to be?

What is performance art?

What were coffee shops like before the internet?

Tell me about Ave A, but did you ever go to Brooklyn?

What about Coney Island?

I do not ask questions or hold you too tight or close. I am thankful that you are here and let your stories slowly transfer into my skin,

I hope I will get every single one of them and am already sad that I will not.

I smile with pride when you tell me I remind you of someone or something that isn't around anymore

The Way It Used to Be Museum was built by old queens, they needed a palace, a place to be worshiped and keep the stories. They built the walls out of heartbreak and resilience.

At The Way It Used to Be Museum, we tell you what to care about because it doesn't exist anymore. The artifacts are old tee shirts, postcards, syringes, press clippings, grains of sand, paintings that never sold, and leases that were not renewed.

The museum was built on hustle, tips, spit, sweat, soul, gut, cum and glitter. It is shiny and cluttered, recovered and constantly in recovery, there will never be enough and no matter how much you have you will feel conflicted somewhere about wanting more.

You will keep wanting. The Way It Used to Be Museum was built on desire.

The museum is not so clean, there is no wifi, it is not up to code, not organic or gluten free, and doesn't know what a cabaret license is.

Come right in and step right up! You need to know why you are how you are. Come to The Way It Used to Be Museum.

Part 2

My Mother notices it is not the way it used to be. She recalls the days when you used to open a bank account and they used to give you real good stuff. "You know real good stuff, microwaves, VCR's, and corning ware, not like the crap the banks try and give you now."

My Mom unapologetically uses high end paper plates

Screams across the house

Speaks of wedding proposals and cancer in exactly the same tone

My Mom seems most at peace after all her guests leave. She immediately takes her shirt off, and eats the carcass from the chicken soup while directing everyone else on how to clean up.

My Mom is a tough broad, and a lone wolf. The few people she keeps close are also the toughest most badass broads. I'm talking women with pasts and secrets.

One night when I was very young and I couldn't sleep, I stumbled into my Mother's room and she wasn't there, so I looked in the next logical place, the kitchen. Looking in I had no idea what I was seeing, but I did know I was seeing something I wasn't supposed to.

Late night in the kitchen, hours after the Mahjong game ended, Fran and Lois and Maxine were still there. It appeared that these women weren't playing with blocks, but canned goods? My Mother was building a wall or a fortress. She was moving quickly, more swiftly than I had ever seen her move, stacking tuna fish cans, more tuna cans than I had ever seen! More tuna cans than were at the supermarket! My mother was creating a wall of tuna cans around herself and her friends. I could barely see what they were doing in these walls made out of tuna cans but whatever it was, was unlike everything else my Mother did. This was not for me.

I felt wrong looking in, but I could not look away. It seemed that inside the tuna fish can walls these mothers saw each other's scars from hair removal procedures and C-sections. They saw that their breasts were shaped in ways they didn't want. In the tuna fish can walls, I think that they actually didn't care that they were fat and they certainly didn't talk about the new diets they were trying because if they talked about that in there what would they talk about in the office or with each other in front of their families. I now know that in that tuna fish room sat Anita, Fran, Lois and Maxine and they just sat and made small spaces for their pasts to sit. They all worked so hard to leave where they were once from and their dissatisfaction with suburban life was in the walls too. It's where they got older in front of each other. I could barely see in the cracks of the cans, but I swear I saw my Mother touch her friends' faces. I saw them touch hers too.

As I got older, ate more canned goods, and met more women, this scene made more and more sense.

You see, growing up we never had any less than maybe 50 cans of tuna fish. The tuna fish cans were on the third shelf of the pantry taking up most of the shelf .

I appreciate how neatly tuna fish cans stack on top of each other. Unlike other canned goods piled high you never feel like they are going to topple over. There is a strange security in this. A feeling that I could stack cans and cans of tuna fish, cans from the floor to the ceiling, that I could build a castle out of tuna fish cans.

We ate the solid white tuna in my house. I didn't realize there were so many different kinds of tuna until I had the task of picking out my own as a grownup. I always bought it on sale and I always stocked up. In my small kitchens in New York City and Brooklyn, I would get alarmed as the tuna fish cans started to slowly take over all my cupboards.

I have built many extravagant and artfully designed tuna fish can projects of my own. Some that are fun to climb up, others just to protect me late at night, and a few that capture the most precious moments between me and some other beasts.

One night, after stacking every tuna can in my kitchen, building walls almost to the ceiling around my bed, a magical queen climbed up my wall, and started peeking through the cracks of my cans.

When the queen finally made it to the top of my can walls, she peeked over and said "I would really love a tuna fish sandwich," and I wanted nothing more than to make her the most delicious tuna sandwich.

I found a love so safe and so good

I made her tuna sandwiches every day.

Sandbox

Azure D. Osborne-Lee

· ·

Cast of Characters --

June: A headstrong girl of 13

Jelly: A dreamer born 11 years ago

Neale: A girl with a job and 14 years of experience

Granny: She's old and she's not having it

Scene -- A dusty yard   Time -- Late afternoon

1

· ·

Lights up on a yard, bare save for a few scraggly clumps of grass and a clothesline. Jelly enters crouching low in a well-worn jumpsuit, holding a pair of toilet-paper-roll binoculars up to her eyes and growling like a tiger. She looks left and right, searching the yard, then darts across the space and hides.

June runs in wearing a threadbare dress a bit too small for her and dusty beaten-up shoes. She looks around, but doesn't see Jelly. June staggers to the far side of the yard, glances behind her, then holds the back of her hand up to her forehead and sways a bit. She waits. Nothing. June looks around again, then goes back to posing with her eyes screwed shut.

JUNE   (shouting) Jelly! I'm waiting on you!

Beat

JELLY!

Jelly peaks out from her hiding spot as Neale enters wearing long shorts and a t-shirt. She's carrying a box, and stops where she is as she sees June frozen in the corner of the yard. June sighs and tries again.

JUNE   You'd better watch out, sister! There's danger! Daannnggerrrrr!

Neale puts the box down and sneaks up June, getting very close to her.

NEALE   Boo!

2
• •

June jumps, uncovering her eyes and spinning around to face Neale. Her face fills with recognition and she pushes Neale's shoulder, taking a few steps back as she does.

JUNE   Stop playin', Neale!

NEALE   *(smirking)* Aww, June, I know you wasn't scared. Not rough & tough June!

Neale's eyes sweep over June, pausing at her hemline and her exposed knees. Embarrassed June uncovers her eyes and yanks her skirt down a bit.

JUNE   No! Not like there was a mouse, was there?

NEALE   That was one time!

JUNE   Uh huh! One loud time.

NEALE   *(kisses teeth)* Anyway, how'd you get out the house? I heard your granny had you locked down.

JUNE   Just 'til I finished my chores.

Beat

What are you doing here anyway? Ain't you got a job now?

NEALE   Yeah, but I always got time for them ashy knees.

JUNE   *(yanking her skirt down a little bit more)*

                They are not ashy, Neale! Get out my yard!

NEALE   Uh uh. Can't.

3.
• •

JUNE   *(narrowing her eyes)* Whatchu you mean you can't?

Neale jumps suddenly and looks around in mock panic, then rushes to June, pressing her body up against hers in a protective manner.

NEALE   Ain't you say we were in danger?

JUNE   (laughing, then becoming serious)

           Shut up, Neale! That wasn't for you.

They realize that they are standing very close to one another.

NEALE   I got somethin for you.

JUNE   (hopefully) What?

Beat

NEALE   (a little out of breath) My aunt sent your granny's laundry.

Neale retrieves the box and returns to June, pushing it into her hands.

JUNE   (taking the box, a little disappointed)
Oh. I'll give it to her when I go back in.

Beat

Do I need to get you some money or something?

NEALE   Nah. It's taken care of.

JUNE   Okay.

NEALE   Okay.

4.
. . . .

*Neale turns to leave, stops, takes a deep breath, and walks back to June and kisses
her awkwardly but sweetly. Jelly gasps from her hiding place.*

NEALE   I gotta go.

*Neale places a note on folded construction paper on top of the box. June leans
forward, ready to speak, but Neale runs offstage. June puts down the box, unfolds
the note, and reads it. She hears something offstage, and so she looks down at her
dress, sees that she has no pockets, and shoves the note into the box of laundry. Jelly
emerges from her hiding place, holding her binoculars up to her eyes with one hand.*

JELLY   I've made a very important discovery!

JUNE   (holding out her hand)

           Jelly, come on! We've got to find shelter!

Jelly looks up at June through her binoculars and doesn't move, then starts to growl a bit.

JUNE   I said we've got to go! Come on! Run, Jelly, run!

June runs to the far side of the yard. Jelly pauses for a beat, growls even more ferociously, then leaps to her feet, and begins to hop around from foot to foot, still holding her binoculars.

JUNE   Not like that! I said run, not double dutch!

JELLY   Okey dokey!

5. . . . .
. . . .

Jelly lets the binoculars dangle from a piece of yarn around her neck and drops to all fours, galloping around the yard. Increasingly exasperated, June puts her hands on her hips and stomps her foot.

JUNE   Jelly! Come on! You gotta run like a person. We're in danger! Daaaaanger!

Jelly stands up abruptly, screams melodramatically and jumps into June's arms, holding on with one arm and holding the binoculars up to her eyes with the other.

JELLY   I saw it!

JUNE   What?!

JELLY   I finally saw it! That darn tiger! IT'S BEEN AFTER ME FOR WEEKS!

JUNE   It's the sun, Jelly, the hot red sun so big overhead that it blocks out everything! You can't see a thing! You can barely breathe. All you can do is keep going, hoping to cross all that sand and pray you find some shade.

Jelly drops the binoculars.
Beat.

JELLY   Wait, where are we?

JUNE   *(exasperated)*

                 We're in the desert today, Jelly. Obviously.

JELLY   I hate the desert! I was on a safari. In the jungle! I was fighting back the wild animals and poisonous flowers and vines covered in sticky thorns!

Jelly leaps in the air and swings an invisible machete around her, vocalizing as she chops and hacks.

6.
. . . .

JUNE   *(putting her hands on her hips)* Oh yeah? Well, I coulda sworn I heard you being growling at me earlier. People on safaris don't growl, Jelly.

JELLY   That wasn't me. It was my sworn enemy, the wild tiger!

Jelly drops back to all fours and stalks around the yard, then suddenly pounces on the box of laundry

JUNE   Jelly! Not the laundry!

June rushes over and tries to right the box. As she focuses on picking up and shaking out the sheets and towels, Jelly discovers the note, which has fallen to the ground.

JELLY   I say! I believe I've discovered a secret treasure map!

JUNE   Jelly, give that to me!

JELLY   No! I found it!

JUNE   Give it to me!

JELLY   NO! I SAW IT FIRST!

JUNE   JELLY! GIVE IT TO ME!

June throws herself into Jelly, grabbing the note and crushing Jelly's binoculars in the process. Silence. Then.

JELLY   *(wailing)*

Graaaaaaaaaaaanny! June's keepin secrets again!

Granny enters, shuffling quickly and cussing under her breath.

7.
. . . .

GRANNY   June! What I tell you 'bout keepin secrets?

JUNE   *(sighing)* Secrets eat the soul.

GRANNY   Don't you sigh at me! What else?

JUNE   Secrets give you bad breath.

GRANNY   Filthy stankin breath! And what else?!

JUNE   The devil sends secrets via the World Wide Web...

GRANNY   What on God's green earth happened to my clean laundry? Lord, what is wrong with you children?!

JUNE   Oh. Well, Jelly and I were just playing and we...

Jelly begins to tiptoe away.

GRANNY   Don't think I don't see you, girl! Get your tail back here and help your sister clean up this mess. And don't neither of y'all even think about comin back in the house until my laundry is hangin up spotless on the line!

JUNE   Yes'm.   JELLY   Yes, ma'am.

Granny exits grumbling under her breath.

GRANNY   Don't make no sense. All that money to clean these clothes and these chirren here...

Jelly and June are alone for a moment. Jelly hands June sheets and towels to shake out.

JUNE   Is she gone?

8.
· ·

JELLY   I think so. I don't see her.

JUNE   Use the binoculars.

Jelly holds up her crushed binoculars.

JUNE   Oh, right. Sorry. I'll make you a new pair. I promise.

JELLY   Okay.

Granny comes back outside just as they finish shaking out and hanging the last of the laundry.

GRANNY   Jelly, girl, go inside and get your granny a glass of water.

JELLY   But, Granny, you just came from in there!

GRANNY   Just do what I say, now!

JELLY   Yes, ma'am.

Jelly exits.

GRANNY   Now, June, you know I expect you to set an example cuz you the oldest.

JUNE   I know, Granny.

GRANNY   You got to help me show your sister what's what.

JUNE   I know, Granny.

GRANNY   I can't afford to be wastin any more money sendin out washin more times than necessary.

JUNE   I know, Granny.

9.
. . . .

GRANNY   So tell your little girlfriend to be a little slicker next time she comes round. I can do my own laundry, you know.

June looks up, shocked, as Jelly runs back out with the glass of water and hands it to Granny.

JELLY   Here you go, Granny.

GRANNY   Oh, thank you, baby. You and your sister go play. And be careful this time.

Granny imitates a tiger growling and swiping at the air as she exits. Lights down. End of play.

Wonderings

YaliniDream

· ·

I wonder if a day will come

when I will stop feeling the need to write about war.

rape.

murder.

injustice.

A day when that task is
left to reminiscent bards

who tease children
with stories of the Dark
Times--

"when gunpowder was used
for weapons instead of
firecrackers."

A time when a child
wakes with

crusted eyes from night-
mared sleep,

And an Amma lulls her
with assured whisper

"ushhh darling, its just a
silly dream.

We are the descendants of

healers & truthseekers.

These are the days of love."

Photo by Nicole Myles of L to R: Jendog Lonewolf
and YaliniDream, 2013.

STEALING FROM THIEVES

Michelle Embree

My father had developed an obsession with the Rubik's cube. It was late 1980 so, he actually shared this obsession with a nation of shoppers in desperate need to prove their individual intelligence. My father was not to be outdone in this regard. The fact of it is—my father was obsessed with his intelligence and its tacit superiority over all others. My father mocked people who played sports or lifted things for a living. My father was obsessed with the Rubik's Cube because he was obsessed with himself and his need to control the world by believing he had an answer for everything.

My father locked himself in his office with the cube, and a stack of books about the cube, for days. This was not unique, he taught himself calligraphy and calculus in this same manner. It was a useful enough predisposition but his desperation turned all his achievements into dull weapons and took our genuine appreciation from our lungs as surely as a punch to the diaphragm will do.

Eventually my father emerged from his den claiming he could solve the famous puzzle like a professional. Despite this man's rather awe inspiring capacity for lies—learning to solve the Rubik's Cube is probably something he did do. He liked that sort of thing.

Neither my mother nor myself would ever witness this feat, but that means nothing. My mother and I were not included in my father's life. Though the three of us lived together—there was no father, no husband, no man at all, really—just a dark sickness that chewed up normal and spat it out in bits.

The Rubik's Cube was a cultural phenomenon; an object tied to a much larger experience. It was a *magical cube* that held the mystery of belonging in and to the world and I was keyed into the presence of the solved puzzle in the way that meant I couldn't stop thinking about it, ever. I was eight and I knew better than to touch it. But, I couldn't stop thinking about it.

I don't know how many days it went on, my father with this *magical cube*. He put it next to him on the nightstand when he slept and carried it back to his office when he worked. No doubt his possessive behavior piqued my already intense desire and quickened me to the breaking point. In a matter of days I could no longer stand it: I *had to have* the cube.

My father was taking an afternoon nap. I peeked into the room and holding myself steady, I listened to the rhythm of his breathing. Once I felt sure he was deep in dream, I snuck alongside his bed and carefully plucked the prize from the table beside him. I stood frozen for a suspended moment watching his scruffy face sleep before I tiptoed backwards out of the room to the front porch where I would breathlessly examine the pure fucking wonder of that thing.

I twisted the sides, whole sides, at first, glancing over my shoulder—waiting to hear sounds of my father stirring—whole sides one at a time, then two at a time, gaining confidence. Then a little more by a little more, I messed-up the puzzle and solved it again. A little more by a little more I messed up the puzzle and solved it again. My heart: thumping, thumping, thumping. Sometimes losing track of rotations and panicking.

If I didn't keep that puzzle solved—intact—and get it back to it's pedestal before my father woke, I was dead. Like, maybe, actually dead. He was like that, sometimes. Homocidal, my father was.

After a particularly close call, my hands sweating onto the squared colors of the stickers, I restored the cube to solved and returned it carefully to its place, next to my napping father.

I feared trouble born of my behavior but a greater desire trumped that fear—my desire to live inside moments of freedom. To live inside moments when terror of my father did not control me. I wanted freedom. So I took it. I tiptoed past the sleeping monster and played with his toys because stealing from thieves is the lightening strike of those who seek their birthrights.

The summer of 1981 was the summer after all the most important things that would ever happen, happened. It was the summer after my father fully lost his mind, and after I contracted the dyslexia, and after I got held back a grade, and after I almost fucking died from a ruptured appendix. It was that summer and I stayed out of the house as much as I could.

I roller-skated and I rode my bike, sometimes I did both at the same time, and I went swimming with my friends in the pool at their respective apartment complexes. On a couple of occasions, we snuck into the pool at the 'rich' complex. It had a sixteen-foot deep end, but we never lasted long at the 'rich' pool. A couple of trips down to the bottom and we'd get kicked out. But, snatching pennies from the bottom of that pool with its clear-blue sixteen feet of deep end, made us feel strong. So we got away with it a few times. We liked anything that made us feel like we could survive a world determined to crush us on every conceivable level. We liked anything that made us feel like we could learn to never feel again.

All kids like to find things and that's what I did for the summer of 1981. All the apartment complexes and the strip malls had big dumpsters, overflowing, sometimes, with interesting things. I found a gel-paint set once, brand new, never opened, new brushes and everything. I turned the box over in my hand, feet sunk into the garbage below, sun refracting against the colored paints. It was pure magic and when I used the paint, it dried shiny like glass, like gems, like jewels I had discovered all on my own. Treasure was everywhere. This much I knew for certain.

The older kids jumped in the K-mart trash and threw t-shirts and sneakers over the side. Brand new. I was amazed by this trick and when I got older, I did the same thing with my friends. We jumped over the rim of the big dumpsters and found clothes and electronics and toys. Everything went into the trash. Everything was garbage and we were scavenger-rats scouring the edges, stoned and furiously curious about the worlds that had put us there.

During the summer after everything that would ever happen, happened— I was nine and everything was already over so becoming an explorer didn't pose any threat to my non-existent future. I was utterly relentless, if not organized, in my pursuit. I scaled, trekked, ducked under, went over, pried open, slipped by, or otherwise got into *everything*—in my super-hero, Wonder Woman-esque bikini, most of the time.

My appendectomy scar was still a raised white line running through a gash of red and toughened skin, surrounded by circular white scars that had held the stitches. The sight of it made adults want to look away, the scar made people afraid of me, just because they didn't want to look at it, and that was fine with me.

One day while at the pool my friends and I got to conspiring a good bit. Now I admit it was my idea, but my two girlfriends required no convincing. I said it. They were into it. And we did it.

The grocery store was *Thor's*. That's right *Thor's*, as in, I supposed, that which belongs to Thor. The plan was a full-spectacle approach. It was a diversion tactic I'd seen in a Mel Brook's film titled *High Anxiety*.

In the film Mel Brooks and Madeline Kahn are trying to sneak a gun on an airplane, rather than try to blend into the crowd they make a spectacle of themselves. They dress in shambles and yell at one another as they wait in line. When the metal detector goes off, the two of them begin shouting: "I'm beeping, I'm beeping!" and "You're beeping, your beeping!" They bicker and feign physical pain, on and on, until security hurries them onto the plane, with the gun. When I saw that scene I thought to myself: *I wanna get away with something.* So I did.

My friends and I went to *Thor's* in our flip-flops and bikinis. We'd bundled our pool towels into one lump and as we went through the store we complained loudly about having to do laundry all the time and chores and one of the girls revealed disgusting details about her grandmother's ill health. It worked, everyone did whatever they could not to look at the loud-mouthed, trash-girls with their cheap bathing suits and scarred bodies and foul language. We left with a sixer of Coors short-boy's and a pack of Eve cigarettes.

We hauled the goods to an empty laundry room at Evergreen Apartments to pop open warm beers we did not drink and light cigs we did not smoke. We went over and over the caper. High on adventure and experiment, high on finding something in defiance of all the fences that surrounded us—all the *backsides* of privacy fences that surrounded our shitty, brutal little girl lives.

We were not the kind of little girls you protected with a fence, we were the little girls you wanted the princess to never know and I was ready to devour every drop of what it meant to be *anything but your fucking baby.*

Over the course of the next few years I would develop my thieving techniques to a fine art. I favored spectacle because I liked to force eyes away from me even more than I liked slinking along the edges of things. Though, don't get me wrong, I liked that too.

I had a theory, and technically, I stand behind it to this day. During the commission of any illegal activity, using a foreign language will add an extra layer of hesitation for anyone who might consider stopping you. Now, this is merely padding, I want to be sure you understand, one should always have a solid plan in such activities, but adding barriers never hurts. A friend and I once robbed the K-Mart blind of Nancy Drew Mysteries and Duran Duran cassettes whilst speaking loudly in French as we did so.

While I do continue to recommend the language barrier approach, I recommend speaking in a language you are, at least, marginally familiar with.

Our French was only gibberish spit out in an accent we likely got from Pepe Le Pew. It did not occur to me during the summer of 1981 that the adults probably knew it was not actually French.

We were children making mischief in a jungle of walls and steel girder beams and cash register machines. We were children making mischief because that's what children do, they find out what makes the world. Children build and rebuild wonderland every time it is destroyed.

We were children and we were in wonderland where everything is backwards, and everything is true, and magic-powers come naturally with imagination. We roamed strange and powerful lands where we encountered strangers who told us confusing and often dishonest things. We often witnessed insanity and plain mean spiritedness. And, on one occasion, while in our most magical bikini-bathing suits—we lifted a sack of goodies from *The God of Thunder*. And *that* is how we learned that we could, because in wonderland only the mischief-makers grow wise.

what the brain forgets and the heart denies, the body remembers...

Heather María ács

. . . .

(Excerpt from a full-length solo performance)

Preset: eggs, two ropes of the "river," bread bags, string, heels, tortilla props, mason jars, broom and dustpan, prom dress, knife, marigolds, table and chair.

*Sound Cue: String Theory Voiceover (with thick West Virginia accent)

(introduce movement vocabulary with the following text)

the body is just a body (waving)

there are no guarantees

no guarantee of safety or even life *(scraping toast)*

the body can get broken *(hand clap game)*

the body can get sick   these are facts

I don't often like facts *(files, smiles, answer the phone movement)*

don't often believe them, but these, these are facts, indisputable

the body can get broken *(making tortillas)*

the body can get sick

the body can die

sometimes slowly *(large hand covering small hand retrieving egg, pause)*

but we are all dying right?

we are all dying, together, in this space right now

thank you for sharing your dying with me tonight *(to entire audience)*

(DS/US running)

i didn't believe she was going to die

no one I loved that much had ever died

i never loved anyone as much as her

i will never love anyone as much as her

i don't want to feel like a piece of my body is missing

(abrupt stop, breath intake contraction)

in some ancient cultures they would cut off a piece of their finger
when a family member died
I don't know if this is a fact
this is what some anthropologists believe
but what the fuck do anthropologists know?
the field of anthropology has a really fucked up history
that, I know, is a fact

i thought about cutting off a piece of my finger
which one will it be?
my mother has beautiful hands
she does her nails herself, clear polish only
I love to get my nails done, I used to get acrylics
hot pink with swirling designs and sparkling rhinestones
(remove "dough" from butterbowl, hand movements-making tortillas)
mi abuelita makes tortillas todas las mañanas con arthritic hands
las manos de mi abuelita are twisted and painful
igual que la historia de mi familia
las tortillas unfurl from her hands like birds flying up from gnarled trees
i think about cutting off a piece of my finger
which one will it be? *(holding up my hand to the audience)*
i will cut off the tip of my smallest finger
of my right hand
will anyone even notice?
have any of you?
does anyone ever notice the tiniest finger of my right hand?
now you will
now you will be watching it for the rest of the performance
imagining that it's not there
(on backdrop-make "handprints" with "flour" from tortillas)
they found cave walls covered in handprints with missing digits
covering the walls

i thought that sounded beautiful

I would cut off the tip of the smallest finger of my right hand

but the part is already missing, see? it's not there

thank you for dying with me today

(rip bread bags from bottom, push feet through and into heels)

my mother is a very busy woman, she works hard

one has to work very hard when one is just one,

not two, like they teach you

one has to do everything on their own when taking care of two

two little chicks

(move to a different location with each line, making a square, sound of heels and how wearing heels affects movement is important)

she gets up in the morning, gets us ready for school

makes breakfast *(abrupt pause)* she always burns the toast

she always burns the toast, she has to scrape the toast

(toast scraping movement with voiced sound affect)

that takes extra time *(move)* and there is no extra time

when there is only one for two, two little chicks

she sends us off to wait for the bus

then she walks to work *(finishing square)*

(stationary office mvmt, answering phone, filing repeated in next section jerky and robotic, wide smile.)

all day long she

answers the phones smiles files files smiles

helps him write his speeches *(a secret)* because my mother's very smart

and she has a great smile, are you seeing where I get it?

smiles files files smiles

i go to the afterschool program *(hand clap movement, crouching down)*

i like it there, it makes me smile

i play, make crafts, have lots of friends, after 5 we listen *(drop down, ear to floor, moment of silence, listening, staying down for next section)*

we listen for the sounds of keys jangling, heels clicking, shoes slapping

because each kid knows which key, which click belongs to their grownup

each key, each click belongs to a grownup who belongs to a child

that's us and we are waiting, listening

(up and moving, circular floor pattern)

I know the sound of my mother's heels,

(aside to audience, breaking performance mode) her sensible heels,

not these heels, these are my heels, they're only a metaphor

(moving again, back to performance)

I know the sound of my mother's heels as she walks down the hall we

run to greet her, then it's off again *(move to points on square again)*

grab some food, strictly drive thru

dance class, boy scouts, play rehearsal

swimming lessons *(end abruptly at edge of river)*

because my mother never learned how to swim

(fill river during this monologue with water (blue, sequinned fabric),
*   dirt (real or sequins), pebbles)*

My family doesn't throw anything away. Spools of string, used twist
ties, aging rubber bands, thunder, hot air, light, radio waves and margarine
containers remain tucked away in drawers. Growing up there was either a
volcanic eruption or meteorite impact on the moon, the results of which
escaped the moon's gravitational field and were captured by that of the earth,
filling my grandparents' basement with rusty tools, mysterious bins, blobs of
molten glass, rotting cardboard boxes and melted terrestrial materials. Glass
canning jars collect dust on the shelves. Their ghostly, tektitic contents lure
me closer like a gawker at an old-time freak show. I squint against the bolide
impact, straining to make out pickled mermaids floating in prisons of briny
vinegar, after the earth splashed like a lake of water hit by cannon fire, the
molten terrestrial materials cooled and solidified to glass, then fell from the
sky to the earth's surface. It was shocking, when my mother moved in and
hauled it all away, to see the empty space, the central tubular void.

(move center, stretch arm out window)

i stretch my arm out the window   pressing against the wind

and we sing along to the radio

Sound Cue: You Don't Own Me *(singing along with music in the car with my mother, alternate bw singing to her and out the window)*

(instrumental continues under next section)

They told me how my mother would dance with the young soldiers. When she was married to my father, they were stationed in Budapest, Hungary. It was a big deal for a little girl from West Virginia to travel so far from home- over the bridge, across the creek, past the henhouse, beyond borders of coun- tries she'd never been to, to live in a place she'd only read about in books-an old city, with no mountains, and buildings like broken teeth. They were playing ABBA in all the European discoteques. And because my mother was terribly, terribly shy, the young soldiers would have to call to her over and over again, laughing and teasing until they coaxed her onto the dance floor, calling out to her and the other military wives-come dance with us, come dance with us, come dance with us... *(back away arm outstretched)*

the body betrays

(back and forth running)

I can't stop her body from breaking   I can't stop my heart from breaking

her body is breaking   my heart is breaking

her body is broken   my heart is broken

her heart stops

(sharp breath in, mvmt stops, move into audience to place their

hands on my heart)

can you feel my heart   can you feel my heart

I need you to feel my heart   I need you to check my pulse

I need you to check my pulse and see if I'm still breathing

I need you to check my pulse and see if I'm still alive

Lighting Cue #1: (Blackout)

is this what it means to be alive, is this what it means to be alive?

heart beating   breath taking

breath making   little puffs of air

in   and out   of my body

is this what it means to be alive

what do you think it means to be alive *(really asking an audience member)*

what do you think it means to be alive *(really asking another audience member)*

we're all dying here, right?

Heather María Ács. Photo by Laura Turley @theglittertiger

we're all dying together in this space right now

can you feel it?

heart breaking

breathtaking

Lighting Cue #2: (Lights Up)
(Re-enter the stage with a faux-casualness, looking for "heart")

Fuck, I'm sorry, you all, I always do this...

I can never find my heart before I have to leave the house

And now I'm late, because that's just how I am, I'm always late

I give myself an extra ten minutes to sleep

Because I can't get out of bed and then

I always need that extra ten minutes

But what's more important

that extra ten minutes to get ready or the extra ten minutes to sleep

And now I can't find my heart and I have to leave the house

Do I even have my metrocard?   Fuck!

(looking at river like a bed)

I was watching you

I know this is silly, and possibly creepy, but

I was watching you while you were sleeping

And I just got nervous for a minute because I

wasn't sure if you were breathing

And I didn't meant to wake you up, but I just got

 nervous for a minute, and I needed to check...

(run to mason jar w/ slip & marigold, pick up jar, using it as a phone)

No please don't go   Please don't get off the phone

Uhm okay yeah, I'm fine, okay I'll talk to you tom...Wait

okay, I'll talk to you tomor..Wait

I'm sorry, I just, yeah okay, goodnight, all right, I'll

talk to you tomorro...Wait   Waitwaitwait

If I was the type of person who carried one bag this wouldn't be a problem

I would have one bag with all my things. Everything would be in one place

But no. I have to be complicated. I have to have this purse or that bag

the one with the polka dots. Or the zebra print

and I have to remember to switch my heart everytime I switch bags

And now I'm fucking late. Because I'm always fucking late

Always fucking late,   FUCK

This is so awkward *(with uncomfortable laughter)*

It is so awkward to walk around with this big gigantic heart

It crowds people on the subway I can't get my shirt on over it

It's very delicate

(screaming)

THIS IS A VERY DELICATE SITUATION HERE

WE HAVE GOT TO REMAIN CALM!!!

So *(slap hand, putting powder on my face from a compact,*
becomes exaggerated, lightly slapping face, then harder)
I'm just gonna put my face on   I'm just gonna put my FACE ON
(abruptly close "compact" with emphasis)
you know you really can't break down because if you break down
then everyone is gonna break down and then where does that leave us??
How do you know?
How do you know?
I'll talk to you tomorrow .   I'll talk to you tomorrow baby
okay   Good night

Sound Cue: Final Voiceover
(Scrape toast during following VO, then transform into my mother in the
driver's seat during "you don't own me", rolling her eyes at me while I
sing and show off, then finally smiling and laughing)
in another dimension, my mother is still scraping the toast
in another universe, my mother didn't get sick again
in another universe, my mother is still alive
in another dimension, another universe,
my mother is smiling, she has a beautiful smile
(spoken live)
somewhere, in another universe, another dimension
my mother
is learning
to swim
and we are singing...
you don't own me, don't try to change me in any way
you don't own me, don't tie me down cuz I'll never stay...
(turn away from audience, exit, swimming backstroke, singing)

The Black Dress Passed Down to Me

Sabina Ibarrola

After Saeed Jones

Cheryl's dress is the amber in a shot glass is liquid heat chasing throat,

is every eye in the room on the rising steam, is still prickling the neck hairs,

is lightning made latex, is gasoline rainbow,

is goodbye in my grandmother's closet set ablaze, is goodbye in a room of golden braziers and burning incense, is the crackle hiss crackle of flame licking bronze,

is the San Andreas Fault is a bedroom door, is the earth

split in two on Avenue C is a requiem, is East 3rd Street's keening,

is southern comfort is a suitcase is a scholarship, is the telephone wires with their hand

at the small of my back, is me a nightwitch under cover of dark,

is disappearing into shadow too divinely black for human eyes, is the sweet shock

as fingers find doorknob, is her guardian streetlamp a constant glow.

Shooting Stars

Dandy Vagabond

a shooting star, they said, is the dust of a comet's tail.

a deep expanse of friction.
of skimming & gliding, of brushing & colliding
pulsing interaction swept in magnetic pulses,
pulses, pulses.
The hum & seduction,
embrace & celebration
a vibrato voyage
tenacious... & coyish.

interstellar arabesque,
atmospheric, luminous.
a shooting star, they said, is the dust of a comet's tail.

the dandy vagabonds are a Baltimore based pair of curious, playful artists who thrive on telling stories of whimsy, adventure, insight & balance through performance art, circus arts, fiber arts, the tactile & the ephemeral.

xander dumas, who has a dramatic passion for Art Nouveau headdresses & elliot mittens, an exquisite observer & equilibrist, makeup the collaborative duo, who moonlight under the name ephemeral fossils.
we invite you to explore & tinker at our website:
ephemeralfossils.com

What Was Coming (excerpt)

Chayele had seen what was coming. Huddled on her little cot in the pantry under the hanging pots and pans, she held the fox - der fuks - to her chest and rocked it. She had woken with its cry in her mind early in the morning, had run to the woods next to the castle where Jews were not welcome, searching for that furry red dot in the dark. She felt toward it in her mind, and there it was, caught in the jaws of a trap, shivering and yelping, gnawing at its foot, with blood on its snout. Chayele struggled to pull apart the teeth of the steel jaw trap, gathering the animal and wrapping it in her skirt. She ran with it bundled against her in the pre-dawn mist, sneaking past her sleeping father, back into the pantry.

She fed it a piece of chicken doused in wine, rubbing its throat until it swallowed, then strapped it down on her low narrow cot and tied off its leg with a strip of hide to keep it from bleeding. She ground plaintain and yarrow leaves with mortar and pestle, added a little water still warm from the embers of the night before, and soaked a strip of cloth to absorb the medicinal properties. She then took a swallow of wine herself, and set about cutting off what was left of the dangling foot, sawing through it with a pair of kitchen shears. She cut through fur and bone and sinew, the animal wriggling and shrieking, baring its teeth, nipping at the air. She wrapped the severed foot in a rag and placed it in an urn full of ash in the corner. She spread the wet yarrow and plantain directly on its wound, and carefully bandaged the remaining limb with the steeped cloth. With tears streaming down her face, she held der fuks and rocked it, rubbed its eyes like a mother cleaning her kit, cooing and clicking her tongue.

Chayele's father Mendl and little brother Aharon woke to the sound of the animal shrieking, and covered their heads with their blankets. It was disturbing, but not altogether unusual. They assumed it was Chayele, whatever she did at night with all that moaning and crying. They had given her the pantry as a bedroom so that Aharon might get some sleep at night, but the house small and sound traveled. They were resigned to this fate, and tried to keep her secret, though the townspeople knew she wasn't right. They called her makhsheyfele - little witch. The men had stopped coming to ask for her hand, though she was still very beautiful. The women did not stop by to gossip or check up on her, though she was a young woman caring for the household all by herself. The townspeople tolerated Mendl, who seemed to be a hardworking and pious man, and forgave Aharon, for it wasn't his fault his sister was a madwoman, why should he be punished? Besides, he seemed quite bright, maybe he still had a decent life ahead of him. But they spit and muttered when Chayele passed - khas-vesholim! - G-d forbid! on the few occasions she let herself be seen out and about on the streets.

Chayele was not resigned to her fate. She embraced it. To be the makhsheyfele meant to wrap herself around the title, to swallow it whole. She no longer had any role models, nobody to learn from, she had to find everything inside herself. She found mentorship in the animals she loved, in the spirits that came to her at night. Her own mother had died in childbirth when Chayele was only ten years old. And though she was not the one whose exit from the womb had sealed her mother's fate, it was Chayele's birth that was said to have written the curse. For on the day of her birth, the sky fell over Pultusk: a heavenly body bright as the sun came crashing through the evening clouds, breaking apart into flaming debris that rained down on the sleepy, snowy town. A cow had caught on fire and crashed into the side of the house as Chayele's body burst into the world screaming. This was her legacy: She was born knowing that the world ended often in Pultusk.

Chayele poured herself a cup of chamomile tea and returned to her chair, rocking herself back into a meditative state. She smiled to herself, thinking about Velvele, how she had taken care of him. She had sewn him several new outfits, and gotten him a new trumpet, and a leather suitcase with the words Kley Zmer emblazoned in the upper right corner. Velvele had come to her over and over, so many times over so many years, softening and opening to her over time. At first he never let her touch him, he would do it all to her, put his hands up under her skirts and rub and push and kiss and squeeze and slide inside, put his other hand around the curve of her waist and pull her up to him. He would bite at her nipples and pull back her hair, nibbling her shoulder, pulsing into her soft wetness. Throw her leg over his shoulder, push her against the wall and find a rhythm where the chaos inside him matched the chaos inside her and their breath came ragged and groaning and he would shake shake shake inside her, and she would grasp around him and wail and clutch...

And then, little by little, he would allow her to put her hands on him, first rubbing his neck, then down his back on the outside of his shirt, and then up the inside, fingernails on his flesh. After years of his visits, her hand would slide up the front of his shirt and trail light fingertips over the soft subtle swell of his chest, pinch his nipple between her first and second fingers, then move her tongue to its tip, taking it into her soft wet mouth. Then, after aeons of this, she would put her other hand between his legs and rub while he thrust toward her. At first he had been so scared, he would push her away, fear burning in his eyes. He would stand up and lecture her, his voice sounding like someone else's, insisting he really only liked to be with innocents, that he should be done with Chayele, now she was all used up.

The first time he did this, she showed him the door. She had wept for days, sure that it was over, that she could never be open to him again. But he had come back sooner than usual, drunk and sorry, professing his undying love. She listened stoically, and finally he confessed: He chased after girls who wouldn't wonder why he didn't take it out of his pants, why he didn't rub it against them, try to get it inside them, make a baby. She assured him she didn't need that, the prodding, demanding rodent of longing. She didn't miss what he wasn't. This seemed to give him relief, but then at other times, this too upset him - because he wanted it, oh he did! Hard evidence of his desire. And his was only very small, and wet, tucked up between soft folds.

ets get this femme on the record

Ezra Berkley Nepon

· ·

Using the ancient chaotic powers, Gay trickster queens of all descriptions keep the matrix of human thought in the disrupted, tumultuous state that prevents stagnation and keeps true creativity and flexibility possible.

-- Judy Grahn, Another Mother Tongue: Gay Words, Gay Worlds.

I met a gay trickster queen named SPREE in 2002, when I first visited her home at a rural Queer Arts land project in Tennessee. I was in full swoon on that visit, experiencing a new-to-me world way back in the woods, full of queer flora and fauna, and glorious sexy weirdos. Now, over a dozen years and as many visits later, I count SPREE as a dear friend, and one of my favorite people.

Today, SPREE is a bearded queen in her late 50s, always decked out with purple hair and beard, flowing pink or purple dresses, arms laden elbow-to-wrist with sparkly bangle-bracelets, jewel-ringed fingers, and painted purple nails. In addition to her glamour as a glimmering pink and purple blur, SPREE is also ailed by a train of devoted medium-sized dog friends – I think of SPREE as "Our ady of the Canines." SPREE prefers to spell her name with all-capital letters, and

Photo by Rosin Bean James

does not have a pronoun preference, but "will use 'she' if forced to choose." SPREE is a longtime survivor of HIV/AIDS who was active in the early years of ACT UP New York before touring the US and Europe with the Eggplant Faerie Players performance troupe and moving to rural Tennessee.

I initially came to adore SPREE for her wit and kindness, but over the years I have also come to learn and gain inspiration from stories of her many decades of performance art and HIV/AIDS activism. With her permission, I share a few of those stories here, drawn from our conversations as well as her interview with the ACT UP Oral History Project. In a time when the legacies of performance art and activism in the 80s and 90s are being archived, analyzed, and applauded, I want to make sure that the story of this Southern, radical, genderqueer femme is on the record.

SPREE grew up in Houston, Texas until the age of ten and then moved to Southern Georgia - "from a bad situation to a worse one" for a young queer. In 1975, at the age of seventeen, SPREE moved to Los Angeles to attend the American Academy of Dramatic Arts. She stayed in LA for the next ten years, working phone jobs to support her acting career. "Some people wait tables, some people bartend, I did phone jobs" says SPREE. She also attended support groups at the Gay Community Services Center, where she and her first boyfriend got up on the roof, and stuck in a sign that said "Lesbian," so that the Center's sign would read "Gay and Lesbian Community Services Center."

SPREE found the newly-emerging Radical Faerie movement in the Summer of 1983. She remembers, "Once I met the Faeries, it became pretty clear to me that it was a lot more important to be who I am as a person than to try to play this Hollywood game of hiding myself [as a gay person] so that I could be a movie star." SPREE got increasingly more involved with the Faeries and in Spring 1985, she attended a Gathering at a Radical Faerie intentional community in Tennessee which led her to move to New York with fellow faeries. She found work at the NBC switchboard at 30 Rockefeller.

The AIDS Coalition to Unleash Power (ACT UP) was founded in March 1987, kicking off with a March on Wall Street. In October of that year, the second National March on Washington for Lesbian and Gay Rights was attended by an estimated half-million people, led by People with AIDS. A few days later, SPREE was one of almost 600 people arrested in the first national lesbian and gay civil disobedience action at the Supreme Court, in protest of the homophobic Bowers v. Hardwick ruling, which affirmed a Georgia Sodomy Law as constitutional – criminalizing gay sex, even in private and between consenting adults. From the New York Times report on the demonstration:

At one point, a group of demonstrators including some AIDS victims [sic] sat down on the steps of the building and began to chant, "We have AIDS, and we have rights." At another, as a group crossed the barricades to be arrested, some police officers at the top of the steps placed white gloves on their hands, ostensibly as a protection against AIDS, prompting the crowd to shout, "Shame, shame!" and "Your gloves don't match your shoes!"

SPREE was not planning to get arrested, but swept up in the excitement she joined the resisting group and was put on a police bus with Ortez Alderson, Gregg Bordowitz, and many other ACT UP members. SPREE was one of two people who refused to plead "not guilty" and instead told the judge, "We plead for a reversal of the Supreme Court's decision of Bowers versus Hardwick." SPREE went to trial, in drag as always, but none of the cops showed up because they were providing security for Russian President Mikhail Gorbachev's Washington DC visit. The judge dropped the charges, and a crowd of activists was there to celebrate with her. That's how she got involved with ACT UP.

Because of her phone switchboard experience and her HIV/AIDS activism, SPREE became one of the first staff members of the National AIDS Hotline, which was advertised on TV with an 800-number to call if you had any questions about HIV. Working the overnight hotline shift, SPREE was on the receiving end of many calls from people who had worked themselves into a frenzy about unlikely ways they might have been exposed to the virus. These calls included queries such as: "If a person from the country visits the big city and gets it, then goes back to the country and gives it to a cow, can I get it from eating a hamburger?" Says SPREE, "This was in the early days when people literally didn't know anything about AIDS."

At ACT UP meetings, SPREE performed dramatic renditions of the most outrageous hotline calls, bringing humor to the crisis of silence and misinformation about AIDS transmission and treatment options. She performed in character as Barbara Broadcast, a tripped-out take on Lily Tomlin's phone-operator character Ernestine. Always in radical-faerie drag, SPREE brought her full self to her life as an AIDS activist, including her trial with the Surrender, Dorothy Affinity Group of ACT UP NY, which took their name from a message sky-written by the wicked witch in The Wizard of Oz.

Surrender, Dorothy was focused on NYC Health Commissioner Stephen Joseph, whose dangerous, irresponsible behavior included suddenly halving the number of estimated AIDS cases in NYC - which would inevitably lead to dramatically reduced funding for AIDS services. ACT UP NY got a copy of Joseph's itinerary and shut him down at every appointment. In her interview with the ACT UP Oral History Project, SPREE describes an action where the affinity group interrupted a meeting between Joseph and a number of city health officials. In a "very lovely black and white polka-dot dress and pink sunglasses," SPREE took Joseph's seat when he got up, screaming protest chants and banging her fists so hard she broke one of her rings.

Eventually that affinity group went to a three week trial, and SPREE had a different glamorous outfit for every day. She and her co-workers/co-defendents Ortez Alderson and Bill Monahan would work all night at the AIDS Hotline and then get off work in the morning, get on the train, and go downtown to the courtroom at 100 Centre Street. In anticipation of the sentencing, and her opportunity to give a sentencing statement, SPREE decided to re-enact the glamour of a scene from the end of Dynasty's first season, where Alexis Carrington (Joan Collins) dramatically enters a courtroom in a big hat. "So I came in with my big hat," says SPREE, "a lovely hat to match my outfit."

The bailiff comes over and he says, "Excuse me, but I'm going to have to ask you to take off that hat." And I just looked at him, and I said, "Well answer me this: if I was a woman would you ask me to take off my hat?" and he said "Actually, yes I would" and I said "Well then, in that case I shall take it off." But if he had said that a woman could wear it, I was gonna pitch a bitch and not willingly remove my hat!"

The Surrender, Dorothy members all made impassioned statements, explains SPREE: Originally when the judge sentenced us she said "You broke the law, and because of that you should be punished, so I'm sentencing you to ten days with the Department of Sanitation." And we were like, "Excuse me, some people have HIV and some people have AIDS and you can not be sentencing those kind of people to shlepping with the Department of Sanitation." I thought "there's no way we're ever gonna get through to this woman," but because of the sentencing statements she literally changed her mind. She said "ok, you have convinced me." The group was sentenced to ten days with AIDS service organization God's Love We Deliver.

Fast-forward to 1996, when SPREE co-wrote and performed a play called "Person Livid with AIDS" about her own experience of developing full-blown AIDS and then experiencing an unexpected recovery due to the advent of protease inhibitors as a treatment option. The show also includes a scene where SPREE performs tongue-in-cheek as New Age character Crystal Debris, offering a critique of those who encouraged people with HIV/AIDS to simply use positive thinking to heal themselves:

[The book] is for our dear viewers out there who are immune impaired. Through the knowledge and information in my book you will be able to learn how to impress your own immune system so much that you will then be able to impress others with it. Now, we try to impress others with our looks, our talents, our knowledge, our personalities. Why not our immune systems? And think about it folks, if you are so impressed with your own immune system that you are able to impress others with it, then there is just no possible way that it could be repressed, oppressed, suppressed, or depressed!

In the show, which toured throughout the South, SPREE tells of the outrageous barriers to competent medical care that she faced. Even despite being an ACT UP activist, an information specialist with the AIDS Hotline, and having a friend who worked at the Center for Disease Control, the layers of Catch-22 drama she had to deal with are exhausting to recount. Finally, she calls in her friends to help her, and they do a fabulous musical clowning number called the "Tenn-Care Shuffle."

After digitizing a number of SPREE's old VHS and Hi-8 tapes, I was able to watch a video of the 1997 event "Night of 1000 Stars" held at SPREE's home, a rural queer arts community in Tennessee. The video opens with a runway walk-off where each partier is announced and promenades to the applause of the crowd. SPREE is the last one out, her arrival hyped by a performer in suit and tie drag announcing into a giant cardboard cell phone: "She's on her way! She's almost here!" After a dramatic entrance, SPREE introduces the party, explaining that it's a fundraiser for both her home and the local HIV/AIDS support group. The acreage of her home's land has been turned into a giant board game and SPREE's partner MaxZine is transformed into a giant board game-spinner, with a big pink triangle pointer strapped-on to land on different game options after each spin.

After much running around and game-playing, the party regroups for another speech by SPREE, who explains that one year ago, on May 11, 1996, she suddenly decided it was Magic Day. That day she had asked each person three questions: Do you believe in faeries? Do you believe in magic? Do you believe in the power of your heart to change the world? She had envisioned that one year later they would hold the Night of 1000 Stars. She doesn't say this in the video, but on Magic Day, 1996, SPREE didn't really know if she'd be alive a year later — and here she is, manifesting her Magic Day vision. In the video, the camera person holds a pink star bubble-blowing wand in front of the camera so that in the camera's frame, SPREE is surrounded by the star. It's a perfect moment. She is a star. We are all stars. The power of our hearts to change the world.

I want this femme on the record because the power of her magic heart has changed my world, and the worlds of so many - through her activism and through making cultural productions and spaces that have widened our perceptions of what is possible. Yes, I do believe in faeries, and I do believe in magic, and I do believe in SPREE!

Heels on Wheels awesome merch. Photo: Damien Luxe.

9 *How We Fly:*
Magic
& Dreams

one by one

Lettie Laughter

· ·

one by one,

i lay down the bones & feathers from the place inside
i didn't want to know i didn't know/corners culminating webs of light in
the saddest moments of my making

i want to make you blue corn cake

tongue turquoise pebbles with every kiss

& fold your hand into the sand of my heart

i want to sing you the sole song i carry until the thing i'm waiting for
happens

maybe i'll find new canyons of verse, soft, course, raw

i want to cover us in wet sand

lick rain from your sweet face

& take naps in the shade of juniper trees

i want to show you dinétah from the top of eagle mesa, show you where
my grandparents are buried, show you where their hogan was/is, show you
where we tried to plant the tree for my baby cousin, but the tree joined
him, too

i want to open a worm hole

traipse you back in time

& share all the stories

i want to sleep beneath the brightest milky way in the back of my uncle's truck like i did all those summers ago, fix us the softest nest of blankets & pillows, & watch the morning sun birth your face red & gold with touch of cloud

i want to introduce myself proper

shake your hand, spirit to spirit

& draw my clan family tree

i want to know the names without looking them up, without asking my mom, without shame or fret—with all the tones & glottal stops in the right place

i want my femmestory to feel like home on my tongue

i want to remember the story of when we were both birds & words, shells & quiet of water, fire & blue blush, back when we were both prayers our ancestors sang.

Audiences at the Opentoe Peepshow

Photos by Nicole Myles, 2013, 201

Just Say Yes

Annie Danger

My eyes are closed. The music is up. My head is tilted, searching for the next secret. I am in spotlight on a dark stage, attending a line of people that extends from the house onto the stage. The audience moves and whispers in unison, like water as the tide pulls it in, up. One by one, their waves lap against the shores of my ears. The secrets range in subject, but much less so in potency for their tellers.

"I hate my face so much I haven't looked in a mirror in years."

"I cry whenever someone touches my chest."

"I don't think I'll ever be in love like you just talked about. Like I hear about. No one can love me like that. No one sees me."

I take each secret, hold it. I whisper an honest moment of support in each teller's ear:

"You never have to look in a mirror again if you don't want to. And I can't see your face, but I know you're beautiful because you have the heart and soul to feel sadness and want joy. Because your face is part of you and you are clearly amazing. Wonderful. You're important."

"I know so many people who have felt that way. And it's such a fucking bum thing, right? Like, can't you just be okay? And your body won't let you. But you still deserve love that makes you feel whole, and it's coming to you. If you can, be patient with yourself. You're perfect."

"I didn't think I could either. But just the fact that you're able to worry about that love and want it means that you have the capacity to have it and to give it. And if you give it, you will someday get it. You are so loveable."

And then I hand them a small, round mirror—one with no corners on which to cut yourself; a new mirror with which to see.

———

It doesn't work for everybody, but by the time we get there from the start of the show forty-five minutes earlier—through jokes and puns and layers and layers of perv-ified church trope. And through my own nakedness/embarrassments/earnestness and much ritual—most of the audience is honest with me and willing to try to let go of one of these barbs. We all hate ourselves. We all learn to hate ourselves.

That piece is called The Great Church of the Holy Fuck. On the surface, the show is a joke church about sex—the whole thing kicks off with a boner joke—but just inside the gates it becomes clear: the joke is that it's not a joke. The line between feel-good funtime and Deep Shit has been removed. We're here to play together and to laugh at our human weirdness. We're here to crack wise about catholic perversion, but we're also here to redefine holiness. We're here to rebraid life into art into activism. We're here to hybridize and break borders. We're here to be queer.

––––––

The Great Church of the Holy Fuck embodies for me the deep collaboration, generosity, and integration of personal and political which defines queer art. Queer art is what I do. Queer art knows in its very bones that you can't stay still on a moving train and it knows precisely where that train is headed.

I came into the word Queer as an explicitly politicized identity. In my understanding, a clear difference lies between gayness (a generalist sexual identity) and queer, a politically intentional reclamation of a not-yet-fully-reclaimed slur. Claiming Queer, for me, is a way of standing out as a person who understands the political context of queerness in a racist, patriarchal, classist, ableist society. ("Not 'Gay' as in 'Happy,' but 'Queer' as in 'Fuck You'!") There's no room in my worldview for political neutrality because to live a life (especially in the United States) is to be part of a complex and oppressive political system. Food production, water and electric resources, jobs, money, location, family, friends, healthcare...every aspect of a life is positioned within a system with people above and people below.

I know we all know this truth of power, but it must be said. The fact that Everybody Knows doesn't end the struggle for a better world, it sparks that struggle. Queer as a politicized term is necessary in a society that by intention and on accident is bent on ignorance, separation, and control. We must name our radical lives to keep radicalism alive; to keep ourselves alive.

And boy how we struggle to keep afloat. What could be more heartbreaking than looking with clear eyes and empathy across a social landscape engineered toward suffering a thousand different ways under the boot of a society that bases its very existence on exploitation. Where do you begin, working in the belly of the beast, when every road leads back to the very structure of the system that makes our lives possible? How do you stop a juggernaut?

My answer is that you begin with hope. Not dependence on false hopes. Not faith in some distant heaven. But real, hard, daily belief that we can make the drastic, bone-deep changes necessary to make our world a better place. Every morning, every evening, rising and resting with hope in our hearts is the only way we can make it through the lifetimes of hard work we have ahead of us as people committed to a better world.

And we've got to learn to love the work. I read a Wendell Berry article a few years back in Harper's that cut deep for me in ways I hadn't expected. Berry talks of change-making as metaphorically related to farming. You can't expect an answer or a single victory at the end of the day. It's not in the nature of the work. To do farming, to get through it well, you have to learn to love the work. You have to enjoy the feeling of shoveling shit, tilling ground, squatting for hours pulling weeds, processing what you've grown, and knowing the whole time that a freak storm or a dry year could topple everything. You have to love the work itself. This is true, as well, for the ultimate crop of the human project: justice. We've got to love the work itself.

Radical art is a vital tool in learning to love the work; learning to tell the story one sentence at a time. Throughout human history, it has been the necessary role of the storyteller to frame our world in terms that help us get by. The spectacle-makers and the narrators help us feel pride in the unending effort necessary to make a good life. And for those of us who know the difference between making the world better for ourselves and our loved ones (also known as Making a Living) and making the world better for everyone (which is not only an impulse at the heart of activism, but which is an implicit commitment to explore paths to utopia), art is the balm that will keep us going until the new world has come. To fight for a better world for everyone is to commit to a lifetime of frustration. We must reclaim the other half of that story—to fight for a better world must also be to commit to building and feeling hope for something more every step of the way. The role of the revolutionary artist is not only to make the revolution seem irresistible, but to make it seem possible. Worthwhile. To remind us what's on the other side. To reflect back to us our progress and keep us on track.

This last bit shows how revolutionary art must, by definition, be made by a wide and deep diversity of voices. The quality of our insight as we step

Photo by Nicole Myles of Annie Danger at the first Opentoe Peepshow, Oct. 2012.

toward a better world is predicated upon a multitude of viewpoints (and thus histories and experiences and struggles) collaborating to give a multilayered view of the road behind us and the road ahead.

To be queer is to be tied to revolutionary art making. We queers—the perpetual hybrids, the intersection of so many oppressions—know in our hearts and souls and on our dance floors and songbooks that the hard work of building a better world must be diverse and must be punctuated by pleasure in order to keep us all afloat. All outsiders know this trick of survival. As queers we are fighting for liberation and we are fighting for joy.

As outsiders, and queers in particular, we learn new ways to love. When families of origin (as well as the wider family of society) reject/eject us, we discover through trauma and trial how to love in radical ways. We learn about the necessity of community in sustaining us through struggle. There is no choice, only the need for support that can drive us toward an enactment of an ideal love which I think is well-defined by bell hooks. In All About

Love, hooks writes "To truly love we must learn to mix various ingredients—care, affection, recognition, respect, commitment, and trust, as well as honest and open communication". The point is that making a truly loving act takes decades of practice. It asks us to grow. She steps further to proposition: what if we endeavored to treat all of humanity with this tricky combination.

———

At the heart of the power structure crushing our world today is the notion of "Yes, but": Power today holds authority to say what is what. To maintain borders. Our civilization is defined by this myth of hard borders. Power today maintains imbalance precisely because it has become expert at separating and containing its subjects. Binarism is about power. Cormac McCarthy wrote in The Crossing about a boy learning to trap a wolf. The wolf expertly dismantles each trap the boy sets and in discussing this with an older trapper, the mentor reminds him that it's not that the wolf is necessarily smarter. It's just that the wolf has nothing else to do. It's got all day to outsmart you.

And so must we spend our time integrating the work of a better world into our play and play into our work for a better world. Right now, the power structure that defines our civilization has spent millenia, all day every day, piecing together how to keep its precious, delicate imbalance.

But the way of nature is balance. Osmosis. Without constant effort, power cedes to nature. The only true antidote to our "Yes, but...." society of exclusion is a lifetime of "Yes, and." The way we build a better world is by welcoming in instead of keeping out. Is by breaking borders. It is through Queering lines. We know that the line between making revolution and making love has never existed. We understand that to love well, we must love everyone. And that is no New Age, groovy sort of task. It is long hard work to learn how to collaborate with everyone in your life. It is generations of work to functionally and fully extract ourselves from under the boot of our oppressive society because that boot is not just on some of our necks, it is also in our every interaction. In the face of such work, the hope in Queer art is vital to our wellbeing.

As Queer artists, we must endeavor to, ahem, fill the gaps. Much activism in the United States has a gaping hole in its strategy because it has set aside pleasure for the sake of righteousness. We queers must fill that gap using our vision and our wit and our understanding of the vitality of pleasure. Our work is our play.

Art in Heaven

Anna Joy Springer

. . . .

...But meanwhile, Lulu's just announced in a stage whisper that all her life she's "longed to see a father out her window," and per the rule, has reached up to touch the flat air, which is my cue to wrap it up, so that's all I'll say about my father for now except that I spent an awful lot of time when I was younger imagining him imagining me and thinking it was emotional telepathy when really it was just art.

Lulu doesn't seem to see that she shares the stage with her father. It's as if they are on two corresponding planes divided by an invisible wall. The chorus silhouettes are no longer visible in their windows. It's not a peepshow anymore.

Lulu fades as Father brightens. "Vanity of Vanities!" says Father smacking his equation. The Congregation of Cats leap arhythmic onto stage in their weird masks. The symbols he's drawn look like nothing; they could be numbers, scribbles, or birds. "What vanity?"

The Cats chant low, "Says this dad-dy, son of a bomb-broker, scrubber of miss-iles, piss-smelling, schiz-oph-renic, self-appointed May-or..."

"Vanitity of vanities! All is Vanity! What profit..."

The Cats echo, "Profit?"

"...has a man of all his labor..."

The Cats say, "Labor?"

"...Which he takes under the sun?"

He wants to know, and so do I. But the Congregation of Cats is not reverent. They taunt him, not in an especially sinister catlike taunting manner, but more like he's taking himself a little too seriously, and they're poking fun to lighten the mood and draw his attention to the absurdity of asking a non-numerical question requiring an answer. They flick their metronomic tales and chant, "Par-a-noi-ac! Par-a-noi-ac! Par-a-noi-ac! Par-a-noi-ac!" Some of them continue this background beat while the others growl in catty falsetto, "Work your fingers to the bone, what do you get?"

"Bony fingers," says dejected Father.

"All pointing back at yourself, yourself, yourself, yourself, your selllllllllf," say the cats.

His volitional fingerrises like a periscope, crooks and turns. Then Father pokes himself in the eye. At the same time he's also trying to defend himself with his other hand, but he keeps being too fast. We want to stop him. He says, "Ouch! Ouch!" but won't stop poking or failing to block the pokes. We are aware of withholding help as we watch.

"Why are you hitting yourself?" The cats ask. We can't tell if they're being facetious. Are they really wanting an answer?

"Ouch." Our father's eyes weep.

"Why are you hitting yourself?"

"Why am I hitting myself?"

"Why are you hitting yourself? Why are you hitting yourself?"

He pokes again and misses, instead stabbing deep into his giant beard. He hooks out a streak with his finger to inspect. "I'm no young Daddy now," he says.

Lulu, the older younger me is 21, the age he was when I was born, not a baby girl the size of a baking chicken or a tiny bag of cat litter like I was when he knew me. She's not the image he keeps of me in his head.

"Where's my tiny star?" He can't find Baby Lulu, so he slumps like a Punch with no stick. He pulls a small square photograph from 1973 out of the bib pocket in his overalls. He's preparing for his sermon back in his apartment in San Pedro, preaching to a room full of cats, passing around the picture of me. In the small square I am a toddler with fine clear hair standing up. I am also wearing overalls, tye dyed green, and little shirt and white baby shoes like an actual toddler. I look surprised but I am also smiling. The photo is shot from above. For the most part, the cats ignore it. Now, my father, not really my father, is already tucking the photo back into the pocket on his chest to get ready for the rest of the sermon.

He's using two different voices to make his hands into two different people. "Mayor Teddy Boy," his left hand says, "There are two opinions on where the babygirl has gone. She is a young San Francisco woman who goes to college and is smart, very smart. Although intelligence and a dime won't get you a phone call." His right hand says, "She's out of the game now; already passed."

"A grown up baby daughter wearing glasses? Wearing sweaters? Doing equations? Filling out government forms?" the Congregation taunts.

"Vanity!" His left hand snaps. The cats, skulk beyond the row of unlit windows, as if receding into undifferentiated consciousness, then his poor right hand turns side to side, searching for cats, but they can't be found, and Father's hand goes limp in despair.

"It is already passed." I lift him from the stage and hang him on his hook. A new Chorus comes out in a line, unfolding out one from behind the other until they extend in a row across the stage. As if they are tied to each other at the wrist, they seem to hold hands, but they don't. Please welcome the Moping Lulu Brigade. They're costumed in worn Mervyn's nightgowns with cartoon images like Garfield and Wonder Woman on their chests and their bellies are still rounded with milk. The ones in headgear spit and lisp when they talk. All but one of the Lulu's face their windows, but the middle one faces out. It feels to her like she's narrating alone on a dry desert on the moon into a punishing interrogation light, except she's attached to the five other girls spiritually so when she moves her arm the others' move with it. Her stagename is Growing Up Lulu, and she's twelve. She's taken Jesus Christ into her heart. He is always there inside her heart, not crucified and suffocating and not imprisoned. Her heart is not hollow she knows, but there is the spiritual body and the visual one, and they overlap. The sweet sacrificial son version of the father of the universe lives inside her heart and anybody else's heart that longs for him and asks him to come in, and he's happily kept, not burdened, so nobody's ever alone and everyone in the Moping Lulu Brigade has a little room where Jesus can live in her heart whenever they want. She lives in a small rural town with her checked-out mother, Mom, and her mother's dumb evil stepfather, Man.

Growing Up Lulu needs to watch her weight or she'll end up like her grandmother. Her teeth are chipped. Growing up Lulu keeps on eating in the living room and curling her hair in the living room and whatever she wants in front of the TV because nobody's around and even if she gets caught, negative attention is still attention, and that's her catchphrase, so that's the new rule. Whenever Growing Up Lulu comes on stage, everyone has to say, "Negative attention is still attention!" all together like a game-show audience or "Naisa" for short. Growing Up Lulu is the stage name for Naisa now. She's always getting in trouble, but she's rebellious and histrionic and she's always cringing when no one's around like when she hears keys in the keyhole or footsteps on the creaking hallway floor.

She watches television, goes to church, and makes friends with the prettiest girl in school. The prettiest girl in school lets her go home with her at lunchtime and they microwave hotdogs. Naisa is in love with the prettiest girl in school; she loves her so much. She never does her homework. When her mother asks about homework, Naisa always says it's already done but she copies it before on the sidewalk outside the classroom door. Everything is boring and depressing except for Jesus and the prettiest girl in school. Mom and Man are nudists so they're naked all the time, which is both natural and disgusting. Naisa cries and cries all the time, from all the hormones and other material factors like the isolation of the so-called "nuclear family" and discovering that as far as points go, she ranks pretty low in her rankless pond though just how low or high she does not know, it's just this looming feeling. And truly, the more she develops, the more everything feels like too much, and this too-muchness feeling won't ever change even though everyone says it will, so what she's doing is becoming acclimated, which is why it's good she's got Jesus. She can't remember the states and the capitals and she can't do math for shit, which everyone says has something to do with being a girl. She can draw and read. Her friend, the prettiest girl in school wears tight Jordache and blue eyeliner inside her eyelids and her hair is like the hair on the women on Dallas and her legs are as skinny as Naisa's arms, and that gives her points.

Naisa is keenly aware of her skin, pinkly blobbing and stretched out around her. Besides Jesus, her inside world is soothed by two actions: laying down and gazing. The light in the living room goes black-light purple; she stays there watching real life fade and return. Reruns. I Love Lucy, Brady Bunch, What's Happening, Eight is Enough, The Jeffersons, Alice, One Day at a Time. Everything is families. Every story has families or cops – the basic units of property management. Naisa picks the family shows not the cops. Every night Naisa watches an average of six different families engaging in repetitions of familyness, which includes little buzz-ings of conflict and little smoothings of alrightness, over and over like the times table. There are brothers and sisters in the families and there is love, and when there's not enough money, "...Naisa is keenly aware of her skin, pinkly blobbing and stretched out around her. Besides Jesus, her inside world is soothed by two actions: laying down and gazing. The light in the living room goes black-light purple; she stays there watching real life fade and return. Reruns. I Love Lucy, Brady Bunch, What's Happening, Eight is Enough, The Jeffersons, Alice, One Day at a Time. Everything is families. Every story has families or cops – the basic units of property management. Naisa picks the family shows not the cops. Every night Naisa watches an average of six different families engaging in repetitions of familyness, which includes little buzzings of conflict and little smooth-ings of alrightness, over and over like the times table. There are brothers and sisters in the families and there is love, and when there's not enough money, there's more than enough love even minus prayer."

On television families never hate each other, except on soap operas and talk shows, which is theater. The evening shows, never have families that hate each other living in the same house, because don't expect fucking Stridex Pads and Lean Cuisine to be your fucking mirror because you're obviously Stridex's and Lean Cuisine's fucking mirror, which is called "growing up," which is another way of saying tilling the flesh soil to get it ready to grow a fine family.

Oh boo hoo hoo. Oh where is my papa? Where is my Red? Oh boo hoo reality, chubby female nothing to sell except hair or virtue, boo hoo hoo screw, excrutiatingly undermedicated, oh where are you med? They have not in history yet started really germinating the SSRIs among the outpatients, so boo hoo dissociate on the boo hoo living room floor to yum family shows and ads for yum udding pops and boo hoo pimple cream waiting for the soothing balm of yum rankless social resolution in twenty-minute yum intervals, boo-papa, yum-papa, hoo-papa-whatev-papa. Pa-dump-bump-ting!

Thank goodness for all the angels or whatever who actually saved us from real cops and families. Thank goodness for the fatherish ghosts, stuffed in our hearts, like a teddybear in an I Love You mug. A store bought sacrificial stuffed toy father best friend. We'll always have someone to talk to and he'll never leave. We'll open our hearts and tell him, tell him we believe. We'll sing, "Well he's knocking and begging and pleading, won't you let him come in? You feel his love and you know that he died for your sin. Well he's begging and pleading and asking won't you open that door? And when you finally do, you know you won't be alone anymore. " I mean we are alone, but we're not ever really alone. We've got this crazy this rushing unstoppable longing for fathers, innocent ones and the ones who've been wrongly accused or undone. Drunk, sad, dumb, irrelevant and embarrassing warriors, holy as hookers, but less necessary, pitiable in the rain outside without an umbrella, hearing voices, nonetheless loving us, so happy when we invited them to live there in our hearts. Happy and humble. Limp plush fathers safe there in our hearts.

Something. Like. Freedom.

Meliza Bañales aka Missy Fuego

I'd like to tell you that freedom came to me. That it came in the form of a girl or a poem. But really, freedom came to me in the form of a little, tiny dog. In an alley my ex and I had no place being in but found ourselves one fine San Francisco day.

My ex, he didn't want me to go near it "it looks really hungry" he said and the little beast kept growling and gnashing her teeth against a heap of trash. But, I'm a gamblin' man by nature. I got closer and discovered four tiny puppies clutched against her

and two dead ones under a newspaper headline that read, "When Doing Your Best Just Isn't Good Enough." And with my last piece of food in the whole world, a piece of beef jerky, she let me save her that day. And it felt good to be good. But the problem was I had a hard time making that habit stick and in another day I was back to all the speed that didn't make me fast for anything but made it easy to forget. And my ex was my dealer, and the

puppies were adopted, but the little dog went home with us and for a moment everything felt simple. "She looks hungry" he would always say and no matter how much I gave her it was never enough

especially for something so small especially for something so delicate. Dogs are the worst judge of character because they will love anyone and do anything to get what they need and I guess that's why I found myself to be one. "I can't keep you anymore" he'd say "you're doing too much" he'd say "this is bad for business" he'd say. And when I thought it would be time to leave, he'd do the reverse and invite me to stay. When I thought there was no arguing left he'd give me the reasons and there were moments I think he felt bad for giving-in to me or maybe he just felt sorry for me. But I had become so good at not caring. "Just a little more" always fell from my lips after I had just had some and as I graduated from speed to opiates to taking and never asking he'd try to make it all stop. Try to hide it from

me. Try to get me to slow down "but you made me this way" I'd say "I'll go down to the Tenderloin and do what I have to do" I'd say "I don't need you" I'd say. Then he'd grab hold of a continence or his anger at my thinking I could leave and lock me in his bedroom so I couldn't further damage myself without him. And I beat the walls. And claw the door. "The best way to train a dog" he'd say "is to break them." And I would fall to the floor losing all track of time thinking that the poison would eventually just spill out of me. "She looks like she's carrying her skeleton and someone else's" he'd say "are you feeding her? She looks so hungry..." And then the door would open and he'd get on the floor with me and finally deliver me with the stash

"Don't look like such a caged animal" he'd say as we got high one last time, always one last time "You're too pretty for that." And I'd always do a little extra afraid I'd sweat or shit it out.

I wanted to be ready for the next time. And then he'd just leave me alone for awhile and then finally the little dog would find me—she'd been hiding under the bed the whole time. And we'd climb into each other all our scars touching and I'd be covered in her kisses and small pleas. He finally dumped me. He told me my stuff and the dog could stay but I— I had to go. And I did a show and all the drugs I had on me and some people who really hated my guts found me on the floor of some bar's bathroom and

their hate turned to pity and they called another ex, one I'd really done a number on, and he came for me. And I was homeless and he gave me a home. And I was sick and in withdrawal from all

the junk and he let me convulse on his floor and held my hair as I puked in his trashcan. And he made me lots to eat because he never wanted me to go hungry. Though dogs don't discriminate,

they are very good at trusting their instincts. They have no problem protecting and dying for what they love. "Maybe that's why God spelled backwards is Dog" my friend said and it was a good enough reason for me to start believing in one and this former lover turned friend took me back which is no surprise to me now—he worked at an animal shelter, he rescued dogs for a living with a little chicken and a fist-full of patience. And we went back to the old house to get my stuff but all I took was the little dog. "I was starting to think you were never gonna come back for her" he said "I didn't know what I was gonna do with her—she peed in my bed while you were gone." And I spent the next few months, then years moving in small steps with a

couple trash bags of clothes and poems and the little dog. But I always felt fed, I always felt full. So I'd like to tell you how freedom came in the form of redemption or a second chance or yes, even a poem. But it was actually four legs, two little brown eyes, and a wet nose. And somehow, we two dogs managed to keep the pack together.

Quiet Come Dawn,
A Sci Fi Aerial Choreopoem (excerpt)

YaliniDream

QUIET COME DAWN follows the queer love story of Rook and Z, lovers living in a post-apocalyptic world where humans require drugs & magic to survive. Rook, a healer, is a refugee from an island nation ravaged during the Great War. She is of the earth and lives in the blighted, polluted and violent Hollows. Z was exiled for having an incurable disease to the Hollows from the protective community of the Conserves which is guarded by a dome synthetic sky and operated by weather machines that simulates perfectly the seasons. Z, mutated by the conditions in the Hollows, can fly and is of the skies. Their connection, however, is marred as Z cannot remain on earth because the atmosphere is too toxic, and Rook cannot ascend to Z. Rook journeys through this dilemma to discover that she too can fly if she learns to heal her own wounds.

Excerpt from Scene 6: Experience

Rook and Z are laying in each others arms after their first time making love.

Z Rook?

Rook Yes?

Z I have to go.

Rook Ok.

Z I want to stay. I just can't.

Rook Better be careful. U might give a girl the wrong idea.

Z Its. I'm. I'm the birds' caretaker. They'll be expecting me. And it's hard for me to stay down here too long.

Rook I get it.

Z gets up to get dressed.

Z Actually. I need your help... They're dying Rook. The birds.

Rook gets dressed.

Rook Z, so many animals are dying. Fuck—we're dying.

Z But these birds raised me they took care of me... Look it's our fault that the animals are dying. Our fault that everything's a mess. We have a responsibility to make things right.

Rook That war was not *my* fault. I didn't have shit to do with it. Though your daddy and kin in the Conserves sure did—with their weather weapons. My people were as fucked by this bullshit as the birds. So no baby, I don't have a duty to make anything right. My conscience is clean. My only responsibility is to my survival. And that's hard enough. Especially on my own. At least the birds got you takin care of them.

Z I want to take care of you. I just can't stay right now.

Rook I'm not asking you to take care of me! I can take care of myself.

Z I'm not saying you don't. I just mean--

Rook Look, Z, I'll help you cuz you help me, but I'm not trying to save the world. Try n save the world on your own it'll cave in on you.

The earth's atmosphere is beginning to weaken Z.

Z, you're shaking.

Z I should go soon.

Rook How do you want me to help you?

Z Rook, don't you know? When you sing—the birds fly. They dance again and the dawn is filled with song. Rook your music can save the birds. You bring them to life. I thought if you sang more—

Rook I can't do that. That's the last thing I want to do.

Z But Rook. You just said—

Rook No! I will not do *that* on purpose.

Z You said you'd help. I've been getting you the nitro-leaf just like I said I would. and have been thinking about if we can make another path through the burning bramble so you could get in without flying. I even feed the worms extra so the soil--

Rook Do you know what you're asking of me?

Z I'm asking for your help. I told you. The first day we met. I need your help.

Rook Do you have any idea what happens when those birds fly? I hate hearing those fucking birds. I pray for a day when they're silent.

Z Rook!

Rook No. I said no.

Z Please I don't understand. I love the birds. You're hurting me.

Rook I'm hurting you? Well when I hurt, your precious birds soar into joyous flight.

Z Rook, I don't know what you're talking about.

Rook Look Z, I can't control when I sing or dance like that.

It's something that just happens.

Z And it hurts you?

Rook It happens when I'm about to be hurt.

Z I don't understand. Rook—

Rook The first time was when I was a kid.

The only way to leave Kunnpaanum was to pay the boatman. Appa didn't have the money, but he thought he could pay him back once we got in a conserve. But the conserves only took asylum seeker from other conserves. When he couldn't pay up—they took me for pay.

Z Oh God Rook. how old were you?

Rook 8. I was 8 years old. Everyone I loved had been killed by the Tsunami generators. All I had left was Appa. And then he was gone. I cried and cried for him to come get me. It got on the boatman's nerves. The first time he hit me I didn't see it coming.

Then this one time—when he was about to beat me—I heard these voices, and I began to dance. I could hear the birds. These shrieking voices telling me what made the boatman the monster he was. I could feel his pain. His misery. Understand him. It hurt so badly I had to heal him. And I did. I calmed him, just enough to keep him from hurting me. Just a little. Just enough. To run.

Z What do you mean by heal him?

Rook I don't know how to explain it. This energy passes through me and whoever's emotions I feel. They calm down and the pain quiets.

I am drowning in pain and fear when those birds fly, Z.

Z Each time it happens you're about to be attacked?

Rook Every time. Your birds are new. I used to hear different birds. But they died. My song doesn't save the birds, Z, They die anyway.

Z You're able to escape... people who want to hurt you. By healing them?

Rook How do you think I run the hollows by myself with no weapons. Have you forgotten what its like out here? I guess if I could fly I'd keep away as much as I could, too.

Z It's not that . If I stay on earth too long I get sick. I have to be in the skies. No solutions or adaptions ever worked on me.

Speaking of which. I need to go back soon.

Rook I'm not used to being the one being left.

Z I want to stay

Rook I know.

Z I'll come back

Rook I'll have to move. I don't get to stay in one place.

Z I'll find you. I gotta bird's eye view. Thank you. For telling me that story.

Rook You really are a beautiful creature, Z.

Z What makes you so sure.

Rook My experience tells me so.

Z Good Bye for now. I'll see you soon...

Z and Rook kiss and Z flies to the sky.

Quiet Come Dawn was performed at Embody Aerial Studio Nov 12-15, 2009. It was choreographed by Keibpoli Calnek of Black Acrobat. The cast included Sego Marchand Lazzaro, Shenelle Eaton Foster, YaliniDream, Kim Howard, and Sunder Ashni.

We Live On An Island

Sabina Ibarrola

This is a performance score for all of us, all of us here in this room tonight. I'd like to read it to you, and I ask for you to please close your eyes and mark it out in your head as I read, so that at some point after I finish reading we can all try it together. You can think of this as a mental rehearsal.

You should know that this score doubles as a magic spell. This score also doubles – triples? – as a recipe, to be tried in your own kitchen, on your own time, with whatever ingredients you happen to have available. This score is also translatable into html code, to be broken and re-broken and programmed and re-programmed as you see fit.

So please close your eyes and try to find a comfortable position.

1.   The piece begins seated. Or standing, if you are standing.

2.   Take a deep breath, in through your nose, and out through your mouth.

3.   Take another deep breath. Let it out slowly, with care.

4.   Bring your awareness down to your feet.

5.   Let your awareness travel slowly up your ankles and calves to your thighs. Up to your hips. Moving up your body without judgment. Your pelvic cradle. Your ass. The small of your back. Move through each and every little part of your body, just checking in and noticing what's true for you right now. Bringing breath up into your belly. Your chest, your heart center. Breathe into the wingspan of your back. The long bones of your arms. Send your breath out to your fingertips. Up into your neck, and the big bones in the back of your skull. Bring your awareness into your face, and finally, the crown of your head.

6.   Expand your awareness out, to feel the presence of the other bodies in this space.

7.   With eyes closed, take in the presence of one person directly in front of you or behind you. With your eyes closed, try to see them. Try to see them with the eyes of a person who loves them unconditionally, with the eyes of their mother or lover or child.

8.   With your eyes closed, take in the presence of the walls around us. With your eyes closed, focus in on one brick. Take care to choose a different brick than the person next to you has chosen. Feel this brick start to change. Something is happening. It starts to feel less solid. Feel the brick disintegrating. Feel it dissolving into powder, moving like sand through an hourglass. Feel the walls start to crumble slowly around us. Feel them disappear completely.

9.   Feel the floor begin to melt, too, like ice cream in the sun on your 7th birthday, or any day when you felt happy, and special, and loved. The floor gives way to earth. Rich, fertile, moist, black earth.

10. You may choose to remove your shoes. You may want to feel the earth between your toes.

11. Now feel the cool night air on your skin. It smells blue green, and feels thick in your nostrils. It tastes delicious.

12. Feel the quiet. It is so quiet. Quiet like the way you sit with someone you trust with all your heart.

13. There are no police sirens. There are no police.

14. There are no cars stuck in traffic. There is no traffic.

15. There are no gunshots. There are no guns.

There is quiet. There is the slowly waning moon. There are the sounds of crickets.

There are stars. Look up at the stars. There are so many, more than we've ever seen in this city, more than we've ever even imagined. There are planets and comets and meteors and other objects we do not have names for - but they are made of the same star-stuff as you and me.

There is the land. Manhattan Schist, glacial till, Inwood marble metamorphosed from limestone. Heat and pressure; fault lines. "Listen to the sound of the fire burning in the center of the earth." The land is awakening. Take a moment to notice where in your body you feel it. Do you feel it? Have you visited this place in dreams? Does it smell the way you remember?

There are the plants. Our grandmothers, our teachers, our kin.

There are the spirits. Spirits above and spirits below.

We are not the only animals here tonight, we are not the only animals looking up at the stars.

We live close to the ocean.

We live on an island.

We live surrounded by water.

Soon the fish will come back. Soon the oysters will come back. Soon our children will dive off the piers on summer nights like this one, and swim in what we used to call the Hudson. They will delight in the way the salt dries on their skin. They will float on their backs and watch heat lightning flicker behind the clouds.

Photo by Nicole Myles of Mette Loulou von Kohl and Sabina Ibarrola at Fuck You Dad: Cabaret to End Patriarchy, 2013.

Twinkle, Twinkle

Ariel "Speedwagon" Federow

twinkle, twinkle

by ariel "speedwagon" federow

you are a star. your light is so perfect and unique.

just like the other 5,999,999,999 people on the planet.

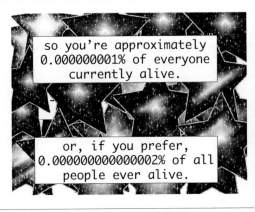

so you're approximately 0.000000001% of everyone currently alive.

or, if you prefer, 0.000000000000002% of all people ever alive.

do you think anyone'll notice when you go?

this is how it will happen:

maybe you'll be having sex, her fingers deep inside you, your back arching...

and your aorta will dissect

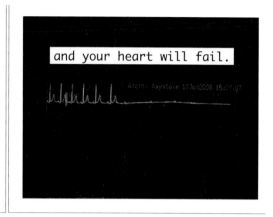

and your heart will fail.

maybe you'll be in an airplane...

something will go wrong, and down you go.

or you'll be walking down the street, minding your own business...

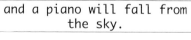

and a piano will fall from the sky.

or you'll wink at the wrong person

;)

at the wrong place

:O

at the wrong time.

X|

or the knot in your stomach will grow heavier and heavier

until it pulls you down to the concrete below.

but I hope when you die you go right up to gay heaven

and there'll be a drag queen at the gate and she'll welcome you home.

and you'll come in, and there's a bar,

and whitney houston and donna summers are hosting karaoke.

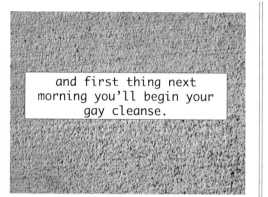

and first thing next morning you'll begin your gay cleanse.

they'll bring bedraggled homophobes up from hell for you to bite and scratch and kick and punch, and they won't complain because they'll know they earned it.

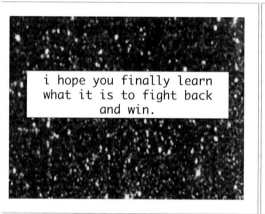

i hope you finally learn what it is to fight back and win.

i hope you do it a lot in gay heaven,

until every time your body feels like home.

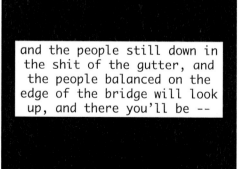

and the people still down in the shit of the gutter, and the people balanced on the edge of the bridge will look up, and there you'll be --

lighting their way home.

HOT PINK MASS:
Divine Fuckery and & Holy Perversity (Selection)

. . . .

Welcome. I am The Reverend Honorable Doctor Madam Miss Damien Luxe and I am a moderate, severe and imperfect weirdo. But this isn't about me. This is *our* Hot Pink Mess of a Mass. So...

PERSONAL INVOCATION

In the name of the Father who will not know my name, of the son of bitches who are fucking up this earth, and of the Holy glowing box watchers who refuse to live, Let the pomposity begin!

A few points of process *[jazz hands]*

You may feel free to sit, be quiet, twitter - I suppose. Otherwise, your involvement in our service is precluded by your presence.

Please look at your bulletins and repeat the Introductory invocation after me:

#1 INVOCATION/PRAYER

It is our will that we manifest:

divine fuckery and holy perversity / holy vengeance and divine liberation / on all fronts.

[darkly]

This is for us.

[spit on ground]

At our service on this stolen land today we will learn about choosing manifestation, hear from several spiritual leaders, sing, pray, partake in the sacraments, participate in confession, and possibly the spirit will move us to a laying on of hands - remember, the Devil goes after the willing, and what is willed is what we get after ugly legal battles. So we shall will cautiously.

[brightly]

But, first, a few announcements.

#1: The becoming a contagious Christian class has been cancelled, as all the members caught it & left.

#2: Youth group next week will take place at *[local arts institution]* The Museum of Sex. Ensure your youth are properly sexed up.

Does the gathering have any community announcements? *[take moment to allow gathered people to speak]*

Excellent, lets move forward - I invite you to join me in prayer.

You may bow your head, clasp your hands, clench your kegels, check your purse for lube, whatever feels appropriate, as I lead us to invoke *my* deity, a most inspiring girlfriend. You can envision whomever you like – I'm not going to tell you about your god, after all.

#2 PRAYER

May the almighty femme bitch Trisha cleanse us of worrying sin, may she lead us right to the face of temptation and show us how to make out with it, and through this mess we celebrate make us worthy to sit at good tables at our favorite bars, finally get healthcare and bring our cousins home from war.

A-choo – a-men has had its run, wouldn't you say?!

LITURGY OF WORDS SECTION

And now, from The Word of my Lord.

[Open to page 15, read: "sex cannot save us." from Macho Sluts]

While Saint Califia/Acker wrote these words many many many many years ago, they still ring so true today: sexual agency, courage, disillusionment, and changer; all this because these people tried to create their desire, to Manifest....no, to femmifest.

Lets us femmifest excellent dance moves and friends beyond facebook. Motorcycle rides with no cars or potholes or steel-grating bridges in sight;

Femmifesting belief in entitlement, a full bottle of Jameson on my counter when I get home, and the return of meaning to flagging.

Let us never forget to honor our fellow perverts and freaks; dropouts, black market workers; hoes and hustlers; People who live without money and people who live without the threat of hell motivating them.

Personally, all my ex-lovers, future dates, and people I will only fuck once. May we all femmeifest.

A space-time rift or some other weird science allows some of us to come through with our brilliance intact. It is threatened that the regime of normals will be unbroken. It is true that so will we.

SUNG - SACRAMENTAL HYMN

Refer to The Liturgy of Sacraments in your bulletins and sing with me, do not worry that there is no hymnal or melody provided, just go for it!

Blessed are you, homos,

Makers of creativity and awesomely complicated sexual positions.

Through your kink we have rough trade and chocolate coating to offer,

Which the bodega has given and human hands have made.

It will become for us the cream of life, and we will eat our way out if we have to.

LITURGY OF CONFESSION/REBUKING:

Congregation: It is now time for our public confession. But we are going to improve on the existing format. Because these hot messes are only partially our fault, and if we can't blame god...we need to pinpoint the culprits

We don't need forgiveness for sin as much as we need to be LIVING in the SPIRIT of liberation, libation, and live action. TRISHA!!

Friends, as we will call out or write down our mistakes, we must also rebuke that which pisses us off, something for which *we* need an apology.

You may derive inspiration from the accusation/confessions listed in your bulletin; use the blanks in your bulletin to take notes.

To motivate us, I call on the messy troublemakers of history:

Mae West, Queen Helene, Mary Magdalene, Lilith, Killer Queen, Little Debbie, The Whore of Babylon, a few select Babymakers and Babykillers, all women with big hair. All the species of Finches, Salome, Delilah, Lola, all the young pups. Jolene, Miss World, All my relatives and friends who can shoot guns and live off the fat of the land around us. And Trisha. Especially Trisha.

Is everyone done writing? you've filled in your bulletins?

I am MOVED to PRAYER!

#4 PRAYER

I believe in the Holy lemniscate, in chaos

That all belief is magical,

The perfection of the Platonic Life Partner,

The communion of community,

The refusal to forgive all the bullshit we've gone through,

The resurrection of a righteous ferocity

And living the dream everlasting.

I am FEELING it! Who is WITH me - the DREAM!!

[Audience cheers!!]

Don't we feel a little better? I do!!

I am FEELING the SPIRIT!! I am MOVED to a GROUP REBUKAL of EVIL!! Let us be saved from their mistakes, let us remember that Jesus died for his own sins, not ours!

[reveal felt cops target]

Today, we are rebuking the state for refusing to grant us full rights of citizenship. For each confession and accusation you made, you may feel the weight of SIN lifting OFF your conscience! NOW! Stand up and reveal **your** confessions and accusations.

[Encourage audience to participate in a group high-heel and purse-throwing at the felt "cops." Explain that we are fighting back against the state and systems, and not the individuals who survive by taking these jobs. Audience members will call out people, situtations, and experiences.]

For example: I rebuke your bullshit work ethic! May the sacrifice years be over. I rebuke you with your bad boundaries, angry people on the subway, you who assault in the name of god or your twisted needs, those who'd claim mere holy tolerance as acceptable.

CLOSING/BENEDICTION

In closing, we will pray once more:

Take me out of the book of life and put me in the arms of the living. Let us manifest tender terrorist jolts, selfless acts of passion intended not to get us into heaven but to get us off; falling in lust as a holy act; sharing our bodies or not sharing our bodies equivocally treated; community as communion. I manifest the holiness of adventure seeking and looking up to really bad ass shitkicking bitches as my heroes. I deserve it. This is my will.

[Sing + exit + shake hands]

I was lost now I get down // my dance floor magic abounds

daily lets all live the dream // as I work it, I will femme close to theeeeeee

Photo by Sophie Spinelle, of Damien Luxe, 2013

And so shall our Heels till the Earth

sunny drake

* *

A love letter to those to whom femininity is forbidden or frowned upon. Effeminate boys & men. Femme trans* & transsexual women and two spirit people. Femme genderqueers. Beloved ho's. And all other femmes who are called "too much" or not meant to exist.

My dearest forbidden Flowers,

Let me stand before you, that you may harvest your bloom. Fishnet stem reaching to tight studded shorts, matching phone case peaking from front pocket. Petals: my blouse hugging boy tits. My stamen: grandmother's plastic pearls repurposed into safety pin qu-earring.

This blossom now, but before I was the spindly weed. Confused not by who I was but by how this gender disordered world sought to manicure me: first into a pretty girl and then later a "manly" man. Lest they betray me, I kept my pink petals tucked under rigid thorny leaves. Until one day that tomboy I was clambered to the top of the hedge, straining to peer over, and I saw...You!

You! Exquisite Haven of forbidden Flowers in every imaginable bloom.

You! The stubborn glitter that lingers weeks after the party.

You who beckon to me in sweeping cement cityscapes with your flashes of fuchsia, glints of gold and streaks of silver. You, prancing studded boots pressing possibility into pavement.

And every micro-bounce to your step is a victory in this plagued world that seeks

> to smash your petals
>
> frost your emotions
>
> wilt your intuition
>
> and rake your ruffles
>
> into row upon row
>
> of clipped hedges

But together, you and I, we will hold the million memories of sweet children separated from boyhood dresses and silenced squeals and cascading tears and long locks of hair and mums' lipsticks, abandoned under threat.

[Have you ever wondered where the snatched sequins drift?]

[Where do the seized satin socks lie their worn out feet?]

[Perhaps there a river of confiscated emotions gushing down into a graveyard of broken lilac dreams. Deep graves crammed with giddy emotions and graceful gloves and girly giggles. Grey gravestones spiked into the treasures beneath.]

This, my pledge to you:

For every crushed frilly boyhood, a thousand manly ruffles will take your place.

For every girl kidnapped into boyhood, a thousand constricting chains will be cracked.

For every femme called "too much", a thousand more will be a thousand much-more-too-much.

For every fallen pansy, a thousand petunias will bloom on your grave.

Photo by Damien Luxe of Zachary Wager Scholl
@ Fuck You Dad Cabaret to End Patriarchy, 2012

And your ashes will be mixed with magenta and painted on the lids of a thousand thousand warriors. War paint. Fierce defiance. Faithful memory. We will not only refuse to forget: we will make the pavements on which you fell our runways, and we will mince! We will strut so fiercely, prides of peacocks will follow our flaming trails. We will saunter until the streets are streaked with silver glitter. We will careen wildly in the highest of heels without caution for what is "practical", because we know that

Every g r o u n d – b r e a k i n g invention

Every u n i m a g i n a b l e innovation

Every r e v o l u t i o n a r y creation

was born from i n g e n i o u s impracticality

And to the hedge makers who would wrestle away our sparkly delights, with stifled snickers or crushing blows, let us tell them this:

Beware.

You are right to fear us. We are dangerous. We are revolutionaries. We are healers. We are mums, dads, brothers, sisters, siblings, cousins, lovers, fighters, artists, visionaries. Some of our lace may be tucked only beneath our pants. Some of our tears fall only behind dry eyes. Some of our pink is worn only in the soles of our feet. But make no mistake.

We are EVERYWHERE!

And our parties are fun-er. Our battle screeches louder. Our dreams brighter.

And our revolution will be the most

SPECTACULAR
FUCKING
GLITTERBOMB
you have ever seen!

It will be waged alongside warrior women & brazen girls & genderqueer grandparents & sex workers & ancestors & queens & studs & femme scientists & tomboys & crips & butches & sharks & faggots & magic makers & peacocks & inventors of delight! Our trenches will be lined with fake fuchsia fur. Our guns will shoot silver glitter. And we will conjure storms of rhinestone studs that will scour the fear from the hearts of the hedge makers until there is nothing left except the naked love that held us all in the seeds of our births...

And when the storm settles,
we
will
dance!
until the sun streaks the sky in persimmon orange and crimson pink

and so shall our Heels till the soil
and so shall our glitter seed the Earth
and you'd better be ready for the exquisite garden which will

s t r e t c h   a l l   t h e   w a y   t o   t h e   s t
a r s !

Yes.
Yes!
This is how it will be, because you, my forbidden flowers,

Dare To BLOOM

Soon, Queerness Will Come to You Like a Gift

Celeste Chan

· ·

Dear me:

I see you walking down the school hallway. 16-year-old self. Manic panic blue hair with baby barrettes. Bell-bottoms you patch-worked into a galaxy of purple velvet stars. Cookie monster in a spiky dog collar safety pinned to your backpack. You walk into the classroom. Hear a dirty blonde in her 30's whisper loudly, "What's wrong with her," and then, "some people dress like they're on drugs." "I'm not homophobic, I just don't need to know about their lifestyle," says a woman with a frosted perm. You keep walking, and take a seat by the window so that you can stare out into space and pretend that you don't hear them. Later, in chemistry, a scraggly man sitting two seats over, playing with his toothpick, says aloud, "Wow, they have high school girls here. And some of them are exotic."

Again, you are reminded that you don't fit in. Prime example: the prank calls from the neighbors across the street, asking for the Wongs and Wangs, even though your family is the only Asian one on the block.

You are a stranger in the hallways of community college. Your classes are on Capitol Hill, Seattle's gay neighborhood. You tell yourself, I'm not gay or anything, I just like being here. And indeed, you are here 10 hours a day on Broadway for school and for work, by choice. Rainbows bursting from your bag as you march down the street, matching the rainbow flags in nearby stores. You wear glitter in your hair and around your eyes - sometimes it mingles with your tears, so that gold sparkles streak down your chubby cheeks.

Every day after school, you go to your job at Value Village. In the thrift store, I see you surrounded by fabrics and sounds of the 60's, 70's and 80's, a time trap machine. You clean out the dressing rooms, filled with mounds of clothing, broken hangers, torn off and crumpled price tags, and dirty tissues. You clean them like dank confession booths, evidence of transgressions. Everyone you work with is queer, thank god for that.

At the library, you pick up a Bikini Kill CD. You listen as Kathleen Hanna screams, "Rebel girl, rebel girl, they say you're a slut, but I know..." You read Randall Kenan's book about a queer teen who comes to understand himself through the theory of relativity.

Soon, queerness will come to you like a gift. Like a telescope view of an alternate reality.

You'll wear your heart on your sleeve, sewn and sutured, tattooed by a rocker chick named Magenta. You will read Sassy and obsessively listen to Riot Grrrl, their growls and screams speaking to the sheer f---ing urgency you feel in your heart. You will not slit your wrists, you will tattoo them with typewritten hope.

You will learn that it's not "what's wrong with you," it's about what is wrong with the lies, manipulation, and abuse of an oppressive culture. Your nerdy, freakiness is a way of seeing outside. Your stacks of library books show you something else exists. You will read and read and read, to save your own life.

You need to know that it is okay to have a heart, one that beats magnetically, that stretches your chest, this ceramic heart thumping outside of your skin, growing 20 feet tall and rising. You need to know that someday soon, you will remove the swords from your throat.

I'm writing to you from twenty years in the future, and I want to hold you. Go forth, brave little one. Let no one and nothing tear you down. Go forth, salt water and sparkles spilling, your head held high.

With love,

Celeste

Publication credit: Previously published in Glitterwolf Magazine: Identity (Issue Eight)

10

Appendix

Who & When of Heels on Wheels

B.H.: BEFORE HOW

March 2009 -- Heather and Damien first travel hangout, in LA. Trisha is discovered. A tour is discussed.

June 2009 -- Acquisition of The Dream [travel van] by Damien.

EMERGENCE

Jan 2010-Damien & Heather say, "Fuck it! We're goin on tour anyway! It can't be that hard to book a tour!" Heather and Damien only book one college. In Texas. the college tour is pretty much...a fail. But, making the Roadshow happens!

January 2010-March 2010 - Damien & Heather mad scramble to book a tour. We did the GRAND GIANT fundraising amount of $800.

March 2010: First Heels on Wheels Glitter Roadshow: Southern exposure! Featuring Heather, Damien, Chicago (Princess Tiny and the Meats) and Sequinette Jaynesfield.

March 2010: How to Build a Fire, our one-gig teaching artist tour, performs in Texas.

All posters and graphic design in this section by Damien Luxe 2010-2015.

Photo by Rebecca Greenberg, 2011

March 2010: Damien stays in Austin with the Van and sends everyone home on flights they have to pay for themselves.

January 2011: How to Build a Fire/ Queer Sans Fin, our workshop + performance format, presented in Montreal.

Jan-March 2011: Booking Tour #2. Hundreds of emails are sent this time.

April 2011: Tour #2: Midwest, a magical tour. The first time we smarten up and include roadie Lizxnn Disaster; now the tour is officially punk. The first time we tour with DJ Shomi Noise, the tour is officially also a party. We all spoon in Heather's Abuelita's bed together & Damien's gramma makes us "texas caviar." Shomi DJs on a washing machine. We party atop the van. Tour ends in us spending our total tour profits of $250 getting matching tattoos in Philly.

Photo by Nicole Kwit

BUILDING COMMUNITY

January 2012: Beyond Visibility, a 100-femme-strong discussion, art, and community building event, featuring skillshares/workshops/discussions, early evening performance event, and late-night performance event + dance party. Booked and built in 2 weeks with community collaborators.

January 2012--March 2012: Booking a mid-atlantic tour.

March -- April 2012: Tour #3: Mid-Atlantic. Heels on Wheels parties so hard at a bar in DC that the bar finds our facebook page the next day and invites us to come back anytime. Later, Shomi DJs on cat litter at one of our fave shows, at B16 in Providence, booked by Ian Cozzens.

NEW WORKS BY QUEER PERFORMERS

KIRYA TRABER & M. LAMAR

+ MORE ARTISTS TBA & A SKILLSHARE ON PA SETUP BY JADE PAYNE!

@ THE SPECTRUM 57 MONTROSE BKLYN, NY $3-10

HEELS ON WHEELS PRESENTS

OPENTOE PEEPSHOW

SUNDAY NOV. 4, 2012, 7 PM

NEW WORKS BY QUEER PERFORMERS: KIT YAN + NCN ADELAIDE WINDSOME, A SKILLSHARE + PATTI SMITH SURPRISE

HEELS ON WHEELS ROADSHOW PRESENTS

OPENTOE PEEPSHOW

SUNDAY JAN. 6, 2013, 8P $3-10

BRANDED SALOON, 603 VANDERBILT AVE. BROOKLYN, NY

June 2012 -- First Annual Cabaret to End Patriarchy: FUCK YOU DAD.

August 2012 -- HOW produces a panel at the Femme Conference, gathering tour organizers YaliniDream, Maggie Crowley, Leah Lakshmi, and more.

Summer 2012 -- swooned by the sweetness of community love & local events, Damien comes up with the idea to do a monthly salon. The search for affordable venues in NYC begins anew.

October 2012 -- First Opentoe Peepshow, monthly salon in Brooklyn. The first event is at the Brooklyn Society for Ethical Culture, featuring Annie Danger, Ivette Alé, and Bevin Branlandingham.

November 2012 -- Opentoe Peepshow #2 is at The Spectrum a few days after Hurricane Sandy. Shomi has to call in, Heather is stuck out of town due to flights being cancelled. Drae Campbell and Ariel Speedwagon present Binders Full of Women: the Performance Song, TL Cowan presents I Disown You Right Back, M. Lamar sings, and we experience our first lesson in archiving: get a camera card with more than 2 gigs of space.

November 2012 -- Heels co-host events at MIXploratorium, a queer film/art event at La Mama Galeria in the LES, and Damien & Heather present HAIRsuite.

Dec 2012 -- Heels on Wheels gets a rehearsal space at the Willie Mae Rock Camp studios in Brooklyn.

HEELS IN FLIGHT

January 2013 -- FEMMEpowerment workshop developed for Willie Mae Rock Camp youth.

January 2013 -- March 2013. We book a tour, actualizing our dream of flying HOW to the West Coast through community fundraising. Yet, Damien is finishing graduate school & Heather is finished with life. We book a two-week tour anyway. We are very much looking forward to this tour as a time of restoration and fun. We dream about slapping people with pizza to deal with stress and conflict.

March 2013 -- Opentoe Peepshow #? An unannounced smoke bomb set off by a performer brings the Fire Department and several asthma attacks after Cristy Road presents on Prudence the Pig [a bunny].

March 2013 -- Group trip to Hampshire College to perform at the Five College Gender and Sexuality Conference, featuring Kirya Traber, Bevin

Branlandingham, Shomi Noise, Heather & Damien. Plus we throw Cristy road in the van for extra fun bc she's presenting at the conference too!

March 22 2013 - April 6 2013 -- Tour #4: West Coast. We're psyched to be flying and very tired from the epic preparations. Our community fundraising reaches its most epic proportion, gaining us almost $3500. We weasel a larger rental car with a $60 tip after realizing 5 adults would not fit into a compact sedan. A few days into our tour, personal tragedy befalls one of our friends and bookers and the tour grinds to a total stop for a few days; we make the difficult decision to continue with most of the latter half of the tours shows. Oakland especially welcomes us with open arms and a packed house. Though we're still dealing with the effects of trauma, we feel so loved.

April 2013 -->end of 2013 -- Heels folks try, try, try to take it easy. Take some time apart. Participate in witchery. Recover slowly.

HEALING AND FLYING

May 2013 -- debut of PIZZA SLAP.

June 2013 -- second annual Fuck You Dad: A Cabaret to End Patriarchy.

June 2013 -- Damien and Heather celebrate Damien's birthday by spending most of the day writing a NYSCA grant application (which we got!) and budget. Then they go have fun.

August 2013 -- PERVER/CITE, Wild Montreal adventure w/ Holotropik. Adventures include: human bowling, a rope workshop, many shots, garden watersports, alley roaming as sun breaks all leading to one tragically hungover community performance in a backyard garden. Later, the van breaks down in a slightly dramatic way as Damien takes everyone to the bus, en route to another art gathering. Community fundraising covers half the cost to fix!

September 2013 -- the first meeting of the Leadership Development crew incarnation of Heels on Wheels; we take adorable photos and newer members name themselves The Kitten Heels.

Oct 2013 -- The 2nd season of the Opentoe Peepshow begins! Branded Saloon becomes the stable home and host venue to the Peepshow. We get a poster illustrated for the Peepshow by Lex non Scripta.

November 2013 -March 2014 -- Booking tour #5, this time featuring more months to stress out. Heels again tries to book colleges and "start

OPENTOE PEEPSHOW

monthly live art salon

Revealing new work by queer artists

the first Sunday of every month at Branded Saloon!

603 Vanderbilt Avenue @ Bergen St., Brooklyn, NY 11238
7p doors / 7:30pm / $3-10 / wheelchair accessible
Curated by Heels on Wheels
heelsonwheelsroadshow.com

booking tour early," this time by recruiting Sabina Ibarrola as a co-producer. We are so grateful for Sabina's fresh energy and curatorial vision.

December 2013 -- Heels gets
our first state funding, from
NYSCA, for $3,000! We use some
of it to pay honorariums to members, and to have an organizing retreat!

March 2014 -- Heels receives our second grant, from the Brooklyn Arts
Council, for $1,100. When Heather, Andie, and Damien attend the ceremony,
our collective babeliness wows all and we get applause when we stand up to
accept our hundreds of community art dollars.

March 2014 -- Group trip to Hampshire College to perform at the CLPP
Conference. Heels get their first comped hotel rooms of touring! Door
handle breaks off inside of passenger door in van. "Mi'lady" develops as the
title of any person in that seat who must now wait to be released from the
van by someone opening the door from the outside.

April 2014 -- Heels on Wheels begins calls for submissions for our anthology.

HEELS ON WHEELS

SHANI NOISE

DAMIEN LUXE

ALVIS PARSLEY

GLITTER ROADSHOW

HEATHER ACS

SABINA IBARROLA

ANGEL NAFIS

LIZXNN DISASTER

QUEER FEMME ART SHOW // APRIL 11 2014
THE ROOT SOCIAL JUSTICE CENTER
BRATTLEBORO / 8PM / $7-15 SLIDING SCALE / ALL AGES
HEELSONWHEELSROADSHOW.COM
DESIGN BY FEMMETECH.ORG / PHOTOS BY MARS HOBRECKER

April 2014 - Tour #5: Northwest/ Canada. Heels crosses the US/Canada border for the second time in their group career. We get to do completely amazing shows in Montreal and Toronto. One of our tour members was turned back at the border, in an act of transphobic, colonialist control. We are, again, heartbroken. We do our best to continue tour and use/offer art as a source of healing.

May 2014-We decide not to tour again next year. We need time to rest and heal. The 2014 tour was supposed to be good.

June 2014 - 3rd Annual Cabaret to End Patriarchy: FUCK YOU DAD, a backyard party. Fire and water balloons and reiki.

July 2014 - Heels on Wheels travels to Montreal to participate in the Hemispheric Institute of Performance and Politics' Encuentro. The conference is a shitshow for political, artistic, and organizational reasons. Damien shouts "Shame!" at a famous male performance artist because he keeps talking over women. With the addition of Mette Loulou von Kohl, Rozele, and Emma we co-create a community art response, FEMME/ifest, to the Encuentro, which collects attendees requests and hopes for what they want from an

art event. The whole experience is not what we wanted.

KEEP HAVIN' FUN

October 2014 -- third season of the Opentoe Peepshow begins, at Branded Saloon in Brooklyn.

February 2015 -- Heels co-hosts LAVAlentines, a queer Valentine's Day alterna-prom at LAVA performance space. Five of us do a collective ritual on radical self-love and collective queendom, guided by James Baldwin's idea that "your crown is bought and paid for; all you have to do is put it on."

March 2015 -- Heels receives our third grant ever, and second grant from the Brooklyn Arts Council.

April 2015-Heels has decided not to tour this year, so HOW artists get to

do other things with their lives

May 2015 -- At Least You Tried: A Mother's Day event is inaugurated at Judson Memorial Church.

June 2015 -- Last Opentoe Peepshow, closing out the third season.

June 2015 - Fourth Annual Fuck You Dad Cabaret to End Patriarchy, this time in a backyard in Ditmas Park. Excitement raised by last-minute tarp pitching.

Summer - Fall 2015 Heels on Wheels produces this anthology.

Learn more at www.heelsonwheelsroadshow.com

Andrea Glik is a femme witch dyke from Missouri. She has organized with Heels on Wheels since 2013. Andrea graduated from The New School with a degree in Gender Studies. She is currently living in Brooklyn, NY and is getting her Masters in Social Work at Hunter College.

Damien Luxe is a Brooklyn-based queer femme liberationist artist, digital technolo- gist, and community organizer who creates, produces and performs political and participa- tory multimedia works all over the US and Canada. She's toured personal and collaborative DIY art consistently since 2004. She is a raised-poor, now hustling/working-class queer, cis, white artist. Damien honors herstories with a cyborg feminist lens. She values community/ socially-engaged arts, working with LGBTQ communities across the continent. Her solo works are: The Whore of Babylon vs. the Lady Pompadour; Not By Bread Alone, mermaids + powdered milk pass poverty; Exorcize, satirical and serious healing aerobics for all bodies; Hot Pink Mass, church for Trisha; and Femmes Fight Back, interactive art honoring queer legacies. She is co-founder and co-artistic director of the performance art group Heels on Wheels and loves this queer femme art extravaganza. She's researching a book on the history of raised fists in US political art: www.raisedfist.femmetech.org. Her sci-fi novel Polyester can be read at www.damienluxe.com. Her open-source technology & design work can be seen at femmetech.org. Her performance, writing & video are at damienluxe.com.

Heather María Ács is a Brooklyn-based theatre artist and cultural worker. She is an independent film actor, high femme drag artist, curator, teaching artist and university pro- fessor. Her work has been featured in festivals, theatres, and galleries internationally. She was born and raised in West Virginia by a single mother, is of mixed-race Anglo-Chicana de- scent, and comes from a working class background on both sides, meaning d.i.y. was a way of life before she came into the subcultural movement. She is a founder and Co-Artistic Director of Heels on Wheels. She co-produced the Heels on Wheels Glitter Roadshow tour for five years and the monthly salon series, the Opentoe Peepshow: Revealing New Work by Queer Artists, in Brooklyn for three years. Heather has worked with Cherríe Moraga, Mx. Justin Vivian Bond, Nao Bustamante, Karen Finley, Lois Weaver, J. Ed Araiza of the SITI Company, and has been a LAMBDA Literary fellow. Selected film, television and web credits include Building No. 7, dir. Steven Soderbergh; blink, dir. Silas Howard, Valencia (the movies): Chapter 9 based on the novel by Michelle Tea; Sunset Stories, an official SXSW selection; HVB with Paula Pell of SNL; and the Emmy Award winning series, Transparent. Heather has been a dedicated teaching artist for over 15 years. "Ms. Heather" uses theatre as a tool for social change with low-income youth in cities across the country and has stud- ied with Cornerstone Theatre Company, Sojourn Theatre, the Living Theatre, and Augusto Boal. "Professor Ács" currently teaches Arts Education at the New School University's New School for Drama. Heather also performs and facilitates workshops at community spaces, colleges and conferences on femmepowerment, femmephobia in queer communities, community arts organizing, and arts education. A selection of past engagements include: Duke University, Hampshire College, Concordia University, SUNY New Paltz, Kingsborough Community College, and multiple Femme Conferences. www.heacheracs.com

Lady Quesa'Dilla AKA Alejandro Rodríguez is a Tejan@ from the El Paso and Ciu- dad Juárez border. Their work is at the intersection of cultural identity, drag, and commu- nity. "The Brown Queen," an autobiographical solo performance about growing up queer

Pictured, L to R: Alejandro, Heather, Sabina, Andrea, Lizxnn, Damien.

Not pictured: LouLou, Nicole.

Photo: 2015, HOW Group.

in the southwest, premiered at HERE Arts Center in the spring of 2010. Most recent solo performances include "My Tia Lupe" and "The Faggot in the Pink House". Quesa is the Volunteer Coordinator for the annual Bushwig Drag & Music Festival, and is also a member of the femme collective Heels on Wheels. Quesa can also be found as an Information and Referral Specialist at the Lesbian, Gay, Bisexual, and Transgender Community Center in Manhattan; and as a Teaching Artist in Brooklyn. They hold a BA in Theater from Eugene Lang College The New School for Liberal Arts, and a MA in Performance Studies from Tisch School of the Arts, New York University. Resides in Brooklyn. Lady Quesa'Dilla is a former Miss Coney Island Queen of Drag.

*Lizxnn Disaster is a Femme Punk Witch. An artist who has worked in visual, musi-*cal, and performance mediums for the last 18+ years, she joined Heels on Wheels as the resident driver/roadie/femme wrangler/yoga teacher/door person/bouncer and merch babe in 2011.

Mette Loulou von Kohl was born from the orange at the center before the new world came. She is a performer and a wanderer. Currently based in New York City, Mette Loulou is a mixed-race queer femme, born to a Lebanese/Palestinian mother and Danish father. She has lived in New York, Romania, Morocco and Denmark. Mette Loulou is fascinated by the intersection between her personal identities as a jumping off point to reveal, dismantle and rebuild realities and dreams. She grapples with her past to complicate and better understand her present. Mette Loulou weaves movement, words, and her love for the unexpected into the exploration of her embodied histories. She exists in two places at once.

Nicole Myles is a photographer, arts administrator, and expert cut-eye giver.

Sabina Ibarrola is a blossoming herbalist, doula, and artist. This bruja finds the meat and magia of her work in the natural world and urban ecosystems of Brooklyn, New York. Inspired by a brilliant galaxy of queer femme artists and instigators, she explores themes of love and heartbreak, mixed-race ancestry, apocalypse and faith. Her work has appeared at LaMama, Brooklyn Arts Exchange (BAX), JACK, LAVABrooklyn,and Bowery Poetry Club. Sabina apprentices with Robin Rose Bennett of Wisewoman Healing Ways. She is Associate Creative Director of Heels on Wheels, and toured with HOW in 2014. www.sabinaibarrola.com

Contributor Bios

Alex Cafarelli is a genderqueer femme Jewish Witch based in Toronto. A lifetime writer and performer, Alex co-founded the Minneapolis-based performance group the Psycick Slutz. She is a member of Body Heat, a touring collective of queer femme artists, and she also works with Sins Invalid, a San Francisco-based performance project on disability and sexuality. Alex is an Amherst Writers and Artists (AWA) Affiliate, certified to lead workshops in the AWA method as described in Writing Alone & With Others by Pat Schneider, Oxford University Press. She has been leading and co-facilitating workshops in North America using this method since 2010. For more information, contact Alex at petals_and_thorns@yahoo.com"

Alex Alvina Chamberland is a Swedish/US trans feminine writer, artist and activist, who lived in Brooklyn in 2014-2015 in order to complete her masters thesis on Trans feminine sisterhood and intersectionality in New York City. Most of her work thus far has been published in Swedish, however this particular piece is a part of her next novel-project which is in English. The tentative working title is "A Hot Temper is it's Own Good Romance" - and it deals with many of the main subjects of Alex-Alvina's work: Emotionality, Intensity, Existentialism, (Trans)Femme-ininity, Failure, Madness, Anti-Capitalism, and things that might lose their meanings if put into neat little categories like feeling so lonely that you strike up conversations with the furniture etc.

Alvis Parsley aka Alvis Choi is an artist, performer, researcher and facilitator based in Toronto. Alvis' work was presented at the SummerWorks Festival, Mayworks Festival, Art of the Danforth, Buddies in Bad Times Theatre, Hemisphere Institute of Performance and Politics – Encuentro, Rhubarb Festival, Videofag, National Queer Arts Festival and Gladstone Hotel. Alvis is named in BLOUIN ARTINFO Canada's "30 Under 30 2014 list. They serve on the Board of the Chinese Canadian National Council Toronto Chapter and the Mayworks Festival, as well as the organizing committee of the Critical Ethnic Studies Conference 2015 at York University, Toronto.

Amber Dawn is a writer from Vancouver, Canada. Author of the memoir How Poetry Saved My Life and the Lambda Award-winning novel Sub Rosa, and editor of the anthologies Fist of the Spider Women: Fear and Queer Desire and With A Rough Tongue.

ANNA JOY SPRINGER, is an artist, performer, and cross-genre writer who investigates the weird intersections of sacredness, perversity, feminist history, and interbeing. She is the author of The Vicious Red Relic, Love (Jaded Ibis, 2011), an illustrated fabulist memoir with soundscape, and The Birdwisher, A Murder Mystery for Very Old Young Adults (Birds of Lace, 2009). Her current research interests are: A graphic text picture puzzle called Thieves' Rebus, and an operatic outer space puppet show memoir called Art In Heaven. An Associate Professor of Literature at UC San Diego and the Director of its MFA Program, she teaches experimental writing, feminist literature & graphic texts. She's played in punk and dyke punk bands Blatz, The Gr'ups, and Cypher in the Snow and toured with Sister Spit.

Annah Anti-Palindrome is a bay-area based musician/Optical Sound-Smith, writer, and queer/femme antagonist who hails from the working-class craters at the base of the Sierra Foothills. Annah performs using a variety of different mediums including a Line 6 (DL4) looping system, kitchen utensils, gas-masks, raw eggs, blood pressure cuffs, found objects, her body (mostly her throat), and more! As part of the 2014 National Queer Arts Festival, Annah co-edited Passage and Place, a queer anthology on the concept of Home. Annah is also the co-editor of 1-2-3 Punch: How Misogyny Hurts Queer Communities, and a collective member of Deviant Type Press (www.devianttype.net). "

Annie Danger is unflinchingly, seamlessly bound to the power of the hybrid to change the world. As a trans woman and a radical, she understands that the only way truly forward into the better world of which we all dream is if we go it together, taking all comers, and building a future that meets all needs. Toward that steep challenge, she makes live art, drawn art, and writing that use humor, weirdness, earnesty, and trickery ("The joke is: it's not a joke.") to frame the way forward in cunningly well-integrated new ways. She believes the revolutionary spirit is one of hope. You can find her work on stage and in the streets in the Bay Area where she lives and around the country when she tours. www.anniedanger.com

*Ariel "Speedwagon" Federow is an interdisciplinary performing artist. Venues: La-*Mama ETC, Dixon Place, the Hemispheric Institute for Performance and Politics, the Bowery Poetry Club, WoW Theater Cafe, Hey Queen!, Rebel Cupcake, In the Flesh, BAX, the Bureau of General Services: Queer Divison. Company member: the Ballez, AO Movement Collective, Butch Burlesque. Works With: Coral Short, Jenny Romaine, Susana Cook, Quito Ziegler, Rosza Daniel Lang/Levitsky, and the Aftselokhis Spectacle Committee. Resident weatherman, Sarah Jenny News Network. Reigning dapperQ of the year. Co-curator of Deadline, a queer works-in-progress series. 2012 Hemispheric Institute Affiliated Emerging Artist. Miss JewSA 5772. Bingo host. Clown about town. Itinerant professor and Powerpoint aficionado. Real nice guy.

*Ashley Young is a poet, writer, teacher and editor. She is a 2010 Voices of Our Na-*tions Foundation Poetry Fellow and a 2011 Lambda Literary Non-fiction Fellow to return the summer of 2016. She writes for Elixher Magazine and has been published in two anthologies published by Seal Press and the University of Wisconsin Press. She is currently working on an Audre Lorde inspired biomythography, a collection of poems and a play on the effects of mental illness on black woman.

Azure D. Osborne-Lee is an award-winning theatre maker and arts administrator living in Brooklyn, NY. Follow his work at http://azureosbornelee.com

bekezela mguni is an abundant bodied Trinidadian femme. she is a reproductive justice & human rights activist, poet and librarian. her work celebrates memory and storytelling as a means of cultural preservation and creation. she believes in destiny, the undeniable genius of Blackness and that grandmothers are magic.

Bevin Branlandingham spreads the message that all bodies are worthy of love exactly as they are. She's a writer, performer, and a body liberation and authenticity coach. She produces nightlife and art events in New York City and tours teaching self confidence and body love. Bevin was one of the 100 Women We Love in Go Magazine, was called a "Warrior for Self Acceptance" by Autostraddle, and was featured in Curve Magazine. Her monthly party, Rebel Cupcake, was called on of the reasons New York City is the best city in the world by Time Out New York. She works to make the world safe for people to love themselves. Blog, calendar of events and booking information: queerfatfemme.com.

Caitlin Rose Sweet explores the intersections between craft, queerness, and pop culture to position queerness as a site for incessant transformation and possibilities. Her playful work resists assimilation and mastery through an intentional disinvestment in finished work and proper use of materials. Sweet has shown internationally from Portland Or, to San Francisco Bay Area, New York City and Berlin. This includes such exhibitions as Mix 26 (NY 2013), Craftivism (NY 2013), Invisible Landscapes (PDX 2014), and Words as Objects(PDX 2014). Sweet received her MFA in Applied Craft and Design from PNCA/OCAC in 2014 and lives in Brooklyn.

*Celeste Chan is a hybrid artist, writer, and organizer. She is a queer student of experi*mentation, schooled by DIY and immigrant parents from Malaysia and the Bronx, NY. A Hedgebrook, Lambda, and VONA alumna, her writing can be found in Ada, As/us journal, cream city review, Feminist Wire, Glitterwolf, Hyphen, Matador, and Writing the Walls Down: A Convergence of LGBTQ Voices (Transgenre Press). Her experimental films have screened in CAAMFest, Digital Desperados, Entzaubert, Frameline, Heels on Wheels, Imperfectu, Leeds Queer Film Festival, MIX NYC, National Queer Arts Festival, Queeristan, and Vancouver Queer Film Festival, among others. Alongside KB Boyce, she co-directs Queer Rebels, a queer and trans people of color arts project. www.celestechan.com and www.queerrebels.com.

Cristy C. Road is a Brooklyn-based Cuban-American illustrator and writer who's been supplying Illustrations for punk, publishing, & activism since 1997. Road published a zine, Greenzine for ten years, and has released three illustrated novels which tackle gender, sexuality, mental health and cultural identity; with a tinge of bathroom humor and curse words: "Indestructible" (2005), "Bad Habits" (2008) and her most recent work, "Spit and Passion" (2013), a graphic queer-coming-out memoir (about Green Day). She's currently working on the Next World Tarot card deck, and her punk rock band The Homewreckers.

*Drae Campbell is an NYC artist who wears many hats: storyteller, emcee, actor, direc*tor, etc. Drae has performed all over NYC and also in Budapest, Thailand and various places in the U.S. The short film Drae wrote and starred in, YOU MOVE ME won the Audience Award for Outstanding Narrative Short at OUTFEST 2010 and has been shown in festivals globally. Drae has performed in every medium, multiple stages and has been spotted once or twice on Conan O'Brien. Drae hosts a monthly storytelling show called TELL & she recently won the grand prize at the first annual San Miguel Storytelling Festival in Mexico. Drae is proud to be included in this collection.

Ezra Berkley Nepon is a performer, writer, and organizer based in Philadelphia, and a recipient of the 2014 Leeway Transformation Award.

After completing the burlesque class series by Defloured Productions, Foxy E Squire gathered her wits and talent to begin performing. Her first performance residence was Rivers of Honey Cabaret and she was a regular performer at Matthew Silver's Circus of Dreams and Crimson Kitty's Cataclysm. Her artistic skill has been shared both nationally and internationally in London, Connecticut, California, Rhode Island, Massachusetts, North Carolina, Georgia (DragonCon), Virginia, Florida, Philadelphia, and NYC. Foxy's first headliner performance was in May 2013 at the DC Gurly Show (Washington, DC). Last year she was proud to be in the original cast of NYC's first all female drag show, Crimson Kitty presents FAUXVASION. She will be doing her first Boston tour at the end of this month. Her motto is EMBRACE YOUR SPECTACLE. Now, she shares her love for deviant art and dark beauty through burlesque.

Gigi Frost is the secret identity of a mild-mannered Boston-based producer, educator and artist who serves up smut with a side of politics. She tours nationally with Body Heat and The Femme Show. Recent publications under a variety of pseudonyms include Second Person Queer, Say Please, and Girl Crazy.

Glenn Marla is a Brooklyn-based performance artist, writer, creative arts therapist, and beauty pageant queen (Miss LES 2006 and the first ever Mr. Coney Island). Glenn's full length solo show Tragic Magic has toured festivals and universities across the country and internationally. When Glenn is not performing original visual and theatrical darings, you may find them playing such roles as the Poppy Flower in Taylor Mac's Obie Award winning epic play The Lily's Revenge, or Pansy Flower in Dave End's F.A.G.G.O.T.S the musical. Glenn is currently working in collaboration with Hana Malia on My Wife's Ass. A full-length theater piece that explores agency over and fear of the fat queer body, the "headless fatty," unabashed consumption, "fat panic," ,and how the "war on obesity" is experienced at street level. while telling the tale of the bravery and imagination required to fall into fat love.

Hana Malia is an artist and educator in New York City.

Hannah Morrow aka Lilac Poussez is a writer, director, performing artist & wrestler based in Montreal. Her processes & works investigate new ways of conceptualizing gendered life through hi-femme consciousness and expression. Her ideas take shape as theatre, political satire, professional wrestling, cabarets, and immersive nights of installation and performance. Currently, she co-writes/directs and stars in the League of Lady Wrestlers Montreal (LOLWM) performance series as her Supreme Femme alter ego, Lilac Poussez. Hannah has completed a Bachelor of Fine Arts from Concordia University, specialization in Theatre and Development.

Johnny Forever Nawracaj vel Joachim Magdalena is a Polish-born genderqueer writer, performer, and visual artist based in Montreal. Their writing, video, fibres installation, and performance work moves through modes of love, loss, and longing. Femme representation figures strongly in their work. Forever's concepts is known for their use of yarn, rope, bright colour, and heavy abstraction. Over the years they have woven their personal symbology through venues in Warsaw, Berlin, Montreal, Toronto, Hong Kong, San Francisco, Glasgow, and Seoul.

Kama La Mackerel is a tio'tia:ke/Montreal-based community organizer, movement builder, cultural worker and femme supreme! With an inter-disciplinary art practice that combines performance, poetry, story-telling, textile, print, film and photography, Kama explores cultural production as modes of anti-colonial resistance. Kama was born in Mauritius, migrated to India as a young adult, and now lives in tio'tia:ke/Montreal on colonized kanien'kehá:ka territory. http://lamackerel.net/

A Trans Justice Funding Project Panelist, and Trans 100 Honoree, & PBS NewsHour feature, Kay Ulanday Barrett aka @brownroundboi, is a poet, performer, and educator, navigating life as a disabled pin@y-amerikan transgender queer in the U.S. with struggle, resistance, and laughter. K. has featured on colleges & stages globally; Princeton University, UC Berkeley, Musee Pour Rire in Montreal, and The Chicago Historical Society. K's bold work continues to excite and challenge audiences. K. has facilitated workshops, presented keynotes, and contributed to panels with various social justice communities. Honors include: 18 Million Rising Filipino American History Month Hero, Chicago's LGBTQ 30 under 30 awards, Finalist for The Gwendolyn Brooks Open-Mic Award, Windy City Times Pride Literary Poetry Prize. Their contributions are found in Poor Magazine, Fusion.net, Trans Bodies/Trans Selves, Make/Shift, Filipino American Psychology, Third Woman Press, Asian Americans For Progress, The Advocate, and Bitch Magazine. K. turns art into action and is dedicated to remixing recipes. Recent publications include contributions in the upcoming anthologies, "Outside the XY: Queer Black & Brown Masculinity" (Magnus Books) and "Writing the Walls Down: A Convergence of LGBTQ Voices" (Trans-genre Press). Their first book of poetry, When The Chant Comes, is due out from Topside Press in winter 2016. Check out their work at kaybarrett.net

Kentucky Fried Woman spent the first 24 years of her life in the Bluegrass State before heading to the west Coast in 1999. Happiest when frying chicken, making grits, sharing recipes and gossiping in the kitchen, KFW is a Dancer, Singer, Writer, Speaker, Event Producer, and Wildcat who has been seen on the stage as a soloist, in collaboration with other queer performing artists, and in troupes such as CHUBB and ButchTap. She feels immense gratitude to those that paved the way for a Southern-bred, kinky, fat, queer, tap-dancing, femme with OCD, Depression and Anxiety to practice her art in the spirit of visibility, connection, tender vulnerability, resilience, and joy. + collaborator **jen valles.**

Kirya Traber is a cultural worker, a nationally awarded writer and performer, a Black queer woman, a high femme, and an Oakland girl with a Brooklyn address. Born and raised in northern California, Kirya relocated to New York in 2011 where she is the current Artist Fellow at Lincoln Center Education. She received her MFA in Acting from the New School for Drama. Kirya is the recipient of the California Governor's Award for Excellence in the Arts, Robert Redford's Sundance foundation award for Activism in the Arts, Congresswoman Barbara Lee's Certificate of Recognition, an Astrea Lesbian Writers Fund award for Poetry, and is a former judge for the LAMDA Literary awards in LGBT Drama. Kirya is an alumnus of the 2010 VONA/Voices retreat for writers of color, and the 2012 EmergeNYC intensive at the Hemispheric Institute, and is a 2014 Space Grantee at Brooklyn Arts Exchange. Kirya has toured the United States and Canada as a poet and solo performance artist, and her written work can be found in the pages of, Other Tongues, an anthology by Inana Press, and in her 2009 chapbook, black chick. She has worked as an arts educator with youth and adults, in school and community based settings, and within the juvenile justice system.

Kit Yan is an Asian American, queer, and transgender slam poet based in Brooklyn, NY and from Hawaii. Kit's poetry has been reviewed by Bitch, Curve, and Hyphen magazines and their work has been in Flickr and Spark and Troubling the Line two queer and trans* poetry anthologies, and they have a forthcoming book with Transgenre Press. Kit has toured with Sister Spit, The Tranny Roadshow, and Good Asian Drivers, and his solo slam poetry show Queer Heartache received the Spirit of Fringe, Artists' Pick, and Audience Choice awards at the 2015 Chicago Fringe Festival. Kit believes in the power of this book and is honored to be among this brilliant group of artists.

Leah Horlick is a writer and poet from Saskatoon. A 2012 Lambda Literary Fellow in Poetry, she holds an MFA in Creative Writing from the University of British Columbia. Her first collection of poetry, Riot Lung (Thistledown Press, 2012) was shortlisted for a 2013 ReLit Award and a Saskatchewan Book Award. She lives on Unceded Coast Salish Territories in Vancouver, where she co-curates REVERB, a queer and anti-oppressive reading series.

Leah Lakshmi Piepzna-Samarasinha is a queer disabled femme writer, performance artist and educator of Burgher/Tamil Sri Lankan and Irish/Roma ascent. The author of the Lambda Award-winning Love Cake, Dirty River, Bodymap and Consensual Genocide and co-editor with Ching-In Chen and Jai Dulani of The Revolution Starts At Home: Confronting Intimate Violence in Activist Communities, her writings on femme of color and Sri Lankan identities, survivorhood, and healing, disability and transformative justice have been widely anthologized, including recent publications in Octavia's Brood, Dear Sister and Undoing Border Imperialism. She is the co-founder of Mangos With Chili, North America's touring queer and trans people of color cabaret, a lead artist with the disability justice incubator Sins Invalid and co-founder of Toronto's Asian Arts Freedom School. In 2010 she was named one of the Feminist Press' 40 Feminists Under 40 Shaping the Future and she is a 2013 Autostraddle Hot 105 member. She lives between Toronto, unceded Three Fires Confederacy Territories and Seattle, unceded Duwamish territories. brownstargirl.org

*Lettie Laughter is a queer indigenous femme babe of the Diné nation & nth genera-*tion community healer, birthworker, & orator. They have spent their whole life collecting stories (most often only told once, twice if they were lucky), trying to make sense of the senseless. As a trauma survivor, Lettie found solace & healing through writing, which is often reflected in the themes woven throughout their body of work. More of their community femme babe healing work can be found at www.highmoonfemme.com.

Matthew de Leon aka Untitled Queen is a visual artist, drag queen, and graphic designer. He received his BFA from the University of Connecticut and his MFA in visual arts from Parsons the New School for Design. He has performed at Triskelion Arts, BAM, La Mama, The Brooklyn Museum, and The Bronx Museum as well as exhibited at Mixed Greens Gallery, NY; Artspace, New Haven, CT; The Kitchen, NY; among others. He received the Brooklyn Nightlife Award for Drag Queen of the Year in 2015.

Mée Rose is a femme gender queer multi-media artist living in Toronto. She has shown work locally, and in various cities, including Montreal, Vancouver, New York, and San Francisco. Her work explores themes of self-love, kink, and sexualityLeanne Powers is a visual artist who lives in Toronto. She currently works in painting, textile, and video making. **+ collaborator Leanne Powers** is a visual artist who lives in Toronto. She currently works in painting, textile, and video making.

Melanie Keller is a mixed race feminist activist, social worker, advocate, performer (as Ursula Unctuous), artist and total shit-kicker. An academic to her core, Melanie is currently investigating the sociopolitical realities of being mixed race and the intersectionality in feminism. She's also been interested in linguistics since her undergrad studies at the College of Charleston in South Carolina. Melanie produced and ran a podcast called The FAP Cast (@TheFAPCast), available on iTunes, as a fun way to initiate feminist dialogue. Melanie likes to take a million photos of her adorable cat, travel all over the place, play music and run around in the outdoors.

Meliza Bañales aka Missy Fuego is the author of Say It With Your Whole Mouth (poems, Monkey Press) and the forthcoming 51 Poems About Nothing At All (poems), Life Is Wonderful, People Are Terrific (fiction), and Laughing to Keep From Crying (Stories and Essays). Her work has also appeared in Without A Net: The Female Experience of Growing-Up Working Class (edited by Michelle Tea), Baby, Remember My Name: New Queer Girl Writing (edited by Michelle Tea), The Encyclopedia of Activism and Social Change, and Word Warriors: 35 Women Leaders of the Spoken-Word Movement (edited by Alix Olson). She was the first Chicana/Latina on the west coast to win a poetry slam championship in 2002, has toured with Sister Spit and Body Heat, and gained national recognition for her appearances on NPR and The Lesbian Podcast. Her short film with J. Aguilar entitled "Getting Off" won the Jury Award at the Los Angeles Transgender Film Festival in 2011 and her spoken-word album, And Now Introducing Missy Fuego, is expected on Crunks Not Dead Records in 2015. She lives in Los Angeles.

Michelle Embree is a novelist, a playwright, a performer, and a Tarot Card Reader. She is currently working on a Tarot Deck and a User's Guide titled: The Book of Keys. To voyeur in on some of this hot project go to: www.bookofkeys.wordpress.com

Muggs Fogarty is a queer poet and teaching artist from Providence, Rhode Island. Since 2007, Muggs has represented Providence at seven inter/national spoken word competitions and is a Brave New Voices finalist. After graduating from The New School in 2013, Muggs has been mentoring with New Urban Arts, ¡CityArts!, ProvSlam Youth, and is now serving as co-director of Providence Poetry Slam. Their work can be found in FreezeRay, Wicked Banshee, Bluestockings Magazine, among others. Send @muggsfogarty crystal ball emojis on Twitter!

niknaz is a time-based artist who uses non-traditional communication strategies to convey ideas of intersubjectiveity and wandering identities. niknaz is obsessed with texture, bicycles, the desert, open source, film, writing on the subway, and yesterday. niknaz can be found on DuckDuckGo.

Nomy Lamm is a writer, singer, illustrator, filmmaker, voice teacher and creative coach. She plays the accordion (backwards), has a crush on the moon, and dedicates herself to anti-racist, embodied, disability-centered movement building. Nomy and her partner, Lisa Ganser, recently relocated from San Francisco back to Nomy's home town of Olympia, WA. "What Was Coming" is a chapter from her unpublished experimental novel, 515 Clues. The only copy of this book is hand-bound in red leather with gilded pages and sits on a wrought iron pedestal in Nomy's bedroom.

rosza daniel lang/levitsky is a cultural worker & organizer based at brooklyn's Glitter House. just another gendertreyf fem who identifies with, not as. can't stop picking things up off the street and making other things out of them - outfits, collectives, cabarets, barricades, puppet shows, meals... never figured out how or why to make art for art's sake; rarely wants to work alone. third-generation radical; second-generation dyke; oysterlish mischling & diasporist apikoyrus. current projects: JUST LIKE THAT (militant research on embodied knowledge in the choreography of justice movements); Critical Reperformance (presenting classic performance scores, often antagonistically); a punk band playing the yiddish anarchist repertoire; investigations of the queer & trans scrapbooks of Carl Van Vechten; custom leatherwork for trans & queer bodies of all sizes & shapes; etc. more at meansof.org

Samantha Galarza is a queer, mixed-raced, Puerto Rican actress/writer/singer/poet/ performance artist/professional ranter/sometimes director. As an art-ivist, her work explores queer identity politics, fluidity, sexuality, systemic and internalized racism, substance abuse, immigration/migration, the U.S. prison industrial complex and policy that disproportionately affects ethnic minorities. Ultimately a storyteller, her dream is to bridge the gap between mainstream media and progressive "anti-colonial" political art.

Sassafras Lowrey is a straight-edge queer punk who grew up to become the 2013 win- ner of the Lambda Literary Emerging Writer Award. Hir books—Kicked Out, Roving Pack, and Leather Ever After—have been honored by organizations ranging from the National Leather Association to the American Library Association. Sassafras lives and writes in Brooklyn with hir partner and five furry beasts. Hir latest novel Lost Boi was released from Arsenal Pulp Press in 2015 www.SassafrasLowrey.com

Siobhan Katherine Flood was born in the second to last year of the seventies, in the Bronx. They have a hard time conceptualizing being able to go home to NYC as a disabled person and until that time they are keeping it real in the unreal beauty of the PNW. They will continue throwing parties and being a magnetic force until they move to the woods and built a hobbit hole. They love their community. Never give up Stay punk.

Shira Erlichman's work has taken her all over the country with various performance poetry ensembles (Spilljoy, 2008; Elephant Engine High Dive Revival, 2009). Her chapbook ""Advertisement for a Human Being"" (Destructible Heart Press) - a personal exploration of mental illness & the socialized alienation of suffering - was nominated for a Pushcart Prize. She has been fortunate enough to have her work included in Muzzle, the Massachusetts Review, Union Station, The Reader, & The Bakery, among others. She has released multiple albums independently & her music has been featured on NPR. She has shared stages with Mirah, Andrea Gibson, Tune-Yards, & Ani Difranco. She counts Wislawa Szymborska, Rumi, Yoko Ono, John Cage, Miranda July & Aracelis Girmay as some of the brightest in her constellation of influences. She currently teaches & creates out of Brooklyn, NY.

Shomi Noise is a musician, writer, DJ, storyteller, dreamer, and tinkerer with an estab- lished reputation in the Brooklyn underground scene. Her work explores narratives of intersectionality, vulnerability, and resilience. She uses music to share empowering messages with the world through a creative mix of stories and sounds. Shomi has DJed nationally and internationally with sets that include a blend of genres ranging from Latin dance music, hip-hop, reggae, pop, and punk rock. She currently produces two parties in Brooklyn: Riot Chica and Telenovela, Riot Chica is a queercore/riot grrrl party that celebrates feminism and DIY culture by sharing empowering live underground music made by ladies and queers, and Telenovela is a party that celebrates Latina culture and Spanish oldies. As a writer, performer, and musician, Shomi is working on original singer/songwriter material and other musical projects with friends including a Selena punk rock cover band. She is the author of "Building Up Emotional Muscles," a coming of age story that incorporates music and storytelling to depict the struggles and triumphs she experienced growing up as a young queer immigrant woman of color in the US. It addresses her experience with the intersectionality of culture, race, class, sexuality and punk rock, and is based on a series of zines sharing the same title. She has had the privilege to share this original work as part of Heels on Wheels. Shomi has DJed nationally and internationally with sets that include a clever mix of genres ranging from Latin dance music, hip-hop, electrohouse, reggae, pop, punk rock etc. Her ability to read crowds and create catchy and original song mashups on the spot makes her DJ work interesting and refreshing. She currently produces three parties in Brooklyn: Riot Chica, Telenovela, and Wretched. Riot Chica is a queercore/riot grrrl party that celebrates feminism and DIY culture by sharing empowering underground music made by ladies and queers, Telenovela is a new party for Spanish oldies and Wretched is a fun 90s party. As a writer, performer, and musician, Shomi is working on original singer/songwriter material and other musical projects with friends. She is the author of ""Building Up Emotional Muscles,"" a coming of age story that incorporates music and storytelling to depict the struggles and triumphs she experienced growing up as a young queer immigrant woman of color in the US. It addresses her experience with the intersectionality of culture, race, class, sexuality and punk rock, and is based on a series of zines sharing the same title. She's had the opportunity to share this original work as part of Heels on Wheels. She is currently working on the 4th and last volume of the series and hopes to one day make a movie or play about it. Shomi's work is best described as unique, sassy, musically eclectic, and fun. She is deeply committed to spreading messages of self-love, empowerment, social justice, and community building."

Sophie Spinelle (www.sophiespinelle.com) is a queer high femme, photographer, and founder of Shameless Photography, a body-positive, feminist pinup portraiture company (www.shamelessphoto.com) with studios in New York and San Francisco. She has done over 600 photo shoots with a range of commercial, journalistic, and individual clients. Her photographic work has been featured in the New York Times, Huffington Post, Buzzfeed, and SFMOMA, among others.

Sossity Chiricuzio is a queer femme outlaw poet, a working class sex radical story-teller. What her friends parents often referred to as a bad influence, and possibly still do. A 2015 Lambda Fellow and contributing columnist at PQmonthly.com, publications include Adrienne, Wilde, Vine Leaves, Glitterwolf, NANO, and Mash Stories. Sossitywrites.com.

Sunny Drake is an Australian born queer trans femme writer, performer & pro-ducer. Now based in Toronto, he's toured his award-winning theatre shows extensively in Canada, Australia, the USA, Puerto Rico and Europe. He is also the author of a blog which weaves trans* and queer politics with personal story (www.sunnydrake.com)

The dandy vagabonds are a Baltimore based pair of curious, playful artists who thrive on telling stories of whimsy, adventure, insight & balance through performance art, circus arts, fiber arts, the tactile & the ephemeral. xander dumas, who has a dramatic passion for Art Nouveau headdresses & elliot mittens, an exquisite observer & equilibrist, makeup the collaborative duo, who moonlight under the name ephemeral fossils. we invite you to explore & tinker at our website: ephemeralfossils.com

The Miracle Whips is a queer femme performance troupe that works to promote models of progressive femininity, create radical erotic possibilities, and disrupt conventional notions of sexiness. We are a feminist collective that provides a healthy dollop of sass with your social commentary.

T.L. Cowan is a Brooklyn-based writer & performer. T.L. got her start in the boom-ing (largely feminist) spoken word scene of Vancouver in the late 1990s and since then have been making work that draws from cabaret, costume-based and alter-ego performance, agit-prop theatre, stand-up comedy, video and sound art, installation and intervention. These performances reflect an ongoing quasi-pseudo-autobiographical meditation on feminine composites, class mobility, sexuality and style.

Tina Horn produces and hosts the sexuality podcast Why Are People Into That?!. She is the author of the nonfiction books Love Not Given Lightly and Sexting; her writing also appears in Coming Out Like A Porn Star, Girl Sex 101, and Best Sex Writing 2015. She is a LAMBDA Literary Fellow and the recipient of two Feminist Porn Awards.

Lankan Tamil Blood, Manchester-Born, Texas-Bred and Brooklyn-Brewed, Yalini- Dream conjures spirit through her unique blend of poetry, theater, song, and dance-- re-shaping reality and seeking peace through justice in the lands of earth, psyche, soul, and dream. She uses performance to open space for heavily silenced issues in Sri Lanka's diaspora including critiques of all armed actors, gendered violence, and Queer sexuality. She is a consultant with Vision Change Win, a specialist with Arts & Wellness organiza-tion EM Techniques, and tours internationally with Hip Hop MC Jendog Lonewolf as part of DreamWolf. YaliniDream was an Artist in Residence at University of Michigan; taught Social Justice Pedagogy and the Arts at the Masters in Human Rights program at University of San Francisco; has shared stages with icons such as Joan Baez, Arch Bishop Desmond Tutu, Harry Belafonte, and Rah Digga; and is represented by awQward Tal-ent-- the first agency representing Trans & Queer Artists of Color.

Zachary Wager Scholl is a writer, performer and organizer. He's a member of the Aftselokhes Spectacle Committee, the Man Meat Collective, the Rude Mechanical Orchestra, and Jews For Racial & Economic Justice.

Final Thoughts

Perfection is Patriarchy

Low Stakes, High Standards

Keep Havin' Fun!

Photo by Tinker Coalescing of Glitter Roadshow Homecoming, 4/20/14
at JACK in Brooklyn.